R Data Structures and Algorithms

Increase speed and performance of your applications with efficient data structures and algorithms

Dr. PKS Prakash
Achyutuni Sri Krishna Rao

BIRMINGHAM - MUMBAI

R Data Structures and Algorithms

First published: November 2016

Production reference: 1141116

Published by Packt Publishing Ltd.
Livery Place
35 Livery Street
Birmingham
B3 2PB, UK.

ISBN 978-1-78646-515-3

www.packtpub.com

Credits

Authors

Dr. PKS Prakash
Achyutuni Sri Krishna Rao

Reviewer

Dr. Vahid Mirjalili

Commissioning Editor

Kunal Parikh

Acquisition Editor

Denim Pinto

Content Development Editor

Siddhi Chavan

Technical Editor

Sunith Shetty

Copy Editor

Sonia Mathur

Project Coordinator

Suzanne Coutinho

Proofreader

Safis Editing

Indexer

Rekha Nair

Graphics

Jason Monteiro
Kirk D'Penha

Production Coordinator

Aparna Bhagat

About the Authors

Dr. PKS Prakash has pursued his PhD in industrial and system engineering at Wisconsin-Madison, US. He defended his second PhD in engineering from University of Warwick, UK. He has provided data science support to numerous leading companies in healthcare, manufacturing, pharmaceutical, and e-commerce domains on a wide range of business problems related to predictive and prescriptive modeling, virtual metrology, predictive maintenance, root cause analysis, process simulations, fraud detection, early warning systems, and so on. Currently, he is working as the Vice President and Practice Lead for data science at Dream11. Dream11 offers the world's largest fantasy cricket, football, and kabaddi games of skill. He has published widely in research areas of operational research and management, soft computing tools, and advanced algorithms in the manufacturing and healthcare domains in leading journals such as IEEE-Trans, EJOR, and IJPR, among others. He has contributed a chapter in *Evolutionary Computing in Advanced Manufacturing* and edited an issue of *Intelligent Approaches to Complex Systems*.

Achyutuni Sri Krishna Rao has an MS in enterprise business analytics (data science) from National University of Singapore. He has worked on a wide range of data science problems in the domain of manufacturing, healthcare and pharmaceuticals. He is an R enthusiast and loves to contribute to the open source community. His passions include freelancing, technical blogs (`http://rcodeeasy.blogspot.com`) and marathon runs. Currently he works as a data science consultant at a leading consulting firm.

Acknowledgments

The completion of this book wouldn't have been possible without the participation and assistance of so many people whose names may not all be enumerated. Their contribution is sincerely appreciated and gratefully acknowledged. However, we would like to express our deep appreciation and indebtedness to all the members of the Packt team involved in this project. The book arose with an idea with an early discussion with Denim Pinto (acquisition editor), so we want to extend special thanks to him; without his input, this book would never have happened. We also want to thank Pooja Mhapsekar and Siddhi Chavan (content editor) and Sunith Shetty (technical editor) for ensuring the timely publication of this book. We would like to extend thanks to Vahid Mirjalili (reviewer), whose feedback has helped us tremendously improve this book.

About the Reviewer

Dr. Vahid Mirjalili is a software engineer/data scientist, currently working toward his PhD in computer science at Michigan State University. His research at the Integrated Pattern Recognition and Biometrics (i-PRoBE) lab involves attribute classification of face images from large image datasets. Furthermore, he teaches Python programming, as well as computing concepts for data analysis and databases. With his specialty in data mining, he is very interested in predictive modeling and getting insights from data. He is also a Python developer and likes to contribute to the open source community. Furthermore, he enjoys making tutorials for different areas of data science and computer algorithms, which can be found in his GitHub repository (http://github.com/mirjalil/DataScience).

www.PacktPub.com

For support files and downloads related to your book, please visit www.PacktPub.com.

Did you know that Packt offers eBook versions of every book published, with PDF and ePub files available? You can upgrade to the eBook version at www.PacktPub.com and as a print book customer, you are entitled to a discount on the eBook copy. Get in touch with us at service@packtpub.com for more details.

At www.PacktPub.com, you can also read a collection of free technical articles, sign up for a range of free newsletters and receive exclusive discounts and offers on Packt books and eBooks.

https://www.packtpub.com/mapt

Get the most in-demand software skills with Mapt. Mapt gives you full access to all Packt books and video courses, as well as industry-leading tools to help you plan your personal development and advance your career.

Why subscribe?

- Fully searchable across every book published by Packt
- Copy and paste, print, and bookmark content
- On demand and accessible via a web browser

Table of Contents

Preface

Data structures represent a way to organize and access particular data efficiently. They are critical to any problem solving and provide a complete solution to implement reusable codes. *R Data Structures and Algorithms* aims at strengthening the data structure skills among R users working in the analytics and intelligence domains. R is a well-designed language and environment for statistical computing and graphics developed at Bell Laboratories (formerly AT&T, now Lucent Technologies). This book will allow users to design optimized algorithms from the computational efficiency and resource usage perspective of an algorithm. This book puts forward the processes of building algorithms by introducing several data structures and their relationship with algorithms, followed by their analysis and evaluation. This book intends to cover not only the classical data structures, but also understand the integrities of functional data structures. We will cover the fundamentals of data structures, such as lists, stacks, queues, and dictionaries, followed by topics such as indexing, sorting, and searching in depth. Readers will also be exposed to advanced topics such as graphs, dynamic programming, and randomized algorithms.

The objective of this book is to build data structure concepts using R.

What this book covers

Chapter 1, *Getting Started*, builds a background for the aspects of data structures that are important to develop basics of R, as well as why they are important.

Chapter 2, *Algorithm Analysis*, talks about motivation, basic notation, and fundamental techniques for algorithm analysis.

Chapter 3, *Linked Lists*, builds a foundation of linked lists and will cover multiple variants of linked lists, such as linear linked lists, doubly linked lists, and circular linked lists.

Chapter 4, *Stacks and Queues*, introduces you to array-based and linked list-based stacks and queues and their implementation in R.

Chapter 5, *Sorting Algorithms*, explains various sorting algorithms, such as insertion sort, bubble sort, selection sort, and shell sort, and provides an empirical comparison between different algorithms.

Chapter 6, *Exploring Search Options*, provides details about search operations carried out on both vectors and lists, including linked lists. It also introduces you to self-organizing lists and hashing concepts.

Chapter 7, *Indexing*, covers indexing concepts, which are essential in file structuring, and organize large amounts of data on disk. It will also cover ISAM, 2-3 trees, B-tree, and B+ tree in detail.

Chapter 8, *Graphs*, builds a foundation for the graph data structure and its implementation. It also covers various algorithms for traversals, shortest-paths problems, and minimum-cost spanning trees in detail.

Chapter 9, *Programming and Randomized Algorithms*, extends the concept of a static data structure to randomize data structure, such as randomized skip lists. The chapter will also introduce programming concepts and several applications of it.

Chapter 10, *Functional Data Structures*, introduces you to functional data structures and lazy evaluation. It will also cover functional stacks and queues in R.

What you need for this book

You will need inquisitiveness, perseverance, and a passion for algorithm design and data science. The scope and application of data structures is quite broad and wide.

You will need a good understanding of R or another programming language. Preliminary experience of programming and data analysis will be helpful as well. You will need to appreciate algorithms that can be applied in scale to build applications.

Who this book is for

This book is for R developers who want to use data structures efficiently. Basic knowledge of R is expected.

Conventions

In this book, you will find a number of text styles that distinguish between different kinds of information. Here are some examples of these styles and an explanation of their meaning.

Code words in text, database table names, folder names, filenames, file extensions, pathnames, dummy URLs, user input, and Twitter handles are shown as follows: "It also enables us to install and compile new R packages directly from the R console using the `install.packages()` command."

A block of code is set as follows:

```
if (test expression)
{
    Statement upon condition is true
}
```

Any command-line input or output is written as follows:

```
pip3 install --upgrade pip
pip3 install jupyter
```

New terms and **important words** are shown in bold. Words that you see on the screen, for example, in menus or dialog boxes, appear in the text like this: "To start a new R Notebook, click on right hand side **New** tab and select **R** kernel as shown in Figure 1.7."

Warnings or important notes appear in a box like this.

Tips and tricks appear like this.

Reader feedback

Feedback from our readers is always welcome. Let us know what you think about this book-what you liked or disliked. Reader feedback is important for us as it helps us develop titles that you will really get the most out of. To send us general feedback, simply e-mail feedback@packtpub.com, and mention the book's title in the subject of your message. If there is a topic that you have expertise in and you are interested in either writing or contributing to a book, see our author guide at www.packtpub.com/authors.

Customer support

Now that you are the proud owner of a Packt book, we have a number of things to help you to get the most from your purchase.

Downloading the example code

You can download the example code files for this book from your account at `http://www.p acktpub.com`. If you purchased this book elsewhere, you can visit `http://www.packtpub.c om/support` and register to have the files e-mailed directly to you.

You can download the code files by following these steps:

1. Log in or register to our website using your e-mail address and password.
2. Hover the mouse pointer on the **SUPPORT** tab at the top.
3. Click on **Code Downloads & Errata**.
4. Enter the name of the book in the **Search** box.
5. Select the book for which you're looking to download the code files.
6. Choose from the drop-down menu where you purchased this book from.
7. Click on **Code Download**.

Once the file is downloaded, please make sure that you unzip or extract the folder using the latest version of:

- WinRAR / 7-Zip for Windows
- Zipeg / iZip / UnRarX for Mac
- 7-Zip / PeaZip for Linux

The code bundle for the book is also hosted on GitHub at `https://github.com/PacktPubl ishing/R-Data-Structures-and-Algorithms`. We also have other code bundles from our rich catalog of books and videos available at `https://github.com/PacktPublishing/`. Check them out!

Downloading the color images of this book

We also provide you with a PDF file that has color images of the screenshots/diagrams used in this book. The color images will help you better understand the changes in the output. You can download this file from `https://www.packtpub.com/sites/default/files/down loads/RDataStructuresandAlgorithms_ColorImages.pdf`.

Errata

Although we have taken every care to ensure the accuracy of our content, mistakes do happen. If you find a mistake in one of our books-maybe a mistake in the text or the code-we would be grateful if you could report this to us. By doing so, you can save other readers from frustration and help us improve subsequent versions of this book. If you find any errata, please report them by visiting http://www.packtpub.com/submit-errata, selecting your book, clicking on the **Errata Submission Form** link, and entering the details of your errata. Once your errata are verified, your submission will be accepted and the errata will be uploaded to our website or added to any list of existing errata under the Errata section of that title.

To view the previously submitted errata, go to https://www.packtpub.com/books/content/support and enter the name of the book in the search field. The required information will appear under the **Errata** section.

Piracy

Piracy of copyrighted material on the Internet is an ongoing problem across all media. At Packt, we take the protection of our copyright and licenses very seriously. If you come across any illegal copies of our works in any form on the Internet, please provide us with the location address or website name immediately so that we can pursue a remedy.

Please contact us at copyright@packtpub.com with a link to the suspected pirated material.

We appreciate your help in protecting our authors and our ability to bring you valuable content.

Questions

If you have a problem with any aspect of this book, you can contact us at questions@packtpub.com, and we will do our best to address the problem.

1
Getting Started

Faster and efficient information retrieval is the primary objective of most computer programs. Data structures and algorithms help us in achieving the objective by processing and retrieving data faster. Information retrieval can easily be integrated with algorithms to answer inferential questions from data such as:

- How are sales increasing over time?
- What is customer's arrival distribution over time?
- Out of all the customers who visit between 3:00 and 6:00 PM, how many order Asian versus Chinese?
- Of all the customers visiting, how many are from the same city?

In the efficient processing of the preceding queries, especially in big data scenarios, data structures and algorithms utilized for data retrieval play a significant role. This book will introduce primary data structures such as lists, queues, and stacks, which are used for information retrieval and trade-off of different data structures. We will also introduce the data structure and algorithms evaluation approach for retrieval and processing of defined data structures.

Algorithms are evaluated based on complexity and efficiency, where complexity refers to an algorithm design which is easy to program and debug, and efficacy ensures that the algorithm is utilizing computer resources optimally. This book will focus on the efficiency part of algorithms using data structures, and the current chapter introduces the importance of data structure and the algorithms used for retrieval of data from data structures.

Introduction to data structure

Moore's law in 1965 observed that the number of transistors per square inch in a dense **integrated circuit** (**IC**) had doubled every year since its invention, thus enhancing computational power per computer. He revised his forecast in 1975, stating that the number of transistors would double every 2 years, instead of every year, due to saturation:

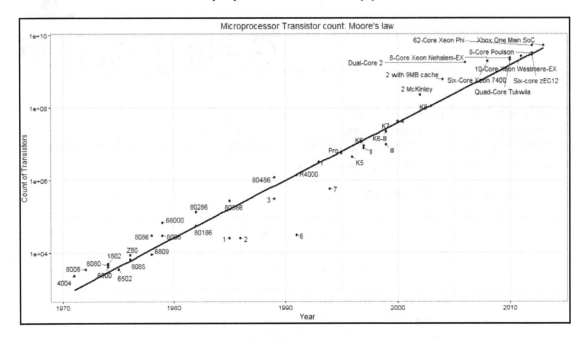

Figure 1.1: Moore's law (Ref: data credit – Transistor count, Wikipedia)

Also, although the computational power has been increasing, problem complexity and data sources have also been increasing exponentially over the decade, enforcing the need for efficient algorithms:

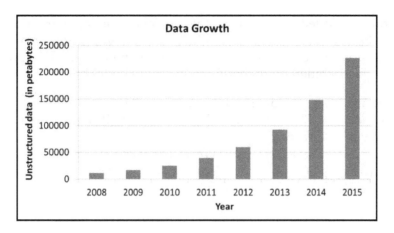

Figure 1.2: Increase in size of unstructured data (Ref: Enterprise strategy group 2010)

This explosion in data from 2008 to 2015 has led to a new field of data science where people put in a lot of effort to derive insights using all kinds of datasets such as structured, semi-structured, and unstructured. Thus, to efficiently deal with data scalability, it is important to efficiently store and retrieve datasets. For example, searching for a word in a dictionary would take a long time if the data is randomly organized; thus, sorted list data structures are utilized to ensure a faster search of words. Similarly, searching for an optimal path in a city based on the input location requires data about road network, position, and so on to be stored in the form of geometries. Ideally, even a variable stored as any built-in data type such as character, integer, or float can be considered as a data structure of scalar nature. However, data structure is formally defined as a scheme of organizing related information in a computer so that it can be used efficiently.

Similarly, for algorithms, given sufficient space and time, any dataset can be stored and processed to answer questions of interest. However, selecting the correct data structure will help you save a lot of memory and computational power. For example, assigning a float to integer data type, such as the number of customers coming in a day, will require double the memory. However, in the real-world scenario, computers are constrained by computational resources and space. Thus, a solution can be stated as efficient if it is able to achieve the desired goal in the given resources and time. Thus, this could be used as a cost function to compare the performance of different data structures while designing algorithms. There are two major design constraints to be considered while selecting the data structure:

- Analyze the problem to decide on the basic operation that must be supported into the selected data structure, such as inserting an item, deleting an item, and searching for an item
- Evaluate the resource constraint for each operation

The data structure is selected depending on the problem scenario, for example, a case where complete data is loaded at the beginning, and there is no change/insertion in data, requires similar data structure. However, similar including deletion into data structure will make data structure implementation more complex.

 Detailed steps to download the code bundle are mentioned in the Preface of this book. Please have a look. The code bundle for the book is also hosted on GitHub at `https://github.com/PacktPublishing/R-Data-St ructures-and-Algorithms`. We also have other code bundles from our rich catalog of books and videos available at `https://github.com/PacktP ublishing/`. Check them out!

Abstract data type and data structure

The **abstract data type** (**ADT**) is used to define high-level features and operations for data structure, and is required before we dig down into details of implementation of data structure. For example, before implementing a linked list, it would be good to know what we want to do with the defined linked list, such as:

- I should be able to insert an item into the linked list
- I should be able to delete an item from the linked list
- I should be able to search an item in the linked list
- I should be able to see whether the linked list is empty or not

The defined ADT will then be utilized to define the implementation strategy. We will discuss ADT for different data structures in more detail later in this book. Before getting into definitions of ADT, it's important to understand data types and their characteristics, as they will be utilized to build an ecosystem for the data structures.

Data type is a way to classify various types of data such as Boolean, integer, float, and string. To efficiently classify a dataset, the following characteristics are needed in any data type:

- **Atomic**: It should define a single concept
- **Traceable**: It should be able to map with the same data type
- **Accurate**: It should be unambiguous
- **Clear and concise**: It should be understandable

Data types can be classified into two types:

- Built-in data type
- Derived data type

Data types for which a language has built-in support are known as built-in data types. For example, R supports the following data types:

- Integers
- Float
- Boolean
- Character

Data types which are obtained by integrating the built-in data types with associated operations such as insertion, deletion, sorting, merging, and so on are referred to as derived data types, such as:

- List
- Array
- Stack
- Queue

Derived data types or data structures are studied on two components:

- Abstract data type or mathematical/logical models
- Programming implementation

ADT is the realization of a data type in software. In ADT, we usually look into high-level features and operations used by users for a data structure, but do not know how these features run in the background. For example, say a user using banking software with search functionality is searching for the transaction history of Mr. Smith, using the search feature of the software. The user does not have any idea about the operations performed, or the implementation details of the data structures. Thus, the behavior of ADT is managed by input and output only:

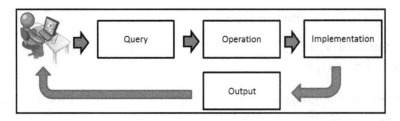

Figure 1.3: Framework for ADT

Thus, ADT does not know how the data type is implemented, as these details are hidden by the user and protected from outside access, a concept referred to as encapsulation. A data structure is the implementation part of ADT, which can be implemented in any programming language. ADT can be achieved by multiple implementation strategies, as shown in *Figure 1.4*:

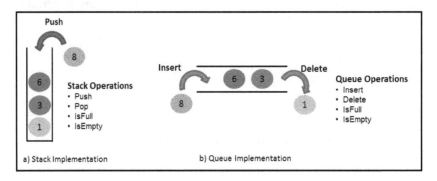

Figure 1.4: Illustration of stack and queue implementation using array with integer data type

The abstraction provided by ADT helps to manage programming complexity. The ADT is also referred to as logical form, as it decides the type and operations required for implementation. The ADT is implemented by using a particular type of data structure. The data structure used to implement ADT is referred to as the physical form of data type, as it manages storage using the implementation subroutine.

Relationship between problem and algorithm

Problem can be defined as the task to be performed. The execution of the task to be performed can be divided primarily into two components:

- Data
- Algorithm

However, there could be other controlling factors which could affect your approach development, such as problem constraints, resource constraints, computation time allowed, and so on.

The data component of the problem represents the information we are dealing with, such as numbers, text, files, and so on. For example, let's assume we want to maintain the company employee records, which include the employee name and their associated work details. This data needs to be maintained and updated regularly.

The algorithm part of a problem represents more of implementation details. It entails how we are going to manage the current data. Depending on the data and problem requirements, we select the data structure. Depending on the data structure, we have to define the algorithm to manage the dataset. For example, we can store the company employees dataset into a linked list or dictionary. Based on the defined data structure to store data approach for searching, insertion, and deletion and so on operations performed on data structure changes which is control by algorithms and implemented as program. Thus, we could state that a program is the step-by-step instructions given to a computer to do some operations:

$$Program = f(Algorithm, Data\ Structure)$$

To summarize, we could state that a program is the group of step-by-step instructions to solve a defined problem using the algorithm selected considering all problems and resource constraints. This book will use program representations using R to demonstrate the implementation of different data structures and algorithms.

Basics of R

R is a statistical programming language designed and created by Ross Ihaka and Robert Gentleman. It is a derivative of the S language created at the AT&T Bell laboratories. Apart from statistical analysis, R also supports powerful visualizations. It is open source, freely distributed under a **General Public License (GPL)**. **Comprehensive R Archive Network (CRAN)** is an ever-growing repository with more than 8,400 packages, which can be freely installed and used for various kinds of analysis.

R is a high-level language based on interpretations and intuitive syntax. It runs on system's or server's active memory (RAM) and stores all files, functions, and derived results in its environment as objects. The architecture utilized in R computation is shown in *Figure 1.5:*

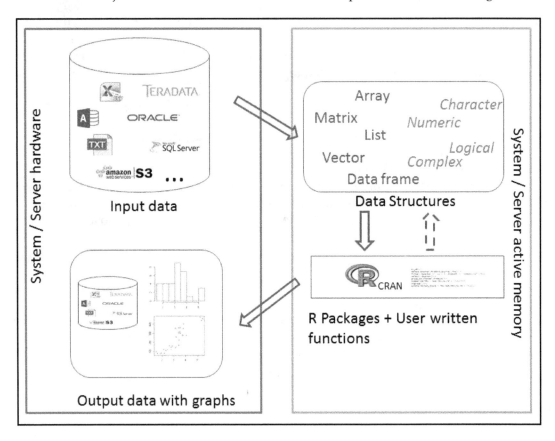

Figure 1.5: Illustrate architecture of R in local/server mode

Installation of R

R can be installed on any operating system, such as Windows, Mac OS X, and Linux. The installation files of the most recent version can be downloaded from any one of the mirror sites of CRAN: `https://cran.r-project.org/`. It is available under both 32-bit and 64-bit architectures.

The installation of `r-base-dev` is also highly recommended as it has many built-in functions. It also enables us to install and compile new R packages directly from the R console using the `install.packages()` command.

Upon installation, R can be called from program files, desktop shortcut, or from the command line. With default settings, the R console looks as follows:

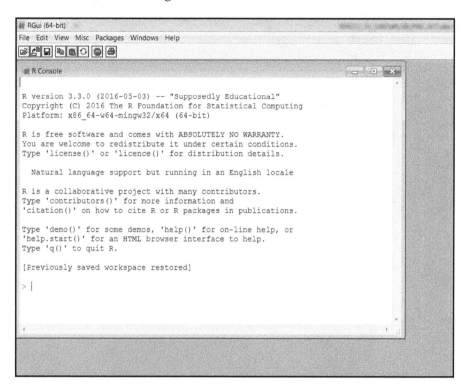

Figure 1.6: The R console in which one can start coding and evaluate results instantly

R can also be used as a kernel within Jupyter Notebook. Jupyter Notebook is a web-based application that allows you to combine documentation, output, and code. Jupyter can be installed using `pip`:

```
pip3 install --upgrade pip
pip3 install jupyter
```

To start Jupyter Notebook, open a shell/terminal and run this command to start the Jupyter Notebook interface in your browser:

```
jupyter notebook
```

To start a new R Notebook, click on right hand side New tab and select **R** kernel as shown in Figure 1.7. **R** kernel does not come as default in Jupyter Notebook with Python as prerequisite. Anaconda distribution is recommended to install python and Jupyter and can be downloaded from `https://www.continuum.io/downloads`. R essentials can be installed using below command.

```
conda install -c r r-essentials
```

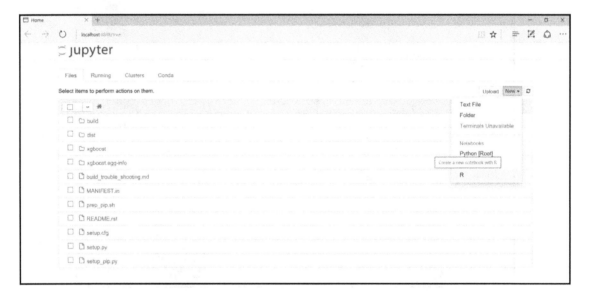

Figure 1.7: Jupyter Notebook for creating R notebooks

Once notebook is opened, you could start organizing your code into cells. As R does not require formal compilation, and executes codes on runtime, one can start coding and evaluate instant results. The console view can be modified using some options under the **Windows** tab. However, it is highly recommended to use an **Integrated Development Environment** (**IDE**), which would provide a powerful and productive user interface for R. One such widely used IDE is RStudio, which is free and open source. It comes with its own server (RStudio Server Pro) too. The interface of RStudio is as seen in the following screenshot:

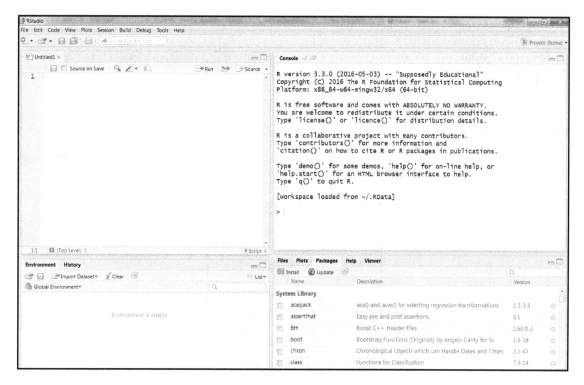

Figure 1.8: RStudio, a widely used IDE for R

Basic data types in R

R supports multiple types of data, which can be organized by dimensions and content type (homogeneous or heterogeneous), as shown in Table 1.1:

	Homogeneous	Heterogeneous
1-D	Atomic vector	List*
2-D	Matrix	Data Frame
n-D	Array	
*List can be converted into *n-D* by composite usage		

Table 1.1 Basic data structure in R

Homogeneous data structure is one which consists of the same content type, whereas heterogeneous data structure supports multiple content types. All other data structures, such as data tables, can be derived using these foundational data structures. Data types and their properties will be covered in detail in Chapter 3, *Linked Lists*.

Operations in R

The syntax of operators in R is very similar to other programming languages. The following is a list of operators along with their explanations.

The following table defines the various arithmetic operators:

Operators	Explanations
+	Addition
-	Subtraction
*	Multiplication
/	Division
** or ^	Exponentiation
%%	Modulus
%/%	Integer Quotient

Table 1.2 Basic arithmetic operators in R

The following table defines the various logical operators:

Operators	Explanations
==	Exact equal to
<	Less than
>	Greater than
<=	Less than or equal to
>=	Greater than or equal to

Table 1.3 Basic logical operators in R

An example of assigned in R is shown below. Initially a column vector V is assigned followed by operations on column vector such as addition, subtraction, square root and log. Any operation applied on column vector is element-wise operation.

```
> V <- c(1,2,3,4,5,6)   ## Assigning a vector V
> V
[1] 1 2 3 4 5 6
> V+10 ## Adding each element in vector V with 10
[1] 11 12 13 14 15 16
> V-1  ## Subtracting each element in vector V with 1
[1] 0 1 2 3 4 5
> sqrt(V)   ## Performing square root operation on each element in  vector V
[1] 1.000000 1.414214 1.732051 2.000000 2.236068 2.449490
> V1 <- log(V)   ## Storing log transformed of vector V as V1
> V1
[1] 0.0000000 0.6931472 1.0986123 1.3862944 1.6094379 1.7917595
```

Control structures in R

Control structures such as loops and conditions form an integral part of any programming language, and R supports them with much intuitive syntax.

If condition

The syntax for the if condition is as follows:

```
if (test expression)
{
   Statement upon condition is true
}
```

If the test expression is true, the statement is executed. If the statement is false, nothing happens.

In the following example, an atomic vector x is defined, and it is subjected to two conditions separately, that is, whether x is greater than 5 or less than 5. If either of the conditions gets satisfied, the value x gets printed in the console following the corresponding if statement:

```
> x <- 10
> if (x < 5) print(x)
> if (x > 5) print(x)
[1] 10
```

If...else condition

The syntax for the if...else condition is as follows:

```
if(test expression)
{
   Statement upon condition is true
} else {
   Statement upon condition is false
}
```

In this scenario, if the condition in the test expression is true, the statement under the if condition is executed, otherwise the statement under the else condition is executed.

The following is an example in which we define an atomic vector x with a value 10. Then, we verify whether x, when divided by 2, returns 1 (R reads 1 as a Boolean True). If it is True, the value x gets printed as an odd number, else as an even number:

```
> x=10
> if (x %% 2)
+ {
+    print(paste0(x, " :odd number"))
+ } else {
+    print(paste0(x, " :even number"))
+ }
[1] "10 :even number"
```

Ifelse function

An ifelse() function is a condition used primarily for vectors, and it is an equivalent form of the if...else statement. Here, the conditional function is applied to each element in the vector individually. Hence, the input to this function is a vector, and the output obtained is also a vector. The following is the syntax of the ifelse condition:

```
ifelse (test expression, statement upon condition is true,
statement upon condition is false)
```

In this function, the primary input is a test expression which must provide a logical output. If the condition is true, the subsequent statement is executed, else the last statement is executed.

The following is example in which a vector x is defined with integer values from 1 to 7. Then, a condition is applied on each element in vector x to determine whether the element is an odd number or an even number:

```
> x <- 1:6
> ifelse(x %% 2, paste0(x, " :odd number"), paste0(x, " :even  number"))
[1] "1 :odd number"   "2 :even number" "3 :odd number"
[4] "4 :even number" "5 :odd number"   "6 :even number"
```

For() loop

A `for` loop is primarily used to iterate a statement over a vector of values in a given sequence. The vector can be of any type, that is, numeric, character, Boolean, or complex. For every iteration, the statement is executed.

The following is the syntax of the `for` loop:

```
for(x in sequence vector)
{
   Statement to be iterated
}
```

The loop continues till all the elements in the vector get exhausted as per the given sequence.

The following example details a `for` loop. Here, we assign a vector x, and each element in vector x is printed in the console using a `for` loop:

```
> x <- c("John", "Mary", "Paul", "Victoria")
> for (i in seq(x)) {
+    print(x[i])
+ }
[1] "John"
[1] "Mary"
[1] "Paul"
[1] "Victoria"
```

Nested for( ) loop

The nested `for` loop can be defined as a set of multiple `for` loops within each `for` loop as shown here:

```
for( x in sequence vector)
{
    First statement to be iterated
    for(y in sequence vector)
{
    Second statement to be iterated
    . . . . . . . . .

}
}
```

In a nested `for` loop, each subsequent `for` loop is iterated for all the possible times based on the sequence vector in the previous `for` loop. This can be explained using the following example, in which we define mat as a matrix (3×3), and our desired objective is to obtain a series of summations which will end up with the total sum of all the values within the matrix. Firstly, we initialize sum to 0, and then subsequently, sum gets updated by adding itself to all the elements in the matrix in a sequence. The sequence is defined by the nested `for` loop, wherein for each row in a matrix, each of the values in all the columns gets added to sum:

```
> mat <- matrix(1:9, ncol = 3)
> sum <- 0
> for (i in seq(nrow(mat)))
+ {
+     for (j in seq(ncol(mat)))
+     {
+         sum <- sum + mat[i, j]
+         print(sum)
+     }
+ }
[1] 1
[1] 5
[1] 12
[1] 14
[1] 19
[1] 27
[1] 30
[1] 36
[1] 45
```

While loop

In R, while loops are iterative loops with a specific condition which needs to be satisfied. The syntax of the while loop is as follows:

```
while (test expression)
{
  Statement upon condition is true (iteratively)
}
```

Let's understand the while loop in detail with an example. Here, an object i is initialized to 1. The test expression which needs to be satisfied for every iteration is i<10. Since i = 1, the condition is TRUE, and the statement within the while loop is evaluated. According to the statement, i is printed on the console, and then increased by 1 unit. Now i increments to 2, and once again, the test expression, whether the condition (i < 10) is true or false, is checked. If TRUE, the statement is again evaluated. The loop continues till the condition becomes false, which, in our case, will happen when i increments to 10. Here, incrementing i becomes very critical, without which the loop can turn into infinite iterations:

```
> i <- 1
> while (i < 10)
+ {
+   print(i)
+   i <- i + 1
+ }
[1] 1
[1] 2
[1] 3
[1] 4
[1] 5
[1] 6
[1] 7
[1] 8
[1] 9
```

Special statements in loops

In R, the loops can be altered using break or next statements. This helps in inducing other conditions required within the statement inside the loop.

Break statement

The syntax for the Break statement is `break`. It is used to terminate a loop and stop the remaining iterations. If a `break` statement is provided within a nested loop, then the innermost loop within which the `break` statement is mentioned gets terminated, and iterations of the outer loops are not affected.

The following is an example in which a `for` loop is terminated when i reaches the value 8:

```
> for (i in 1:30)
+ {
+    if (i < 8)
+    {
+      print (paste0 ("Current value is ",i))
+    } else {
+      print (paste0 ("Current value is ",i," and the loop breaks"))
+      break
+    }
+ }
[1] "Current value is 1"
[1] "Current value is 2"
[1] "Current value is 3"
[1] "Current value is 4"
[1] "Current value is 5"
[1] "Current value is 6"
[1] "Current value is 7"
[1] "Current value is 8 and the loop breaks"
```

Next statement

The syntax for a Next statement is `next`. The `next` statements are used to skip intermediate iterations within a loop based on a condition. Once the condition for the `next` statement is met, all the subsequent operations within the loop get terminated, and the next iteration begins.

This can be further explained using an example in which we print only odd numbers based on a condition that the printed number, when divided by 2, leaves the remainder 1.

```
> for (i in 1:10)
+ {
+    if (i %% 2)
+    {
+      print (paste0 (i, " is an odd number."))
+    } else {
+      next
+    }
```

```
+ }
[1] "1 is an odd number."
[1] "3 is an odd number."
[1] "5 is an odd number."
[1] "7 is an odd number."
[1] "9 is an odd number."
```

Repeat loop

The `repeat` loop is an infinite loop which iterates multiple times without any inherent condition. Hence, it becomes mandatory for the user to explicitly mention the terminating condition, and use a `break` statement to terminate the loop.

The following is the syntax for a `repeat` statement:

```
repeat
{
   Statement to iterate along with explicit terminate condition
   including break statement
}
```

In the current example, `i` is initialized to 1. Then, a `for` loop iterates, within which an object cube is evaluated and verified using a condition whether the cube is greater than 729 or not. Simultaneously, `i` is incremented by 1 unit. Once the condition is met, the `for` loop is terminated using a `break` statement:

```
> i <- 1
> repeat
+ {
+    cube <- i ** 3
+    i <- i + 1
+    if (cube < 729)
+    {
+      print(paste0(cube, " is less than 729. Let's remain in the
         loop."))
+    } else {
+      print(paste0(cube, " is greater than or equal to 729. Let's exit
         the loop."))
+      break
+    }
+ }
[1] "1 is less than 729. Let's remain in the loop."
[1] "8 is less than 729. Let's remain in the loop."
[1] "27 is less than 729. Let's remain in the loop."
[1] "64 is less than 729. Let's remain in the loop."
[1] "125 is less than 729. Let's remain in the loop."
```

```
[1] "216 is less than 729. Let's remain in the loop."
[1] "343 is less than 729. Let's remain in the loop."
[1] "512 is less than 729. Let's remain in the loop."
[1] "729 is greater than 729. Let's exit the loop."
```

First class functions in R

R is primarily a functional language at its core. In R, functions are treated just like any other data types, and are considered as first-class citizens. The following example shows that R considers everything as a function call.

Here, the operator + is a function in itself:

```
> 10+20
[1] 30
> "+"(10,20)
[1] 30
```

Here, the operator ^ is also a function in itself:

```
> 4^2
[1] 16
> "^"(4,2)
[1] 16
```

Now, let's dive deep into functional concepts, which are crucial and widely used by R programmers.

Vectorized functions are among the most popular functional concepts which enable the programmer to execute functions at an individual element level for a given vector. This vector can also be a part of dataframe, matrix, or a list. Let's understand this in detail using the following example, in which we would like to have an operation on each element in a given vector V_in. The operation is to square each element within the vector and output it as vector V_out. We will implement them using three approaches as follows:

Approach 1: Here, the operations will be performed at the element level using a for loop. This is the most primitive of all the three approaches in which vector allocation is being performed using the style of S language:

```
> V_in <- 1:100000      ## Input Vector
> V_out <- c()          ## Output Vector
> for(i in V_in)        ## For loop on Input vector
+ {
```

```
+    V_out <- c(V_out,i^2)   ## Storing on Output vector
+ }
```

Approach 2: Here, the vectorized functional concept will be used to obtain the same objective. The loops in vectorized programming are implemented in C language, and hence, perform much faster than `for` loops implemented in R (*Approach 1*). The time elapsed to run this operation is instantaneous:

```
> V_in <- 1:100000      ## Input Vector
> V_out <- V_in^2        ## Output Vector
```

Approach 3: Here, higher order functions (or nested functions) are used to obtain the same objective. As functions are considered first class citizens in R, these can be called as an argument within another function. The widely used nested functions are in the apply family. The following table provides a summary of the various types of functions within the apply family:

Function	Input data type	Output data type
apply	dataframe or matrix or array (with margins)	vector, matrix, array, list
lapply	vector, list, variables in dataframe or matrix	list
sapply	vector, list, variables in dataframe or matrix	matrix, vector, list
mapply (multivariate sapply)	vector, list, variables in dataframe or matrix	matrix, vector, list
tapply	ragged array	array
rapply	vector, list, variables in	list

Table 1.4 Various types of functions in the apply family

Now, lets' evaluate the first class function through examples. An `apply` function can be applied to a dataframe, matrix, or array. Let's illustrate it using a matrix:

```
> x <- cbind(x1 = 7, x2 = c(7:1, 2:5))
> col.sums <- apply(x, 2, sum)
> row.sums <- apply(x, 1, sum)
```

The `lapply` is a first class function to be applied to a vector, list, or variables in a dataframe or matrix. An example of `lapply` is shown below:

```
> x <- list(x1 = 7:1, x2 = c(7:1, 2:5))
> lapply(x, mean)
```

The use of the `sapply` function for a vector input using customized function is shown below:

```
> V_in <- 1:100000 ## Input Vector
> V_out <- sapply(V_in,function(x) x^2) ## Output Vector
```

The function `mapply` is a multivariate `sapply`. The `mapply` function is the first input, followed by input parameters as shown below:

```
mapply(FUN, ..., MoreArgs = NULL, SIMPLIFY = T, USE.NAMES = T)
```

An example of `mapply` to replicated two vector can be obtained as:

```
> mapply(rep, 1:6, 6:1)
```

The function call `rep` function in R with input from 1 to 6 and is replicated as 6 to 1 using the second dimension of the `mapply` function. The `tapply` applies a function to each cell of the ragged array. For example, let's create a list with a multiple array:

```
> dat<- list(c(4, 2, 6, 1, 5), c("P", "S", "N", "K", "K"))
> tapply(1:5, dat, sum)
   K  N  P  S
1  4 NA NA NA
2 NA NA NA  2
4 NA NA  1 NA
5  5 NA NA NA
6 NA  3 NA NA
```

The output is a relationship between two vectors with position as a value. The function `rapply` is a recursive function for lapply as shown below:

```
> X <- list(list(a = pi, b = list(c = 1:1)), d = "a test")
> rapply(X, sqrt, classes = "numeric", how = "replace")
```

The function applies sqrt to all numeric classes in the list and replace it with new values.

Exercises

1. Can you think of ways in which we can extract a few attributes (columns) and observations (rows) based on a certain condition?

    - Dataset – El Nino dataset from UCI KDD (`https://kdd.ics.uci.edu /databases/el_nino/el_nino.html`)
    - Filter for latitude and longitude with humidity > 88% and air temperature < 25.5 degree Celsius
    - 10,000 iterations for evaluating each expression

2. Can we add multiple arguments within a function in the `apply` family? If yes, what is the syntax for assigning multiple arguments?
3. A general notion states that `for` loops are slower than the `apply` functions. Is it true or false? If false, what are the conditions in which the notion gets negated?
4. Define ADT for calculating the area of any geometrical object, such as a circle, square, and so on.

Summary

Computational power has been continuously increasing in the last couple of decades, and so does the amount of data captured by different industries. To cope with data size, faster and efficient information retrieval is an eminent requirement.

In this chapter, you were introduced to ADT and data structure. ADT is used to define high-level features and operations representing different data structures, and algorithms are used to implement ADT. A data type should be atomic, traceable, accurate, and have clear and concise characteristic properties for efficiency along with unambiguity. You also learned the basics of R, including data type, conditional loops, control structure, and first class functions.

The computational time taken by an algorithm is most important objective considered while selecting data structures and algorithms. The next chapter will provide the fundamentals for the analysis of algorithms.

2
Algorithm Analysis

An algorithm can be defined as a set of step-by-step instructions which govern the outline of a program that needs to be executed using computational resources. The execution can be in any programming language such as R, Python, and Java. Data is an intricate component of any program, and depending on how data is organized (data structure), your execution time can vary drastically. That's why data structure is such a critical component of any good algorithm implementation. This book will concentrate primarily on running time or time complexity and partly on memory utilization and their relationship during program execution. The current chapter will cover following topics in detail:

- Best, worst, and average cases
- Computer versus algorithm
- Algorithm asymptotic analysis
    - Upper bounds evaluation
    - Lower bounds evaluation
    - Big Θ notation
    - Simplifying rules
    - Classifying functions
- Computation evaluation of a program
- Analyzing problems
- Space bounds
- Empirical analysis

Getting started with data structure

Data structure is a critical component in any algorithm. Before we go into details; let's illustrate this with an example; a sorting algorithm for positive integer for a finite length needs to be programmed using user input, and the output is to be displayed in ascending order. The sorting algorithm, which acts as a connector between the user-defined input and user-desired output can be approached in multiple ways:

- Bubble sort and shell sort, which are simple variants of sorting, but are highly inefficient
- Insertion sort and selection sort, primarily used for sorting small datasets
- Merge sort, heap sort, and quick sort, which are efficient ways of sorting based on the complexities involved in an average system runtime
- Distributed sorts such as counting sort, bucket sort, and radix sort, which can handle both runtime and memory usage

Each of these options can, in turn, handle a particular set of instances more effectively. This essentially reduces the concept of **good algorithm**. An algorithm can be termed as good if it possesses attributes such as the following among many others:

- Shorter running time
- Lesser memory utilization
- Simplicity in reading the code
- Generality in accepting inputs

In general, a problem can be approached using multiple algorithms, and each algorithm can be assessed based on certain parameters such as:

- System runtime
- Memory requirement

However, these parameters are generally affected by external environmental factors such as:

- Handling of data structures
- System software and hardware configurations
- Style of writing and compiling codes
- Programming language

As it is almost impossible to control all external parameters, it becomes difficult to estimate the system runtime of multiple algorithms for performance comparison (ideal scenario analysis). Ideal scenario analysis requires algorithms to be implemented and executed for evaluating algorithm performance. However, in a scenario where the user is trying to design an algorithm, asymptotic analysis is utilized to evaluate algorithm performance.

Asymptotic analysis assesses algorithm's efficiency without actually coding and compiling the entire program. It is a functional form representing pseudo system runtime based on the size of input data and number of operations. It is based on the principle that the growth rate of input data is directly proportional to the system runtime. For example, in the case of insertion sorting, the size represents the length of the input vector, and the number of operations represents the complexity of sort operations. This analysis can only be used to gauge the consideration of implementing the algorithm rather than evaluating the comparative merits and demerits of algorithms. The following table represents the most widely used growth rate functional forms. The details are mentioned in later parts of the chapter.

Size of Input data n	Double log form $\log\log n$	Single log form $\log n$	Linear form n	N times log form $n*\log n$	Quadratic form n^2	Cubic form n^3	Exponential form 2^n
4	1	2	2^2	2^3	2^4	2^6	2^4
16	2	4	2^4	2^6	2^8	2^{12}	2^{16}
256	3	8	2^8	2^{11}	2^{16}	2^{24}	2^{256}
512	~3.2	9	2^9	~2^{12}	2^{18}	2^{27}	2^{512}
1,024	~3.3	10	2^{10}	2^{13}	2^{20}	2^{30}	2^{1024}
5,000	~3.62	~12.28	2^{12}	~2^{16}	~2^{24}	~2^{36}	2^{5000}
10,000	~3.73	~13.28	2^{13}	~2^{17}	~2^{26}	~2^{39}	2^{10000}
50,000	~3.96	~15.61	2^{16}	~2^{20}	~2^{32}	~2^{49}	2^{50000}
100,000	~4.05	~16.61	2^{17}	~2^{21}	~2^{34}	~2^{51}	2^{100000}
1000,000	~4.31	~19.93	2^{20}	~2^{24}	~2^{40}	~2^{60}	$2^{1000000}$

Figure 2.1: Different growth rate functional form used for complexity evaluation

The most widely used functional forms of growth rates are based on the size of input data, which are used to analyze the performance of algorithms. These are also considered as pseudo-functional forms to evaluate algorithm's system runtime.

Memory management in R

Memory management primarily deals with the administration of available memory and the prediction of additional memory required for smoother and faster execution of functions. The current section will cover the concept of **memory allocation**, which deals with storage of an object in the R environment.

During memory allocation R allocates memory differently to different objects in its environment. Memory allocation can be determined using the `object_size` function from the `pryr` package. The `pryr` package can be installed from the CRAN repository using `install.packages("pryr")`. The package is available for *R (≥ 3.1.0)*. The `object_size` function in `pryr` is similar to the `object.size` function in the base package. However, it is more accurate as it takes into account the:

- Environment size associated with the current object
- Shared elements within a given object under consideration.

The following are examples of using the `object_size` function in R to evaluate memory allocation:

```
> object_size(1)    ## Memory allocated for a single numeric vector
48 B
> object_size("R")  ## Memory allocated for a single character vector
96 B
> object_size(TRUE) ## Memory allocated for a single logical vector
48 B
> object_size(1i)   ## Memory allocated for a single complex vector
56 B
```

The storage required by an object can be attributed to the following parameters:

- **Metadata**: Metadata of an object is defined by the type of object used such as character, integers, logical, and so on. The type can also usually be helpful during debugging.
- **Node pointer**: The node pointer maintains the link between the different nodes, and depending on the number of node pointers used, memory requirement changes. For example, a doubly linked list requires more memory than a singly linked list, as it uses two node pointers to connect to the previous and next nodes.
- **Attribute pointer**: Pointer to keep reference for attributes; this helps to reduce memory allocation, especially the data stored by a variable.
- **Memory allocation**: Length of the vector representing the currently used space.
- **Size**: Size represent the true allocated space length of the vector.

- **Memory padding**: Padding applied to a component, for example, each element begins after an 8-byte boundary.

The `Object_size()` command is also used to see the inherent memory allocation as shown in the following table:

S. No.	Data Type	Package	Memory allocation (Bytes)
1	Numeric	base	40
2	Character	base	40
3	Logical	base	40
4	Complex	base	40
5	Vector	base	40
6	List	base	40
7	Matrix	base	208
8	Data Frame	base	560
9	Data Table	data.table	846

Figure 2.2: Memory allocated during initialization of different data types in R

The preceding table shows inherent memory allocated by each data structure/type.

Let's simulate scenarios with varying lengths of a vector with different data types such as integer, character, Boolean, and complex. The simulation is performed by varying vector length from 0 to 60 as follows:

```
> vec_length <- 0:60
> num_vec_size <- sapply(vec_length, function(x) object_size(seq(x)))
> char_vec_size <- sapply(vec_length, function(x)
object_size(rep("a",x)))
> log_vec_size <- sapply(vec_length, function(x)
object_size(rep(TRUE,x)))
> comp_vec_size <- sapply(vec_length, function(x)
object_size(rep("2i",x)))
```

`Num_vec_size` computes the memory requirement for each numeric vector from zero to 60 number of elements. These elements are integers increasing sequentially, as stated in the function. Similarly, incremental memory requirements are calculated for character (`char_vec_size`), logical (`log_vec_size`), and complex (`comp_vec_size`) vectors. The result obtained from the simulation can be plotted using code:

```
> par(mfrow=c(2,2))
> plot(num_vec_size ~ vec_length, xlab = "Numeric seq vector", ylab =
"Memory allocated (in bytes)",
+ type = "n")
```

```
> abline(h = (c(0,8,16,32,48,64,128)+40), col = "grey")
> lines(num_vec_size, type = "S")
```

The result obtained on running the preceding code is shown in *Figure 2.3*. It can be observed that memory allocated to a vector is a function of its length and the object type used. However, the relationship does not seem to be linear rather, it seems to increase in step. This is due to the fact that for better and consistent performance, R initially assigns big blocks of memory from RAM and handles them internally. These memory blocks are individually assigned to vectors based on the type and the number of elements within. Initially, memory blocks seem to be irregular towards a particular level (128 bytes for numeric/logical vector, and 176 bytes for character/complex vectors), and later become stable with small increments of 8 bytes as can be seen in the plots:

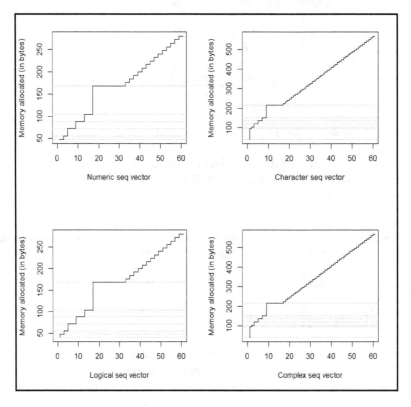

Figure 2.3: Memory allocation based on length of vector

Due to initial memory allocation differences, numeric and logical vectors show similar memory allocation patterns, and complex vectors behave similarly to the character vectors. Memory management helps to efficiently run an algorithm however before the execution of any program, we should evaluate it based on its runtime. In the next sub-section, we will discuss the basic concepts involved in obtaining the runtime of any function, and its comparison with similar functions.

System runtime in R

System runtime is essential for benchmarking different algorithms. The process helps us to compare different options, and to pick the best algorithm. Benchmarking of different algorithms will be dealt with in detail in subsequent chapters.

The `microbenchmark` package on CRAN is used to evaluate the runtime of any expression/function/code at an accuracy of a sub-millisecond. It is an accurate replacement to the `system.time()` function. Also, all the evaluations are performed in C code to minimize any overhead. The following methods are used to measure the time elapsed:

- The `QueryPerformanceCounter` interface on Windows OS
- The `clock_gettime` API on Linux OS
- The `mach_absolute_time` function on MAC OS
- The `gethrtime` function on Solaris OS

In our current example, we will be using the `mtcars` data, which is in the package datasets. This data is obtained from *1974 Motor Trend US* magazine, which comprises of fuel consumption comparison along with 10 automobile designs and the performance of 32 automobiles (1973-74 models).

Now, we would like to perform an operation in which a specific numeric attribute (**miles per gallon (mpg)** needs to be averaged to the corresponding unique values in an integer attribute (carb means no of carburetors). This can be performed using multiple ways such as `aggregate`, `group_by`, `by`, `split`, `ddply(plyr)`, `tapply`, `data.table`, `dplyr`, `sqldf`, `dplyr` and so on. For illustration, we have used the following four ways:

- `aggregate` function:

    ```
    aggregate(mpg~carb,data=mtcars,mean)
    ```

- `ddply` from `plyr` package:

    ```
    ddply( mtcars, .(carb),function(x) mean(x$mpg))
    ```

- `data.table` format:

```
library(data.table)
mtcars_tb = data.table(mtcars)
mtcars_tb[,mean(mpg),by=carb]
```

- `group_by` function:

```
library(dplyr)
summarize(group_by(mtcars, carb), mean(mpg))
```

Then, `microbenchmark` is used to determine the performance of each of the four ways mentioned in the preceding list. Here, we will be evaluating each expression 100 times.

```
> library(microbenchmark)
> MB_res <- microbenchmark(
+   Aggregate_func=aggregate(mpg~carb,data=mtcars,mean),
+   Ddply_func=ddply( mtcars,  .(carb),function(x) mean(x$mpg)),
+   Data_table_func = mtcars_tb[,mean(mpg),by=carb],
+   Group_by_func = summarize(group_by(mtcars, carb), mean(mpg)),
+   times=1000
+ )
```

The output table is as follows:

```
> MB_res
Unit: microseconds
             expr       min         lq        mean    median         uq        max neval
   Aggregate_func   851.489   913.8015   1001.9007   944.775  1000.4905   6094.209  1000
       Ddply_func  1370.519  1475.1685   1579.6123  1517.322  1575.7855   6598.578  1000
  Data_table_func   493.739   552.7540    610.7791   577.495   621.6635   3125.179  1000
    Group_by_func   932.129  1008.5540   1095.4193  1033.113  1076.1825   4279.435  1000
```

The output plot demonstrating distribution of execution time from each approach is shown in *Figure 2.4*:

```
> library(ggplot2)
> autoplot(MB_res)
```

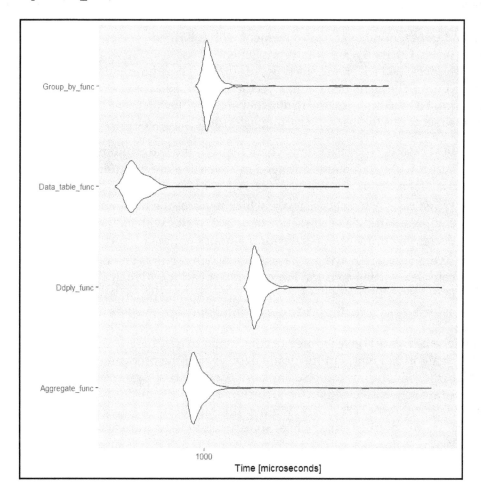

Figure 2.4: Distribution of time (microseconds) for 1000 iterations in each type of aggregate operation

Among these four expressions and for the given dataset, `data.table` has performed effectively in less possible time as compared to the others. However, expressions need to be tested under scenarios with a high number of observations, high number of attributes, and prior to finalizing the best operator.

Best, worst, and average cases

Based on the performance in terms of system runtime, a code can be classified under best, worst or average category for a particular algorithm. Let's consider a sorting algorithm to understand this in detail. A sorting algorithm is used to arrange a numeric vector in an ascending order, wherein the output vector should have the smallest number as its first element and largest number as its last element with intermediate elements in subsequent increasing order. Currently, we will be implementing insertion sorting, however Chapter 5, *Sorting Algorithms*, will cover various types of sorting algorithms in detail. In insertion sorting algorithm, the elements within a vector are arranged based on moving positions. The best, worst and average cases are data dependent. Now, let's define best, worst and average case scenarios for insertion sorting algorithm.

- **Best case**: A best case is one which requires the least running time. For example–a vector with all elements arranged in increasing order requires the least amount of time for sorting.
- **Worst case**: A worst case is one which requires the maximum possible runtime to complete sorting a vector. For example–a vector with all the elements sorted in decreasing order requires the most amount of time for sorting.
- **Average case**: An average case is one which requires an intermediate time to complete sorting a vector. For example–a vector with half elements sorted in increasing order and the remaining in decreasing order. An average case is assessed using multiple vectors of differently arranged elements.

Generally, the best-case scenarios are not considered to benchmark an algorithm, since it evaluates an algorithm most optimistically. However, if the probability of occurrence of best case is high, then algorithms can be compared using the best-case scenarios. Similar to best-case, worst-case scenarios evaluate the algorithm most pessimistically. It is only used to benchmark algorithms which are used in real-time applications, such as railway network controls, air traffic controls, and the like. Sometimes, when we are not aware of input data distributions, it is safe to assess the performance of the algorithm based on the worst-case scenario.

Most of the time, average-case scenario is used as a representative measure of algorithm's performance; however, this is valid only when we are aware of the input data distribution. Average-case scenarios may not evaluate the algorithm properly if the distribution of input data is skewed. In the case of sorting, if most of the input vectors are arranged in descending order, the average-case scenario may not be the best form of evaluating the algorithm.

In a nutshell, realtime application scenarios, along with input data distribution, are major criterions to analyze the algorithms based on best, worst, and average cases.

Computer versus algorithm

This section primarily deals with details on the trade-off between a computer's configuration and an algorithm's runtime. Let's consider two computers A and B, with B being 10 times faster than A, along with an algorithm whose system runtime is around 60 minutes in computer A for a dataframe of 100,000 observations. The functional form of algorithm's system runtime is n^{3*}. However, this functional form can be considered as an equivalent to the growth in the number of operations required to complete the running of the algorithm. In other words, the functional form of system runtime and the growth rate is same. The following situations will help us understand the trade-off in detail:

Situation 1: Will computer B, which is ten times faster than computer A, be able to reduce the system runtime of the algorithm to six minutes from the current 60 minutes?

This is perhaps yes, provided the size of the dataset remains consistent in both computers A and B. However, if we increase the size of the dataframe by 10 times, the following situation arises.

Situation 2: Will the algorithm in computer B be able to run the increased dataframe of 1,000,000 observations in 60 minutes, as computer B is 10 times faster than computer A?

This becomes tricky, as we are dealing not only with a change in computer configuration but also change in the size of input data, which makes the algorithm perform non-linearly (in our case-cubic form). The following table elucidates the capacity of computer B, which is 10 times faster than computer A, to handle the increase in size of the input dataframe, which can be run in a fixed time period for a given functional form of the algorithm's growth rate. Assume that computer A can perform 100,000 operations in 60 minutes, whereas computer B can perform 1,000,000 operations in 60 minutes. The *k is a constant positive real number ~ same time period of x minutes for computer A and computer B.

Functional form of growth rate f(n)	~Size of dataframe to perform 100,000 operations in computer A (n_1)	~Size of dataframe to perform 1,000,000 operations in computer B (n_2)	Methodological change of n_1 towards n_2	Ratio of n_2 upon n_1
k * n	100,000 / k	1,000,000/k	$n_2 = 10 * n_1$	10
$k*Log_{10}(n)$	$10^{100,000/k}$	$10^{1,000,000/k}$	$n_2 = \sqrt[k]{10}\, n_1$	$\sqrt[k]{10}$
$k*nLog_{10}(n)$	$10^{100,000/k}$ > $n_1 > \sqrt{(100,000/k)}$	$10^{1,000,000/k}$ > $n_2 > \sqrt{(1,000,000/k)}$	$\sqrt{10} * n1 < n_2 < k * n_1$	$\sqrt{10}$ to 10
$k*n^2$	$\sqrt{(100,000/k)}$	$\sqrt{(1,000,000/k)}$	$n_2 = \sqrt{10} * n_1$	$\sqrt{10}$
$k*n^3$	$\sqrt[3]{100,000/k}$	$\sqrt[3]{1,000,000/k}$	$n_2 = \sqrt[3]{10} * n_1$	$\sqrt[3]{10}$
$k*2^n$	$Log_2(100,000/k)$	$Log_2(1,000,000/k)$	$n_2 = Log_{10^5/k}(10^6/k) * n_1$	$Log_{10^5/k}(10^6/k)$

Figure 2.5: Performance comparison of widely used growth rate functions using two different sizes of dataframes

Let's understand each functional form of algorithm's growth rate:

- **Linear form**: From *Figure 2.5*, it can be seen that for any constant k, computer B can process 10 times bigger input dataframe within the same time period of 60 minutes. In other words, the processing speed of an algorithm with a linear runtime functional form is independent of the constant k, which affects the runtime behavior of the absolute size of input data. Also, for a given fixed runtime, if a system is i times faster than another system, then the data handling capacity of the faster system is also i times higher than the slower system. Hence, relative performance of the two computers is independent of the algorithm's growth rate constant k.

- **Square and cubic form**: We can see that for any constant k, computer B can process only the square root of 10 (3.16) and cube root of 10 (2.15) times the input dataframe within the same time period of 60 minutes. Here also, the performance of computer B is not affected by the constant k, which affects the absolute size of the input data size. In other words, computer B, which is 10 times faster than computer A, can run only 3.6 (square root of performance increase in case of square function form) times of the data in a given fixed time period, unlike 10 times as in the case of linear form. Hence, as computers perform much faster, the benefit attained towards the size of input data becomes highly disproportionate due to the inherent nature of ith *root (where i is 2,3,4, and so on).*

- **Logarithmic form**: For this functional form two variants are widely used:
  - **Log(n)**: The increment in size of the input dataframe is dependent on two factors–one being the increment in the system's computing performance, and other being the constant k. However, disparity between the system's increase in computing configuration and its performance continues as the increase in size of input data is directly proportional to k^{th} root of increment in the system's performance.
  - **nLog(n)**: The enhancement in handling higher input data size upon increase in the system's computing performance is greater than the improvement obtained using the quadratic functional form, but lower than algorithms with a linear functional form.

- **Power form (exponential)**: In power form, the system runtime of the algorithm increases exponentially upon increase in size of input data. For $k= 1$, the size of the input data to perform 100,000 operations in computer A is ~11. Similarly, the size of the input data to perform 1,000,000 operations in computer B is ~14. Hence, $n_2 = n_1 + 3$. This clearly shows that a system with 10 times increase in performance can handle only a marginal increase in data size within a given, fixed runtime period. The increase in size of the input data for an algorithm with an exponential or power functional form is almost additive rather than multiplicative. In other words, if the algorithm in computer A has a system runtime of 60 minutes for a data size of 100,000 observations, then computer B, which is 10 times faster than computer A, can run only an input data of size 100,003 observations in 60 minutes. Thus, the performance of algorithms with an exponential functional form is much different than the remaining growth functional forms.

Now, let's dive deep into situation 3, which deals with comparing the trade-off between algorithms and computers.

Situation 3: Which scenario is better for an algorithm with a growth rate functional form of n^3– to increase the computer's performance capability, or to reconfigure the algorithm to change its growth rate functional form?

As we have already assessed the scenario of increasing the system's performance capability under *Situation 2*, let's now try to analyze the situation of reconfiguring the algorithm's growth rate functional form.

Currently, our algorithm possesses a functional form of n^3. For an input data of size 1,000, the total number of operations required is $1,000^3$. Suppose, if the current algorithm can be reconfigured to $nLog_{10}(n)$, then the total number of operations would reduce to 3,000, which is much lower than $1,000^3$. As the number of operations using n^3 is more than 10 times the number of operations using $nLog_{10}(n)$ for every $n>2$, it is more advisable to reconfigure the growth functional form of the algorithm rather than increase the computational performance capability by 10 times.

To summarize the trade-off:

- Algorithms with slower growth rate show a better performance in handling larger data observations upon upgrading the computer's computational configuration
- The rate of handling larger data sets by algorithms with a faster growth rate may not be proportionately handled upon increasing the computer's computational capability

Algorithm asymptotic analysis

As we learned earlier, an algorithm is a step by step procedure designed to analyze and compute a given problem in a language understandable by a computer. Asymptotic analysis of an algorithm is a mathematical representation to determine its runtime performance or growth rate with the necessary boundary conditions. The boundary conditions depend on factors such as computer configurations, growth in the size of input data, coefficient of the growth rate function (also referred to as constant (k) in section *Computer versus algorithm*), and others. However, the capability to handle larger data sets is more dependent on the increment in computational performance of computers rather than on the constant term in the growth rate functional form. Also, the curves of different growth rate functional forms do intersect irrespective of the value of the constant in those equations. Thus, the constants in the growth rate or system runtime functional forms are generally ignored while comparing performances at computer level or at the algorithm level. Nevertheless, it is desirable to consider constants in the following situations:

- If the data size is very small, and the algorithm is designed optimally for larger datasets.
- If we need to compare algorithms whose constants differ by a very large factor. However, this happens very rarely, since the algorithms with a very slow growth rate are generally not considered.

Asymptotic analysis is also used to determine the best, worst, and average case of an algorithm, as it is a function of input size which evaluates the runtime of the algorithm. For example, the performance of a sorting algorithm can be evaluated using the incremental length of input vectors. The following are asymptotic functions for standard insertion sorting and merge sorting:

- **Standard insertion sorting**: $f(n) = \alpha + c*n^2$
- **Standard merge sorting**: $f(n) = \alpha + c*n*log_2(n)$

In the preceding two functions, α and c are constants and n is the length of the input vector.

One needs to bear in mind that asymptotic analysis provides only a ballpark estimation of the algorithm's performance in terms of system runtime consumption.

The following asymptotic notations are commonly used to determine the complexity in calculating the runtime of an algorithm.

Upper bounds or Big O notation

The upper bound of an algorithm's running time is denoted as O. It is used in evaluating worst-case scenarios, and determines the longest running time for any given length of an input vector. In other words, it is the maximum growth rate of an algorithm.

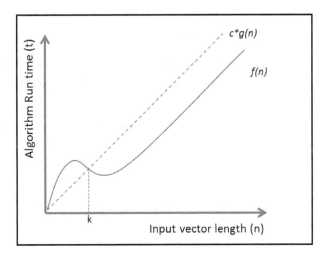

Figure 2.6: f(n) is Big O of g(n) for all n>k

Let us consider two functions, f and g, which determine an algorithm's runtime *t* based on varying input vector length *n*. These functional forms *f(n)* and *g(n)* should be non-negative or non-decreasing, because as the length of the input vector increases, the running time of the algorithm practically increases. These functional forms are equivalent to the running time of best, average, and worst-case scenarios of any given algorithm.

As we can see, initially $c*g(n)$ is lower than *f(n)* for values of *n<k*, and subsequently, $c*g(n)$ is higher than *f(n)* for *n>k*. Thus, the upper bound of the algorithm can be represented as follows:

$f(n) = O(g(n))$ that is–$f(n) < c*g(n)$ for *n>k>0* and *c>0*.

Therefore an algorithm with a growth rate *f(n)* is known as Big O of *g(n)* only when *f(n)* executes faster than *g(n)* for all possible inputs *n* (*n>k>0*) and any constant *c* (*c>0*).

Now, let's consider an algorithm whose running time can be expressed as *f(n)* of polynomial order 2, and we need to determine *g(n)*, which represents the upper bound for *f(n)*:

$f(n) = 25 + 12n + 32n^2 + 4*log(n)$

Now, for every *n>0*:

$f(n) < 25\ n^2 + 12\ n^2 + 32n^2 + 4\ n^2$

$f(n) < (25 + 12 + 32 + 4)n^2$

$f(n) = O(n^2)$, wherein *g(n)* is n^2 and *c=(25+12+32+4)*

However, there exists a limitation with this approach. If the coefficient of the linear function is very high, then a polynomial of higher order or an exponential with a smaller coefficient is preferred in practical scenarios.

The following are some of the growth orders widely used to assess an algorithm's performance. Both $2^{O(n)}$ and $O(2^n)$ yield different results and different interpretations as shown in the following figure:

Type of growth order	Representation using Big O notation
Constant	$O(1)$
Linear	$O(n)$
Quadratic	$O(n^2)$
i^{th} order	$O(n^i)$
Logarithmic	$O(\log_2 n)$
$n \log_2(n)$	$O(n \log_2 n)$
Polynomial of order i	$n^{O(i)}$
Exponential	$2^{O(n)}$ or $O(2^n)$ *

Figure 2.7: Big O representation of various growth order functions

Lower bounds or Big Omega notation (Ω)

The lower bound of an algorithm's running time is denoted as Ω. It is used in evaluating the least running time of an algorithm, or the best-case scenario for any given length of input vector. In other words, it is the minimum growth rate of an algorithm.

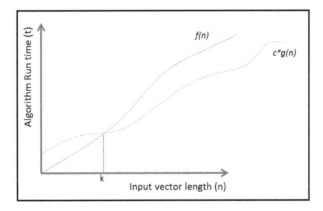

Figure 2.8: f(n) is Big- Ω of g(n) for all n>k

Let us consider two non-negative and non-decreasing functions *f(n)* and *g(n)*, which determine an algorithm's runtime *t* based on a varying input vector length *n*. These functional forms are an equivalent to the running time of best, average, and worst-case scenarios of any given algorithm.

As we can see, initially $c*g(n)$ is higher than $f(n)$ for values of $n<k$, and subsequently, $c*g(n)$ becomes lower than $f(n)$ for $n>k$. Thus, the lower bound of the algorithm can be represented as follows:

$f(n) = \Omega\ (g(n))$ that is—$f(n) > c*g(n)$ for $n>k>0$ and $c>0$.

Hence an algorithm with growth rate $f(n)$ is known as Big O of $g(n)$ only when $f(n)$ executes faster than $g(n)$ for all possible input n $(n>k>0)$ and any constant c $(c>0)$.

Now, let's consider an algorithm whose running time can be expressed as $f(n)$ of polynomial order 2, and we need to determine $g(n)$, which represents the lower bound for $f(n)$:

$f(n) = 25 + 12n + 32n^2 + 4*log(n)$

Now for every $n>0$, the largest of the lower bound is as follows:

$f(n) > 25\ n^2$

$f(n) > \Omega\ (n^2)$ wherein $g(n)$ is n^2 and $c=25$

The smallest of lower bound is as follows:

$f(n) > 25$

$f(n) > \Omega\ (25)$

Here, $g(n)$ is a constant and $c=25$.

Big θ notation

As you just learned, about O and Ω, which describe the upper (maximum) and lower (minimum) bound of an algorithm's running time respectively, θ is used to determine both the upper and lower bound of the algorithm's runtime, using the same function. In other words, it is asymptotically tight bound on the running time. Asymptotically because it is significant only for large number of observations, and tight bound because the running time is within constant factor bounds:

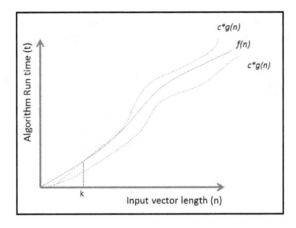

Figure 2.9: f(n) is Big- θ of g(n) for all n>k

Let us consider two non-negative and non-decreasing functions *f(n)* and *g(n)* which determine an algorithm's run time *t* based on varying input vector length *n*.

Then, for every *n>k>0* and *c>0*,

f(n) = *θ(g(n))* if and only if *O(g(n))* = *Ω (g(n))*.

Simplifying rules

Big O (upper bound), Big Omega (lower bound), and Big Theta (average) are the simplest forms of functional equations, which represent an algorithm's growth rate or its system runtime. Simplifying rules can be used to determine these simplest forms without worrying much about formal asymptotic analysis. These rules are applicable to all the three simplest forms. However, the examples shown in the following table are based on the Big O asymptote.

Property	Rule definition	Interpretation
Transitive	If $f(n) = O(g(n))$ and $g(n) = O(h(n))$, then $f(n) = O(h(n))$	Upper bound of an upper bound is always an upper bound to any growth rate function f(n).
Constants	If $f(n) = O(c*g(n))$, then $f(n) = O(g(n))$ for any constant c>0	Constants can be ignored while determining simplest forms for any growth rate function f(n).
Sequence	If $f_1(n) = O(g_1(n))$ and $f_2(n) = O(g_2(n))$, then $f_1(n) + f_2(n) = O(max(g_1(n),g_2(n)))$	The most costly part of the simplest forms is considered when two parts of a growth rate functions run in sequence.
Loop	If $f(n) = O(g(n))$ then $n*f(n) = n*O(g_1(n))$ where n is number of repeat iterations within a loop	The cost associated with each iteration can be simply added when a growth rate function runs within a loop.

Figure 2.10: Definition of simplifying rules along with their interpretations

These simplifying rules are widely used in the following chapters while evaluating costs for an algorithm's growth rate or system runtime functional form.

Classifying rules

Let's consider two algebraic growth rate functions *f(n)* and *g(n)*. The classifying rules are then used to determine which functional form has a better performance over the other. This can be evaluated using the limit theorem, which is as follows:

$$\lim_{n \to \infty} \frac{f(n)}{g(n)} = \frac{\lim_{n \to \infty} f(n)}{\lim_{n \to \infty} g(n)}$$

The following three scenarios are used to classify f(n) and g(n):

Condition	Observation	Comparison in terms of simplest form
If limit tends to infinity	Then, f(n) has faster growth rate than g(n)	f(n) = Ω(g(n))
If limit tends to zero	Then, f(n) has slower growth rate than g(n)	f(n) = O(g(n))
If limits tends to a constant greater than zero	Then, f(n) has a comparable growth rate as g(n)	f(n) = θ(g(n))

Figure 2.11: Classifying rule forms

Computation evaluation of a program

Let's' evaluate the computations of different components within a program or algorithm using asymptotic analysis.

Component 1 – Assignment operator

Assigning an element (numeric, character, complex, or logical) to an object requires a constant amount of time. The element can be a vector, dataframe, matrix and others.

```
int_Vector <- 0:60
```

Hence, the asymptote (Big Theta notation) of the assignment operation is *θ(1)*.

Component 2 – Simple loop

Consider a simple `for` loop with assignment operations.

```
a <- 0
for(i in 1:n)
a <- a + i
```

The following are asymptotes for each line of execution in the code:

Line wise	System run time	Simplifying rule	Asymptotes (big Theta notation)
a <- 0	Constant	Constant	$\theta(1)$
for(i in 1:n)	---		
a <- a + i	Constant (repeats n times)	Loop	$\theta(n)$

Figure 2.12: Asymptotic analysis of a simple for loop

Hence, the total cost of this `for` loop using simplifying rules is $\theta(n)$.

Component 3 – Complex loop

Consider a complex loop using a `while` loop, and a nested `for` loop using assignment operations.

```
a <- 1
i <- 1
b <- list()
while(i<=n )
{
  a <- a + i
  i<- i+1
}
for(j in 1:i)
for(k in 1:i)
{
  b[[j]] <- a+j*k
}
```

The following are asymptotes for each line of execution in the code:

Line wise	System run time	Simplifying rule	Asymptotes (big Theta notation)
a <- 1 i <- 1 b <- list()	Constant	Constant	$\Theta(c_1) \sim \Theta(1)$

while(i<=n)
{
    a <- a + i
    i<- i+1
}
	--- 	
	Constant (repeats n times)
		
		Loop
			
			$\Theta(c_2 * n) \sim \Theta(n)$

for(j in 1:i)
    for(k in 1:i)
{
    b[[j]] <- a+j*k
}
	--- 	
	
	Constant
	(For each j, k iterates n times)
		
		Nested Loop
			
			$\Theta(c_3 * n^2) \sim \Theta(n^2)$

Figure 2.13: Asymptotic analysis of a complex loop

Hence, the total cost of this complex loop using simplifying rules is $\Theta(n^2)$.

Component 4 – Loops with conditional statements

Consider a *for* loop with a nested `if...else` condition, as shown in the following example code:

```
a <- 1
for(i in 1:n)
{
  if(i <= n/2)
  {
    for(j in 1:i)
    a <- a+i
  }else{
    a <- a*i
  }
}
```

The following are the asymptotes for each line of execution in the code:

Line wise	System run time	Simplifying rule	Asymptotes (big Theta notation)
a <- 1	Constant	Constant	$\theta(c_1) \sim \theta(1)$
for(i in 1:n) {... }	---		
if(i <= n/2) { for(j in 1:i) a <- a+i }	Constant (repeats n(n+3)/8 times)	Nested Loops when if condition is True	$\theta(c_2 * n(n+3)/8) \sim \theta(n^2)$
else{ a <- a*i }	Constant (repeats n/2 times)	Simple Loop when if condition is False	$\theta(c_3 * n) \sim \theta(n)$

Figure 2.14: Asymptotic analysis of a conditional loop

The total cost of this loop with if...else conditions using simplifying rules is $\theta(n^2)$. The cost assessment of an if...else condition is evaluated using the worst-case scenario. Here, the worst-case scenario is when the if condition is True, and the nested for loop is executed instead of a simple for loop in the else condition. Hence, maximum growth rate (or system runtime) is considered for evaluating the asymptote of the conditional statements.

Component 5 – Recursive statements

A statement which iterates in a loop using the same function till a condition is satisfied is called a recursive statement. The most commonly used recursive statement is the factorial function. The following code calculates the factorial of an integer n.

```
fact_n <- 1
for (i in 2:n)
{
   fact_n <- fact_n * i
}
```

The following are the asymptotes for each line of execution in the code:

Line wise	System run time	Simplifying rule	Asymptotes (big Theta notation)
fact_n <- 1	Constant	Constant	$\theta(c_1) \sim \theta(1)$

for(i in 2:n)
{...
}
	--- 			

fact_n <- fact_n * i	Constant (repeats n times)	Loop	$\theta(c_2 * n) \sim \theta(n)$

Figure 2.15: Asymptotic analysis of a recursive statement

The total cost of a recursive statement using simplifying rules is $\theta(n)$.

Analyzing problems

Algorithms form an intrinsic base for analyzing a problem, and each problem can be analyzed using multiple algorithms. These algorithms are further evaluated based on their functional performances, as covered under previous sections. However, there arises a basic question–how to evaluate a problem which has many solutions vis-à-vis many algorithms.

Consider a problem with *m* number of algorithms, where *m* tends to infinity. Then, the upper bound or the worst-case scenario cannot be lower than the upper bound of the best algorithm, and the lower bound or the best-case scenario cannot be higher than the lower bound of the worst algorithm. In other words, it is easier to define the lower and upper bounds for an algorithm, but it becomes tricky when it is to be defined for a problem, since there might be algorithms which might not have been explored at all.

More details along with examples will be covered in subsequent chapters.

Space bounds

So far, the performance of an algorithm was evaluated using only its functional form of system runtime. Another functional form can be a key constraint for algorithm developers in system space or available memory. The space functional form depends on both the type and size of data structure unlike the runtime functional form, which depends primarily on the size of the input data structure. As an example, a vector of n elements requires $k*n$ ($\theta(n)$) bytes of memory provided that each element requires k bytes. The space required by each data structure depends on the mode of data storage for efficient data access within.

For example, a linked list not only stores a list of elements but also pointers for easy navigation within. These pointers are additional storage elements, which act as overheads and require additional space allocation. Thus, a data structure with lower overheads *can* enhance the performance of algorithms in terms of space functional form.

However, there needs to be a trade-off between the system's runtime and space requirement for effective evaluation of an algorithm. The best algorithm is one which requires less space and less runtime. But in reality, satisfying both criteria is difficult for algorithm developers. In order to reduce space requirement, developers tend to encode data information, which, in turn, requires additional time to decode, thereby increasing the system runtime. On the other hand, developers tend to restructure data storage information while executing algorithms to decrease the system runtime at the expense of greater space.

More details along with examples will be covered in subsequent chapters.

Exercises

1. The following are some growth-rate functional forms. Can you arrange them in the order of slower to faster performance?

   - $10n^3$
   - $3(\log_e n)^2$
   - $10n$
   - $100n$
   - $Log_2 n^2$
   - $Log_2 n^3$
   - $Log_3 n^2$
   - $Log_3 n^3$
   - $n^{1.5}$

2. Answer the following questions:

   - How can we evaluate the total memory currently being used by a given R environment? What is the purpose of garbage collection (GC) in the context of R?
   - Which occupies more size—a matrix with 10 numbers of categorical attributes, or a dataframe with 10 numbers of corresponding factors?
   - Can you evaluate and plot the memory allocation for dataframes and

matrices with an increment of five observations for a fixed number of attributes (15 columns)?

- Why does `data.table` occupy more memory than `data.frame`?

3. Is `data.table` scalable in terms of performance (faster execution of operations) related to data pre-processing and transformations?

(Hint: `microbenchmark` using large number of variables and observations with a higher number of iterations for each scenario).

4. What are the best, worst, and average-case scenarios for the factorial n ($n!$)?

5. Consider two computing systems A and B, where B is 100 times faster than A. Suppose an algorithm requires 100,000 iterations in system A in a given time t. The following are the functional forms which represent system runtime:

- $10n\log_2 n$
- $5n^3$
- $8\log_3 n^2$

Calculate the following:

- Time required by system B to complete 100,000 iterations
- Number of iterations processed by system B in the given time t

6. Determine the relationship between the following functional forms $f(n)$ and $g(n)$ based on the asymptotic analysis using suitable limits for the input size n.

- $f(n) = n\log n$; $g(n) = n^2\log n$
- $f(n) = n^2$; $g(n) = 2^n$
- $f(n) = 25$; $g(n) = 2^{10}$
- $f(n) = 2^n$; $g(n) = 3^n$
- $f(n) = n\log n$; $g(n) = (\log n)^2$

7. Evaluate Big θ for the following code snippets:

- First snippet:

```
for (i in 1:100)
{
    a = i*10
    b = a+50}
```

- Second snippet:

```
i=1; a=0
while(i<100)
{
   a = c(a,i)
   i=i+1}
```

- Third Snippet:

```
a= data.frame(i=0, j=0)
for(i in 1:100){
for(j in 1:100)
{a[i,1] = i
   a[j,2] = j}}
```

- Fourth snippet:

```
a=50
for(i in 1:100)
{
   if(i <= a)
   print("i is less than or equal to a")" else print("i
   is greater than a")}"
```

Summary

This chapter summarizes the basic concepts and nuances of evaluating algorithms in R. We covered the conceptual theory of memory management and system runtime in R. We discussed the best, worst, and average-case scenarios to evaluate the performance of algorithms. In addition, we also looked into the trade-off between a computer's configuration and algorithm's system runtime, algorithm asymptotic analysis, simplifying and classifying rules, and computational evaluation of programs. The next chapter will cover fundamental data structure and the concepts of lists in R.

3
Linked Lists

This chapter will cover element and homogeneous data type vectors in more detail. The chapter will move from contiguous memory allocation to a non-contiguous memory allocation data type such as a linked list. The linked list data structure collects data and orders them relative to the other elements that come before and after it. The linear data structure can be thought of as having two ends, and the way an item is added or removed from the linear structure distinguishes one structure from another. The chapter will cover multiple variants of linked lists, such as linear linked lists, doubly linked lists, and circular linked lists. The chapter will introduce below mentioned topics in detail:

- Built-in data types in R, such as vector, and element data types
- Writing object-based programs using R S3, S4, and references classes
- Array-based list implementation
- Linked lists
- Comparison of list implementations
- Element implementations
- Doubly linked lists
- Circular linked lists
- Vector and atomic vector

Data types in R

Before we get into data structure concepts, let's look into data types provided by the R programming language. A basic data structure with a homogenous data type is based on a contiguous sequence of cells to enable fast access to any particular dataset. All homogeneous types support a single data type.

For example, in *Figure 3.1* we have a numeric, logical, and character data type, however, it is stored as character.

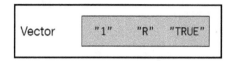

Figure 3.1: Example of vector stored as character

Similarly, a matrix with multiple data types, as shown in *Figure 3.2*, will be coerced and stored as character data type. The array is an extension of the matrix from 2-D to n-D.

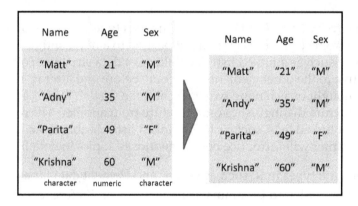

Figure 3.2: A matrix with numeric and characters are stored as 2D matrix with characters data type

All elements of a homogeneous data structure must be the same type, so R attempts to combine the different data types to the most flexible type in a priority order as shown in *Figure 3.3*:

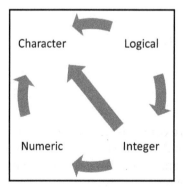

Figure 3.3: Priority order of data types during coercion

Based on *Figure 3.3*, you can see that the character data type gets most priority in homogeneous data type. Logical gets converted into integer, and integer gets converted into numeric if the data type is homogenous. All these are built-in data structures. The following table shows coercion of different data types:

Operators in R	Mode Conversion		Examples	
	From	To		
as.numeric	Character	Numeric	"1", "2.5","3" ---> 1, 2.5, 3	
			"A","B","C" ---> NA, NA, NA	
	Logical	Numeric	TRUE ---> 1	
			FALSE ---> 0	
as.character	Numeric	Character	1, 2, 3, 4 ---> "1", "2", "3", "4"	
	Logical	Character	TRUE ---> "TRUE"	
			FALSE ---> "FALSE	
as.logical	Numeric	Logical	0 ---> FALSE	
			Non-Zero ---> TRUE	
	Character	Logical	"F", "FALSE" ---> FALSE	
			"T", "TRUE" ---> TRUE	
			Others ---> NA	

Figure 3.4: The table shows different types of vector coercions

Vector and atomic vector

The vector representation stores elements in contiguous memory allocation, and the cells are accessed through indexing such as *v[2]* denotes second element of vector *v*. R has six basic atomic vectors.

The following table lists all six basic atomic vectors with their modes and storage modes:

typeof	mode	storage.mode
logical	logical	logical
integer	numeric	Integer
double	Numeric	double
complex	complex	complex
character	character	character
raw	raw	raw

Figure 3.5: The table shows different modes and storage modes of atomic vector types

Contiguous memory allocation and access through indexing makes any insertion or deletion quite expensive. For example, say a company wants to manage the current working employees' details such as name, gender, age, department, and so on. For simplicity, let's only consider that we want to use a vector representation for storing the employee name. Let's assume m employees are currently present in the company, and a new employee named **Navi** joins the company. As employee names are stored in a sorted order, they have to store it after **Bob,** as shown in the following figure:

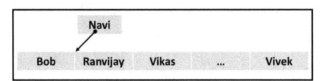

Figure 3.6: An example of insertion in vector

To perform this operation, all employee names need to be shifted by one, leading $m-k$ operations to be performed where k is the insertion position in the vector. Similarly, in a deletion operation, all elements needs to be shifted back as shown in figure below:

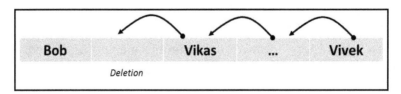

Figure 3.7: An example of deletion of element from vector

Element data types

R supports various element data types, which have unique properties associated with them. Atomic vectors are the most elemental data types as covered under the preceding section. Other forms of data types are as follows:

Factor

A factor is a vector of integer values labeled to each corresponding set of unique characters in a categorical vector. The content within a factor can be of numeric or character format. The content can be of multiple forms such as character, numeric, logical, and complex.

The following example shows how the characters within a categorical vector have been uniquely auto-assigned to an integer (factors). The integer levels are assigned based on the sequence of occurrence of unique character elements within a vector.

```
> fact1 <- factor(c("a","b","c","c","a","b"))
> fact1
[1] a b c c a b
Levels: a b c
> str(fact1)
Factor w/ 3 levels "a","b","c": 1 2 3 3 1 2
```

However, it is possible for a user to define levels as per requirements:

```
> fact2 <-
factor(c("a","b","c","c","a","b"),labels=c(1,2,3),levels=c("c","a","b
"))
> fact2
[1] 2 3 1 1 2 3
Levels: 1 2 3
> str(fact2)
Factor w/ 3 levels "1","2","3": 2 3 1 1 2 3
```

Matrix

A matrix is a two-dimensional array vector defined as rows and columns with homogenous content, which can be of multiple forms such as character, numeric, logical, and complex.

The following example shows a numeric and a character matrix. A mode () is used to check the data type as present in the R environment.

```
## Numeric Matrix
> mat1 <- matrix(1:10,nrow=5)
> mat1
        [,1] [,2]
[1,]     1    6
[2,]     2    7
[3,]     3    8
[4,]     4    9
[5,]     5   10
> mode(mat1)
[1] "numeric"
## Categorical Matrix
> mat2 <- matrix(c("ID","Total",1,10,2,45,3,26,4,8),ncol=2,byrow=T)
> mat2
        [,1]  [,2]
[1,]  "ID"  "Total"
[2,]  "1"   "10"
[3,]  "2"   "45"
[4,]  "3"   "26"
[5,]  "4"   "8"
> mode(mat2)
[1] "character"
```

Array

An array is an *n* dimensional vector with homogenous content, which can be of multiple forms such as character, numeric, logical, and complex.

The following example shows how to generate a three-dimensional array:

```
> arr1 <- array(1:18,c(3,2,3))
> arr1
, , 1
        [,1] [,2]
[1,]     1    4
[2,]     2    5
[3,]     3    6
, , 2
        [,1] [,2]
[1,]     7   10
[2,]     8   11
[3,]     9   12
, , 3
        [,1] [,2]
```

```
[1,]    13    16
[2,]    14    17
[3,]    15    18
```

The `c(3, 2, 3)` column vector defines the dimension of array in such a way that length of the column vector defines the dimension of the array and the values of the column vector define grid size. In this case, *X* has 3 units, *Y* has 2 units and *Z* dimension has 3 units.

Dataframes

A dataframe is a two-dimensional table with combinations of multiple forms of vectors (heterogeneous content) of equal length. It possesses properties of both list and matrix. The content can be of multiple forms such as character, numeric, logical, and complex.

The following is a dataframe with five observations and four attributes:

```
> Int <- c(1:5); Char <- letters[1:5];
Log <- c(T,F,F,T,F); Comp <- c(1i,1+2i,5,8i,4)
> data.frame(Int,Char,Log,Comp)
    Int Char    Log Comp
1    1    a   TRUE 0+1i
2    2    b  FALSE 1+2i
3    3    c  FALSE 5+0i
4    4    d   TRUE 0+8i
5    5    e  FALSE 4+0i
```

List

A list is a way of grouping all possible objects (including lists themselves) and assigning them to a single object. It has a one-dimensional property, which can take in heterogeneous objects. It is also called recursive, as it can contain multiple lists within one. The content can be of multiple forms such as character, numeric, logical, and complex.

The following code explains how to create a list, and what it it looks like in the R environment:

```
> list1 <- list(age = c(1:5), #numeric vector
+ name = c("John","Neil","Lisa","Jane"), #character vector
+ mat = matrix(1:9,nrow = 3), #numeric matrix
+ df = data.frame(name = c("John","Neil","Lisa","Jane"), gender =
c("M","M","F","F")), #data frame
+ small_list = list(city = c("Texas","New Delhi","London"), country   =
c("USA","INDIA","UK"))) #list
> list1
```

```
$age
[1] 1 2 3 4 5
$name
[1] "John" "Neil" "Lisa" "Jane"
$mat
      [,1] [,2] [,3]
[1,]    1    4    7
[2,]    2    5    8
[3,]    3    6    9
$df
  name gender
1 John      M
2 Neil      M
3 Lisa      F
4 Jane      F
$small_list
$small_list$city
[1] "Texas"   "New Delhi" "London"
$small_list$country
[1] "USA"     "INDIA" "UK"
```

R also supports multiple ways to implement data types using **object-oriented programming** (**OOP**) such as S3, S4, and R5 classes. The next section provides the basics on OOP, which will later be used for implementing different data structures.

Object-oriented programming using R

As you already know, R is primarily a functional language; it also supports OOP. OOP in R is an archetype wherein objects and their interactions are used to design various generic functions. It defines the process of constructing modular bits of code, which can be integrated to form a large function. Some key concepts related to OOP are as follows:

- **Object**: An instance of a class or an output of a function in R
- **Class**: Used to define type and attributes of objects in R
- **Method**: An implementation of a generic function for an object of a particular class
- **Generic function**: A generalized function which calls multiple methods without performing any computation itself

R supports three forms of OOP systems based on different objects, classes, and methods:

- **S3**: An informal, simple, interactive, and widely used OOP system in R. Basic packages such as base and stats are primarily built using the S3 system. The following are some generic functions built for multiple objects such as dataframes, vectors, or the output of `lm()` function for its corresponding method:

Methods	Generic function
Print any object	*print()*
Extract summary of any object	*summary()*
Plotting multiple objects	*plot()*

Figure 3.8: Generic S3 functions for different methods

- **S4**: Unlike S3, S4 is much more formal, robust, and provides a uniform mode to create objects. Also, the generic function can be dispatched multiple times to pick methods based on the class of any number of arguments. In S4, new objects are created using the `new()` function, and class components are defined using the `setClass()` function. A class has three main properties:

  - **a name**: This is an alphanumeric string used to identify the class.
  - **a representation**: This is used to define a list of attributes (or slots) along with their data types. For example, an `employee` class of shop will be represented by a `name` represented as `character`, age as `numeric`, and `gender` represented as `character` as shown below:

    ```
    representation(name="character", age="numeric",
    gender="character")
    ```

  - **contains or character vector**: a vector of classes used for multiple inheritance. Caution should be taken while using `contains` in S4 as it makes method lookup intricate.

- **R5 (Reference classes)**: Unlike S3 and S4 which implement generic functions, R5 implements message passing object-oriented programs similar to other object-oriented programs such as Java, C++, and C#, where methods belong to classes rather than functions. R5 objects are also mutable, as they are not dependent on R's modify semantics.

The following table compares the S3, S4, and R5 systems:

Properties	S3	S4	R5 (Reference class)
Identify class of an object	pryr::otype()	pryr::otype() or isS4()	(is(x,"refClass")).pryr::otype()
Identify class of a generic function and method	pryr::ftype()	pryr::ftype() or isS4()	(is(x,"refClass")).pryr::ftype()
Define classes using	Not applicable	setClass()	setRefClass()
Create new objects using	Class attributes	new()	Generator functions
Access attributes using	$	@	$
Methods belong to	Generic functions	Generic functions	Classes
Follows copy on modify semantics	Yes	Yes	No

Figure 3.9: A comparison between S3, S4 and R5 OOs

Linked list

A list can be defined as a collection of a finite number, or as sequence of data items known as elements. Each element of a list will have a specific data type-in the simplest scenario, all elements of a list have the same data type. In R, list implementation is essentially arrays of R objects (SEXP). The array-based implementation of lists will be discussed in the next section. To implement the list data structure, we will use environments, also known as objects in R:

```
# Example list with array, data.frame, matrix, and character
> elist <- list(vec=1:4,df=data.frame(a=1:3, b=4:6),mat=matrix(1:4,
nrow=2), name="pks")
> elist[["vec"]]
[1] 1 2 3 4
```

In a linked list, each item holds a relative position with respect to the others. In a list, there is no requirement for contiguous memory, thus, data can have non-contiguous allocation. For example, *Figure 3.6* shows the implementation of contiguous and non-contiguous memory allocation:

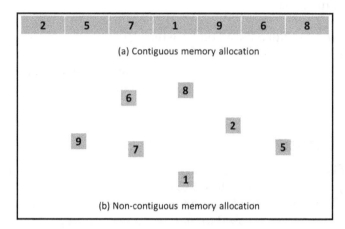

Figure 3.10: Memory allocation

In non-contiguous memory allocation, data is stored at random locations. To effectively use non-contiguous memory allocation, the data structure needs to be embedded with the file system, as shown in *Figure 3.7*. Linked lists store this collection by linking each cell in an ordered format. The start and end of a linked list are also referred to as head and tail respectively.

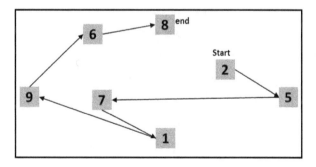

Figure 3.11: An example of a linked list

Linked lists can be of different types such as:

- Linear linked list
- Doubly linked list
- Circular linked list

Also, a linked list can be defined based on how the elements are arranged. For example, a linked list positioning the elements in a sorted order is known as a sorted list, whereas a linked list with no pattern between the element value and its position is referred to as an unsorted linked list.

Linear linked list

A linear linked list is also known as one-way list or singly linked list. A singly linked list is a sequence of nodes, where each node stores an element and a link to the next node, as shown in *Figure 3.12* The elements in a singly linked list may or may not be stored in consecutive memory locations, so pointers are used to maintain a linear order.

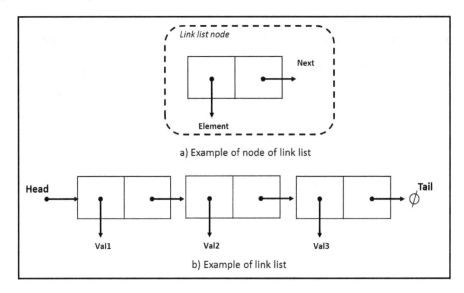

a) Example of node of link list

b) Example of link list

Figure 3.12: Singly link list building block and example

Each node in a linked list consists of an element field and a next field. The **Element** field of a linked list stores the item value and **Next** points to the next node. In the last node, **Next** points to NULL value. Before getting into implementation of singly linked lists, we should focus on defining the ADT requirements for linked lists.

S. No.	Operation	Input	Output
1	Create new empty list	None	Empty list
2	Boolean Check if link list is empty	List	Return Boolean value {True, False}
3	Get size of list	None	Return size as an integer
4	Add an item to existing list	Item to be added	Modified list
5	Remove an item from existing list	Item to be deleted	Modified list
6	Searches for an item in the list	Item to be searched	Return Boolean value {True, False}

Figure 3.13: An example of ADT for linked list

The ADT may depend on the problem requirement. The first item in ADT is to set up an environment:

```
create_emptyenv <- function() {
  emptyenv()
}
```

The linked list can also be represented as an ordered tuple $<e_n>_{n \in N}$ where e_n is the nth term in the linked list. The empty link is represented by the tuple notation <>. The `create_emptyenv()` function creates an empty environment, which can hold a collection of named objects and a pointer to an enclosing environment. Before creating a new list, the `isEmpty()` function checks if the list is empty or not, using an identical function from R.

```
isEmpty <- function(llist) {
  if(class(llist) != "linkList") warning("Not linkList class")
  identical(llist, create_emptyenv())
}
```

The next step is to define a linked list node as shown in *Figure 3.6(a):*

```
linkListNode <- function(val, node=NULL) {
  llist <- new.env(parent=create_emptyenv())
  llist$element <- val
  llist$nextnode <- node
  class(llist) <- "linkList"
  llist
}
```

In the `linkListNode()` function, an element contains `element` and `nextnode`. The `element` field stores the item value, and `nextnode` points to the next linked list node. An example of a linked list can be created using the `linkListNode` function as follows:

```
LList <-linkListNode(5,linkListNode(2,create_emptyenv()))
```

The constructed list can be dynamically expanded by adding and deleting nodes. The elements and nodes in a linked list can be accessed using functions, as follows:

```
setNextNode<-function(llist){
  llist$nextnode
}
setNextElement<-function(llist){
  llist$element
}
```

The next part of ADT is to get the size of the linked list. The size of a linked list requires a pointer to scan through the linked list. The scanning is implemented using recursion in R.

```
sizeLinkList<-function(llist, size=0){
  if (isEmpty(llist))
  {
    return(size)
  } else
  {
    size<-size+1L
    sizeLinkList(llist$nextnode, size)
  }
}
```

The `sizeLinkList` function starts from the first position, and keeps scanning the list nodes till it finds an empty environment. Similarly, the addition of an item can be performed at the start, end, or at any position in the linked list. To add a linked list node at the start, just connect the pointer to the existing linked list as shown in *Figure 3.14* Similarly, add a linked list node at the end by updating the empty pointer to the newly created node. To add an element in between, the node needs to be updated as shown in *Figure 3.15*.

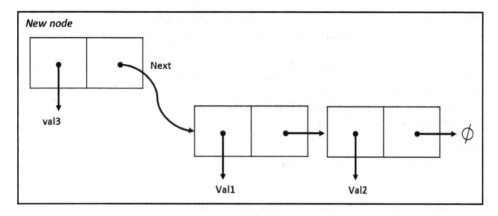

Figure 3.14: Addition of an element to an existing link list

The implementation of insertion at start is done as follows:

```
addElement<-function(new, llist)
{
  if (isEmpty(llist)) {
    llist<-linkedlist(new)
  } else
  {
    llist<-linkListNode(llist, new)
  }
  llist
}
```

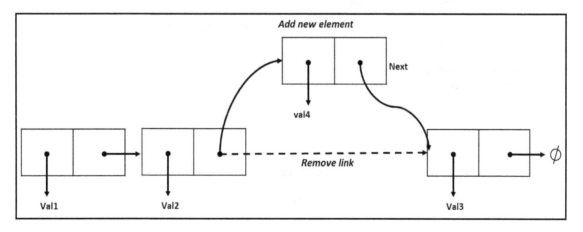

Figure 3.15: Addition of an element in between items in the list

The deletion implementation follows a similar principle as addition (shown in *Figure 3.15*) by skipping the node to be deleted, and updating links accordingly:

```
delElement<-function(llist, pos=NULL){
  if(is.null(pos)) warning("Nothing to delete")
  listsize<-sizeLinkList(llist)
  if(pos>listsize) stop("Position greater than size of list")
  if (isEmpty(llist)) {
    warning("Empty List")
  } else if(pos==1){
    PreviousNode<-llist$nextnode
  } else
  {
    PreviousNode<-linkListNode(llist$element)
    for(i in 1:(listsize-1)){
      if(pos==(i+1)){
        PreviousNode$nextnode<-setNextNode(llist$nextnode)
      } else
      {
        PreviousNode$nextnode<-llist$nextnode
        llist<-llist$nextnode
      }
    }
  }
  return(PreviousNode)
}
```

Searching for an `item` can be implemented by recursively scanning through the linked list from the starting position till the end:

```
findItem<-function(llist, item, pos=0, itemFound=FALSE){
  if (itemFound==TRUE)
  {
    return(itemFound)
  } else if(isEmpty(llist)){
    return(FALSE)
  } else
  {
    pos<-pos+1L
    if(llist$element==item) itemFound<-TRUE
    findItem(llist$nextnode, item, size, itemFound)
  }
}
```

The function will return TRUE if it finds an item, otherwise it will return FALSE.

Doubly linked list

A doubly linked list extends a linear linked list by including pointers to the previous and the next node, as shown in *Figure 3.16*:

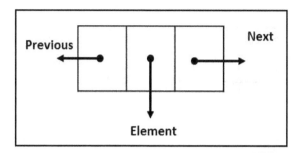

Figure 3.16: Doubly-linked list node

The pointers on both sides allow moving in both directions. For a one-node linked list, the previous and next pointers are set to NULL. The two pointers make this data structure more memory intensive as compared to a single linked list. Similar to singly linked list, a doubly linked list's start and end locations are referred to as the head and tail respectively. The dlinkListNode function provides the definition to create a doubly linked list node.

```
dlinkListNode <- function(val, prevnode=NULL, node=NULL) {
  llist <- new.env(parent=create_emptyenv())
  llist$prevnode <- prevnode
  llist$element <- val
  llist$nextnode <- node
  class(llist) <- "dlinkList"
  llist
}
```

An example of a doubly linked list created using the preceding node structure will look like what is shown in *Figure 3.17*:

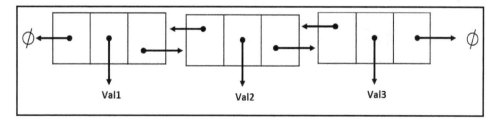

Figure 3.17: An example of doubly link list

Circular linked list

A circular linked list extends both singly and doubly linked lists by connecting the null connection with the tail and head accordingly. The circular linked list extension from a singly linked list and doubly linked list is shown in *Figure 3.18*:

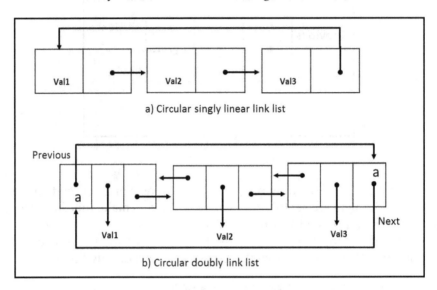

Figure 3.18: An example of circular linked lists

This can be obtained by passing the list to the null node of the linked list. For example, a singly linked list can be converted into a circular linked list by passing the head of the linked list to the tail node:

```
cicularLinkList<-function(llist, val){
  if(isEmpty(llist)){
    llist<-linkListNode(val)
    head<-llist
  } else
  {
    llistNew<-linkListNode(val)
    llistNew$nextnode<-head
    llist<-linkListNode(llist, llistNew)
  }
  llist
}
```

The circular linked list has usage in multiplayer games such as the bridge card game, where the pointer keeps moving from one player to another player in a circular fashion till the game ends.

Array-based list

The array-based list, also known as array list, is a resizable array implementation. Thus, as more elements are added to the linked list, its size increases dynamically. The array-based list assigns an element to the assigned array; however, if a new element is assigned some data, and there is no space in the array, then it allocates a new array, and moves all the data to the newly allocated array. For example, as shown in *Figure 3.19*, since the array is full, all of the data is reassigned to a bigger array by increasing the size by a default value.

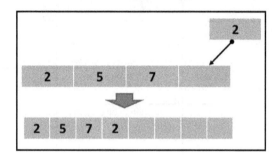

Figure 3.19: Example array-based link list

Let us set up a reference class `ALinkList` for an array list in R. To set up an array linked list, the class fields required are as follows:

- `Alist`: To store the dataset
- `listsize`: Pointer to the current location in the array; this can also be used to get the current list size
- `arraysize`: Default expansion size
- `maxSize`: Maximum array size

The defined class initializes an `arraysize` of 100 elements, thus `Alist` is initialized for 100 elements with `listsize` initialized to 0 and `maxSize` to 100.

```
ALinkList<-setRefClass(Class = "ALinkList",
    fields = list(
        Alist="array",
        listsize="integer",
        arraySize="integer",
```

```
      maxSize="integer"
  ),
  methods = list(
    initialize=function(...){
      listsize<<-0L
      arraySize<<-100L
      Alist<<-array(dim = arraySize)
      maxSize<<-arraySize
    }
  )
)
```

Methods to `ALinkList` class can be added based on the defined ADT. Let's define the basic ADT for the `ALinkList` class as shown in *Figure 3.20*:

S. No.	Operation	Input	Output
1	Create new empty array list	None	Empty array list
2	Get size of array list	None	Return size as an integer
3	Add an item to existing array list and expand if it's filled	Item to be added	Modified list
4	Remove an item from existing array list based on position	position to be deleted	Modified list
5	Searches for an item in the array list	Item to be searched	Return Boolean value {True, False}

Figure 3.20: An example of ADT for array list

The length of an array can be obtained by returning `listsize` into the method:

```
listlen = function()
{
  return(listsize)
}
```

Adding an item into the array list requires an additional check on size of list. If `listsize` is greater than `maxSize,` then the array needs to be expanded based on `arraySize`.

```
updateArrayList=function(){
  Alist<<-c(Alist, array(dim=arraySize))
  maxSize<<-maxSize+arraySize
},
addItem=function(item){
  if(maxSize<=listsize){
    updateArrayList()
```

```
  }
  listsize<<-listsize+1L
  Alist[listsize]<-item
  return(listsize)
}
```

An item can be removed from the list based on the array index:

```
removeItem = function(i)
{
  Alist[i] <<- NULL
  listsize <<- listsize - 1L
}
```

Deletion or searching of an item in array list can be performed by scanning through it. For example, searching for a position based on item is shown in the following code snippet:

```
searchItem = function(val){
  pointer<-1L
  while(pointer!=listsize){
    if(Alist[pointer]==val){
      break
    }
    pointer<-pointer+1L
  }
  return(pointer)
}
```

The searchItem function scans the array list, and returns the position once it finds the value.

Analysis of list operations

The complexity of list operations depends on traversal. For a linked list of n nodes, the isEmpty() method is $O(1)$, as it only compares the first node to see if it is an empty environment. Similarly, the sizeLinkList() method requires $O(n)$ operations to determine the length of a linked list, as the linked list has to traverse through all the nodes for length determination.

The deletion and searching for an item in the linked list in worst case will take $O(n)$ operations, as the pointer may have to scan through all the nodes before it finds the item for deletion. On the other hand, the addElement () method will take $O(1)$ time as it is directly adding a new element to the head of the linked list. Insertion based on position will take $O(p)$ time, as the linked list has to traverse through p nodes before performing an insertion. For example, say we want to insert 11 at the third position in the list <1, 2, 5, 4>. The current insertion operation will require the pointer to move from the head to the third position. In the worst case, where insertion needs to be done after the last node, it would require $O(n)$ computational effort.

In an array list, moving to any position requires $O(1)$ operations, as the elements can be accessed directly. The insert and delete operations are quite straightforward in array list implementation, and require $O(1)$ computational effort if performed at the tail of the list, as no data needs to be moved in the array list. However, if an element is deleted from or inserted in between items in a list, then all the elements need to be moved one position towards the head or tail respectively. For example, insertion of an element in the example shown in the next image requires all the other elements to move towards the tail. So, if an element is inserted at the pth location, it will require n-p elements to be moved to the tail as shown in *Figure 3.14*, thus requiring $O(n)$ computational effort.

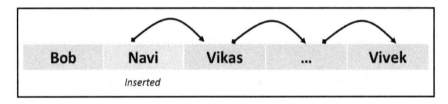

Figure 3.21: Insertion in an array list

To summarize, array lists are very efficient in accessing a dataset with $O(1)$ computational effort, whereas linked lists are just average in accessing a dataset with $O(n)$ computational effort. However, insertion and deletion require $O(n)$ computations in array lists and $O(1)$ computations in linked lists, making linked lists more efficient in handling insertion and deletion if the pointer is at the location of insertion or deletion.

Exercises

1. Modify the `addElement` function of a singly linked list to add an item at any position.
2. Write a function for reversing a singly linked list.
3. Write the ADT for circular linked lists.
4. Write an R function for creating, inserting, and searching for a circular linked list.
5. Write a function which will return the index of an item for a linear linked list.

Summary

The current chapter covered the fundamental data structures built-in in R, and also covered the concepts of lists and their implementation in R. The chapter introduced built-in data types in R such as vector, and element data types. Also, object-based programming, including S3, S4 and reference classes was introduced. The chapter also introduced one of the most fundamental data structures, link list, and its different variation, such as circular link list and array-based list. The next chapter will introduce stacks and queues data structure.

4

Stacks and Queues

This chapter will extend the linked list implementation to stacks and queues. Stacks and queues are special cases of linked lists with less flexibility in performing operations than linked lists. However, these data structures are easy to implement and have higher efficiency where such structures are needed. For example, *Figure 1.4*, in Chapter 1, *Getting Started* shows the implementation of an array with integer data type using stacks and queues. An item can be added (PUSH) or deleted (POP) from a stack from one side only, whereas a queue is an implementation of linear data structure, which allows two sides for insertion (enqueue) and deletion (dequeue). The current chapter will cover array-based and linked list-based implementation of stacks and queues in R. This chapter will cover below topics in detail:

- Stacks
    - Array-based stacks
    - Linked stacks
    - Comparison of array-based and linked stacks
    - Implementing recursion
- Queues
    - Array-based queues
    - Linked queues
    - Comparison of array-based and linked queues
- Dictionaries

Stacks

Stacks are a special case of linked list structures where data can be added and removed from one end only, that is, the head, also known as the top. A stack is based on the **Last In First Out** (**LIFO**) principle, as the last element inserted is the first to be removed. The first element in the stack is called the top, and all operations are accessed through the top. The addition and removal of an element from the top of a stack is referred to as **Push** and **Pop** respectively, as shown in *Figure 4.1*:

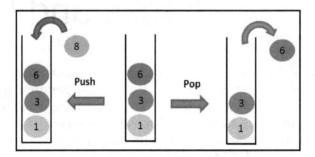

Figure 4.1: Example of Push and Pop operation in stacks

A stack is a recursive data structure, as it consists of a top element, and the rest is either empty or another stack. The main ADT required to build a stack is shown in *Table 4.1*. This book will cover two approaches–array-based stack and linked stack–to implement the ADT mentioned in *Table 4.1*. The implementation is covered using reference classes in R:

S. No.	Operation	Input	Output
1	Create new empty stack	None	Empty stack
2	Check if stack is empty	stack	Return Boolean value {True, False}
3	PUSH an element to the stack	Item to be PUSHED	Modified Stack
4	POP an element from stack	None	Modified stack
5	Size of stack	stack	Return size of stack
6	Top value in the stack	Stack	Return top value of stack

Table 4.1 Abstract data type for queue

Array-based stacks

Array-based stack implementation uses the array data structure to store data. Similar to an array-list, an array-based stack uses a fixed size. Thus, the class definition for an array-based stack would be similar to an array-based list, as shown in the following code:

```
Astack <- setRefClass(Class = "Astack",
  fields = list(
    Maxsize="integer",
    topPos="integer",
    ArrayStack="array"
  ),
  methods = list(
    # Initialization function
    initialize=function(defaultSize=100L, ...){
      topPos<<-0L
      Maxsize<<-defaultSize # 100L
      ArrayStack<<-array(dim = Maxsize)
    },

    # Check if stack is empty
    isEmpty=function(){},

    # push value to stack
    push=function(pushval){},

    # Pop value from stack
    pop=function(){},

    # Function to get size of stack
    stacksize=function(){},

    # Function to get top value of stack
    top=function(){}
  )
)
```

In reference classes, fields are modified using <<- (global operator), and all functions are accessible to objects created using the defined class. The preceding class implements a stack with a default array size of 100 cells. The pointer `topPos` points to the top element of the stack, and `Maxsize` refers to the maximum size of the array. To check whether the stack is empty or not, we can use the top position in an array stack, as follows:

```
isEmpty=function(){
  if(topPos==0) {
    cat("Empty Stack!")
    return(TRUE)
```

```
  } else
  {
    return(FALSE)
  }
}
```

The push and pop operation of an array stack can be performed by working with the `topPos` pointer of the class to update the array index:

```
push=function(pushval){
  if((topPos+1L)>Maxsize) stop("Stack is OUT OF MEMORY!")
  topPos<<-topPos+1L
  ArrayStack[topPos]<<-pushval
}

pop=function(){
  # Check if stack is empty
  if(isEmpty()) return("Empty Stack!")
  popval<-ArrayStack[topPos]
  ArrayStack[topPos]<<-NA
  topPos<<-topPos-1L
  return(popval)
}
```

Pushing an element to a stack which is completely full is known as overflow, whereas removing an element from a stack which is empty is referred to as underflow of stack. Thus, both these conditions are added as exceptions in the current class using the `isEmpty` function `Maxsize` variable. The size of the array stack can be obtained by returning the `topPos` variable:

```
stacksize=function(){
  stackIsEmpty<-isEmpty()
  ifelse(stackIsEmpty, return(0), return(topPos))
}
```

Similarly, the top value of a stack can be returned by returning the value pointed to by `topPos` into `ArrayStack`:

```
top=function(){
  stackIsEmpty<-isEmpty()
  if(stackIsEmpty) {
    cat("Empty Stack")
  } else
  {
    return(ArrayStack[topPos])
  }
}
```

Due to the simplicity of the structure and implementation of stacks, it is possible to implement multiple stacks within the same initialized array. However, the current implementation is recommended if stacks have an inverse relationship, or if there is a functional relationship which could be used to minimize the array memory. For example, a two-stack system in which the first stack gets data from the pop operation performed on the second stack can be utilized to develop a multi-array stack within the same array, as shown in *Figure 4.2*.

In *Figure 4.2*, **Stack1top** and **Stack2top** represent the pointers to the first and second stacks, respectively. As **Stack1top** moves toward the right, **Stack2top** moves toward the left, and vice versa. For other scenarios where the memory required is not predefined, a linked stack can be used, as discussed in the next subsection:

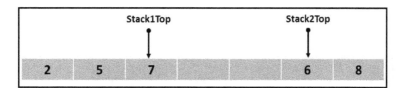

Figure 4.2: Example of a multi-array stack

An example of the use of an array-based stack with multiple push and pop operations is as follows:

```
> array_stack_ex<- Astack$new()
> array_stack_ex$push(1)
> array_stack_ex$push(2)
> array_stack_ex$push(3)
> array_stack_ex$pop()
> array_stack_ex$push(5)
> array_stack_ex$pop()
> array_stack_ex$pop()
> array_stack_ex$top()
[1] 1
> array_stack_ex
Reference class object of class "Astack"
Field "Maxsize":
[1] 100
Field "topPos":
[1] 1
Field "ArrayStack":
[1]   1 NA NA NA NA NA NA NA ... NA NA NA
```

Initially, we push three elements into the stack {1, 2, 3}. We then pop one element out using the LIFO principle, and are, thus, left with the set {1, 2}. We then push another element 5 into the stack, updating the set as {1, 2, 5}. Finally, we pop the top two elements, leaving the stack with only one element, {1}.

Linked stacks

Linked list-based stacks utilize the concept of linked lists with the flexibility to add and remove elements dynamically from the head of a linked list, which is equivalent to the top in an array-based stack. The top points to the first member of the linked list, as shown in *Figure 4.3*:

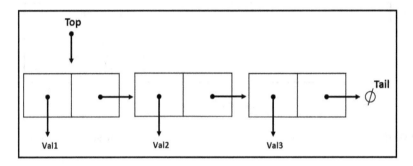

Figure 4.3: A linked stack with the top pointing to the head node of a linked list

The reference class definition of a linked list-based stack is shown as follows:

```
Linkstack <- setRefClass(Class = "Linkstack",
  fields = list(
    Lsize="integer",
    Lstacktop="environment"),
  methods = list(
    # Initialization function
    initialize=function(...) {
      Lsize<<-0L
    },

    # Check if stack is empty
    isEmpty=function(){},

    # Function to create empty R environment
    create_emptyenv=function(){},

    # Function to create node
```

```
    Node = function(val, node=NULL) {},

    # push value to stack
    push=function(pushval){},

    # Pop value from stack
    pop=function(){},

    # Function to get top value of stack
    top=function(){}
  )
)
```

As nodes are created dynamically, memory allocation is not required; thus, `Lstacktop` is defined as an environment variable, and points to the top location of the stack. The `Lsize` variable stores the stack's size. The fundamental node of a linked list comprises the value and address of the next node. Let's use the same ADT as defined earlier for the array-based stack. We could utilize the same `isEmpty` function defined for the array stack by replacing `topPos` with `Lsize`:

```
isEmpty=function(){
  if(Lsize==0) {
    cat("Empty Stack!")
    return(TRUE)
  } else
  {
    return(FALSE)
  }
}
```

The node in the linked stack can be defined as an environment object similar to a linked list as defined in `Chapter 3`, *Linked Lists*:

```
create_emptyenv = function() {
  emptyenv()
}
Node = function(val, node=NULL) {
  llist <- new.env(parent=create_emptyenv())
  llist$element <- val
  llist$nextnode <- node
  llist
}
```

The `node` method consists of `element`, which stores the value, and `nextnode`, which points to next node of the linked list. The `push` method will add a node to the stack, whereas the `pop` method will remove the top node of the stack:

```
push=function(val){
  stackIsEmpty<-isEmpty()
  if(stackIsEmpty){
    Lstacktop<<-Node(val)
    Lsize<<-Lsize+1L
  } else
  {
    Lstacktop<<-Node(val, Lstacktop)
    Lsize<<-Lsize+1L
  }
}
```

The `push` function initially checks whether the stack is empty or not. If the stack is empty, it creates a new node, otherwise it adds the newly created node to the top position of the linked list. As accessing the top position or head node of a linked list is quite straightforward, we do not require to define a separate top variable pointing to the head node in R; thus, top is used as a reference to the head node in linked list stack definitions.

```
pop=function(){
  stackIsEmpty<-isEmpty()
  if(stackIsEmpty){
    cat("Empty Stack")
  } else
  {
    Lstacktop<<-Lstacktop$nextnode
    Lsize<<-Lsize-1L
  }
}
```

The `pop` function also checks for the empty condition, and moves the top position to `nextnode` using the address pointer if the stack is non-empty. The other functionality of stacks can be built around their basic ADT, such as getting the top value of a stack:

```
topVal=function(){
  stackIsEmpty<-isEmpty()
  if(stackIsEmpty){
    cat("Empty Stack")
  } else
  {
    return(Lstacktop$element)
  }
}
```

The preceding function returns `element` from the top node of a stack. This function can be used to set up a list stack. The following is an example of the use of a linked list stack with multiple push and pop operations:

```
> link_stack_ex<-Linkstack$new()
> link_stack_ex $push(1)
> link_stack_ex $push(2)
> link_stack_ex $push(3)
> link_stack_ex $pop()
> link_stack_ex $push(5)
> link_stack_ex $pop()
> link_stack_ex $pop()
> a$topVal()
[1] 1
> link_stack_ex
```

```
Reference class object of class "Linkstack"
Field "Lsize":
[1] 1
Field "Lstacktop":
<environment: 0x00000000405fc248>
```

The preceding example is similar to the array-based implementation. After all the operations have been performed in this last example, `array_stack_ex` object has one value in the stack, as shown in the output stored in environment `0x00000000405fc248`.

Comparison of array-based and linked stacks

From the perspective of time computation, both array and linked list implementations of stacks are quite comparable. For example, the cost of appending and deleting in both arrays and linked list stacks is $O(1)$-worst-case. In a linked list-based implementation, appending and deletion is performed by the head pointer, which can be accessed directly. Similarly, in an array-based implementation, each push and pop is performed through the `topPos` index variable, which keeps moving making access in constant time.

In terms of space, in an array-based stack implementation, preallocation of memory is required during array initialization; thus, $(n-m)$ cells are wasted, where m is the number of elements stored in the array. On the other hand, a linked list stack implementation dynamically allocates and deallocates memory with every push and pop operation respectively, and thus, no memory is wasted. However, a linked list implementation requires an extra `nextnode` field to store the address of the next node.

Implementing recursion

Recursion is used to implement an iterative process, where each state of a variable in a subroutine is registered by the controller. The primary memory, while executing the code, utilizes four main components, as shown in *Figure 4.4*:

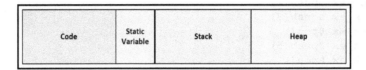

Figure 4.4: Memory allocation

The code part of the memory stores instructions and functions from the program. The static variable stores any global and static variable from the program. The stack stores the variables and data of the function. The heap is used for dynamic memory allocation. For example, a subroutine with data and instructions will register into memory, as shown in *Figure 4.5*. The subroutine variables **x** and **y** are stored in the **Stack**, whereas instructions are stored in the **Code** section of memory allocation. When implemented as a recursion, the machine executes a subroutine repeatedly by changing the contents of the registers until the termination condition is reached. At each step, the state of the subroutine is determined based on the register content in the stack, which comprises variable states:

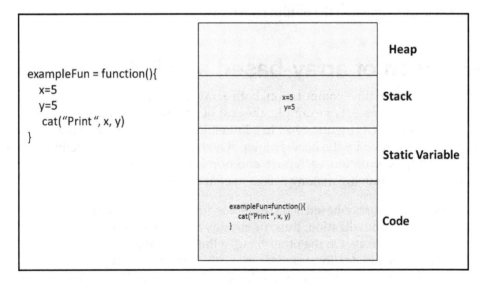

Figure 4.5: Example of memory allocation

The recursive function should always have a termination criterion to be used in real-world applications. Anything which has a self-similar structure with repetition can be implemented using recursion. For example, the factorial of any non-negative integer for any number *n* is represented as *n!*, and can be expressed as follows:

factorial(n) = n*factorial(n-1) where *factorial(0)=1*.

The factorial function is self-similar, as it calls itself until it reaches a value *factorial(0)*. The following represents the R implementation of factorial using recursion:

```
recursive_fact<-function(n) {
  if(n<0) return(-1)
  if(n == 0) {
    return(1)
  } else {
    return(n*recursive_fact(n-1))
  }
}
```

The preceding factorial function uses recursion for evaluation, and uses a stack for computation. For example, for the factorial of **3**, the preceding function will keep pushing values to the stack until the termination condition is achieved (as shown in *Figure 4.6*) before calculating the factorial by popping the stored value from the stack. The function will create a stack of all the values to be multiplied before popping these values from the stack to perform the final multiplication operation to give the factorial value for the given integer:

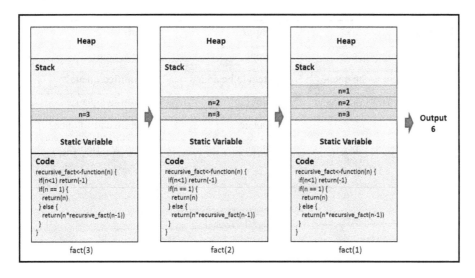

Figure 4.6: Example of recursion for factorial of 3

The recursion approaches are quite efficient in implementing algorithms that require multiple branching, such as binary trees. The details of these algorithms will be covered in a later part of this book.

Queues

A queue is an ordered collection of elements as shown in *Figure 1.4(b)* in `Chapter 1`, *Getting Started*. In queues, addition is restricted to one end, referred to as **rear**, and deletion is restricted to another end, which is known as the **front**. Queues follow the **First In First Out (FIFO)** principle, also known as the first-come-first-served approach. Thus, an element pushed into a queue will wait until all the elements in front are removed. The queue data structure can be applied to any shared resources scenario. For example, in a network printer case where multiple users are sending printing jobs to the same printer, the jobs are arranged in a queue, and are processed in order of arrival. Another example of a queue from our day-to-day life is a shop counter serving multiple people–they use a queue for serving and, thus, follow the FIFO principle in serving the people in the queue. Also, databases accessed by multiple departments/users also use queues to process their queries on data in the order of their arrival. Thus, queues have a lot of application in different domains.

The major operations required by a queue are adding an element (enqueue), deleting an element (dequeue), and size of the queue as defined as ADT requirement in *Table 4.2*:

S. No.	Operation	Input	Output
1	Create new empty queue	None	Empty queue
2	Add an element to the queue	Item to be added	Modified queue
3	Delete an element from queue	None	Modified queue
4	Size of queue	Queue	Return size of queue
5	Check if queue is empty	Queue	Return Boolean value {True, False}

Table 4.2 Abstract data type for queue

Array-based queues

The array-based implementation of queues is not an efficient implementation, as we select one side of a queue to add an element and other side to remove. The task can be accomplished by using two pointers–front and rear. An element is added to the front and removed from the rear of the queue. This leads to a drifting issue, as shown in *Figure 4.7*:

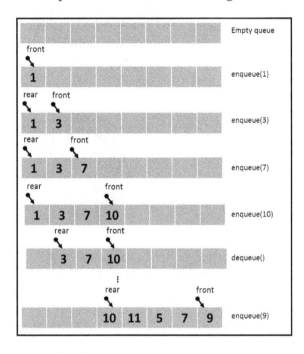

Figure 4.7: Drifting issue with queue implementation using array

In *Figure 4.7*, it can be seen that there could be a situation when the queue is full, yet there is free space available in the array:

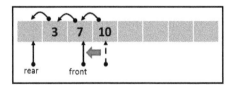

Figure 4.8: Approach 1 to address drifting issue in queue

The problem can be resolved by keeping the rear at the first position, and moving the rest of the array towards the rear by one unit, as shown in *Figure 4.8*. However, this makes the removal operation *O(n)*, which is computationally inefficient. Another way to tackle this problem is by using a circular implementation of queue, as shown in *Figure 4.9*. Circular implementation allows reusing of empty cells once the array length ends. This implementation makes addition and removal operations *O(1)*, which is quite efficient computationally. However, this introduces another challenge related to determining whether the queue is full or empty, as in both situations, empty and full queue, the rear will hold a position less then the front pointer. The current problem can be addressed by keeping track of the number of elements in the queue, or creating an array with *n+1* to store *n* elements:

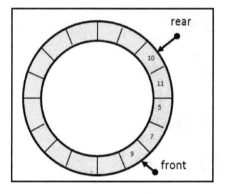

Figure 4.9: Circular array implementation of queue

Let's implement a queue using reference classes in R. The ADT implementation of a queue in R is shown as follows:

```
aqueue<-setRefClass(Class = "aqueue",
  fields = list(
    Alist="array",
    queuesize="integer",
    maxSize="integer",
    rear = "integer",
    top = "integer"
  ),
  methods = list(
    initialize=function(qSize, ...){
      queuesize<<-0L
      rear<<-1L
      top<<-0L
      maxSize<<-as.integer(qSize)
      Alist<<-array(dim = maxSize)
    }
```

```
# Queue is empty
isEmpty = function() {},
# Add element to the queue
enqueue = function(val){},
# remove element from queue
dequeue = function() {},

# size of queue
size = function() {}
  )
)
```

The new reference class can be generated using `setRefClass()`, and the method can be created using a method list within `setRefClass`. The new queue can be created using the `new()` function:

```
> q<-aqueue$new()
> q
Reference class object of class "aqueue"
Field "Alist":
[1] NA NA NA NA NA NA NA NA NA NA NA NA NA ... NA NA NA NA NA
Field "queuesize":
[1] 0
Field "arraySize":
[1] 100
Field "maxSize":
[1] 100
Field "rear":
[1] 0
Field "top":
[1] 0
```

The other implementation from ADT can be added to the queue class by adding methods. That the queue is empty can be checked using the `queuesize` variable, as follows:

```
isEmpty = function() {
   return(queuesize==0L)
}
```

For adding and deleting an element in a queue, the methods `enqueue()` and `dequeue()` can be used respectively in the method list of `setRefClass`:

```
enqueue = function(val){
  if(queuesize<maxSize){
    if(top==maxSize) top<<-0L
    top<<-top + 1L
    Alist[top]<<-val
    queuesize<<-queuesize+1L
```

```
    } else
    {
       cat("Queue Full!")
    }
},

dequeue = function() {
   if(queuesize>0L){
      Alist[rear]<<-NA
      ifelse(rear==maxSize, rear<<-1L, rear<<-rear+1L)
      queuesize<<-queuesize-1L
   } else
   {
      cat("Empty Queue!")
   }
}
```

The preceding function is a circular implementation; thus, the top and rear position is reset to the start of the array once the top and rear pointer hits the maxSize index.

Linked queues

Linked queues are a much simpler implementation, as nodes are dynamically created and destroyed. In linked list queues, an element is inserted at the rear and removed from the front, as shown in *Figure 4.10*:

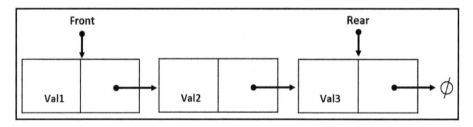

Figure 4.10: Example of link list queue

The class implementation of the queue ADT in R using reference classes for a linked list-based queue is shown as follows:

```
ListQueue <- setRefClass(Class = "ListQueue",
   fields = list(
      Lsize="integer",
      front="environment",
      rear = "environment",
      Lqueue="environment"),
```

```
methods = list(
  initialize=function(...) {
    Lsize<<-0L
  },

  # Check if list is empty
  isEmpty=function(){},

  # create empty environment
  create_emptyenv = function() {},

  # Create node
  Node = function(val, node=NULL) {},

  # Function to add value to link list
  enqueue=function(val){},

  # Function to remove node from link list
  dequeue=function(){}

  # Function to get link list size
  size=function(){}
 )
)
```

The function `isEmpty` checks whether the linked list is empty using the `Lsize` variable, as shown in the following code snippet. For an empty linked list, `Lsize` has zero value:

```
isEmpty=function(){
  if(Lsize==0) {
    cat("Empty Stack!")
    return(TRUE)
  } else
  {
    return(FALSE)
  }
}
```

The link list node in R is represented using environment; thus, the `create_emptyenv` function creates an empty environment:

```
create_emptyenv = function() {
  emptyenv()
}
```

The node representation is similar to the linked list node, and consists of `element` and `nextnode`.

```
Node = function(val, node=NULL) {
  llist <-new.env(parent=create_emptyenv())
  llist$element <- val
  llist$nextnode <- node
  llist
}
```

As the elements in a queue are added to the rear of the queue, the rear pointer is used to capture the environment location for the last node as follows:

```
enqueue=function(val){
  ListIsEmpty<-isEmpty()
  if(ListIsEmpty){
  Lqueue<<-Node(val)
  Lsize<<-Lsize+1L
  rear<<-Lqueue
  } else
  {
    newNode<-Node(val)
    assign("nextnode", newNode, envir = rear)
    rear<<-newNode
    Lsize<<-Lsize+1L
  }
}
```

The `assign` statement is used to attach the reference of a new node using the rear pointer reference. As elements are deleted from the front node, the front pointer is not necessary, and the first element can be accessed and removed directly, as shown in the following code snippet:

```
dequeue=function(){
  stackIsEmpty<-isEmpty()
  if(stackIsEmpty){
    cat("Empty Queue")
  } else
  {
    Lqueue<<-Lqueue$nextnode
    Lsize<<-Lsize-1L
  }
}
```

The size of the linked list is contained in the `Lsize` variable of the class function.

Comparison of array-based and linked queues

The linked list implementation of queues require *O(1)* (worst-case) computation effort, where enqueuing is performed by appending to the rear, and dequeuing is implemented at the head of the linked list. However, new allocation is required with every operation, which may make it slow.

The enqueuing operation in array-based queues is implemented by using a circular buffer, which works as inserting element at the next free position. The implementation can be a dynamic array implementation, where a new array is created with a bigger size when the max memory is reached in the current array. The enqueuing and dequeuing operations are performed using front and rear references, thus requiring *O(1)* computational effort. In terms of memory allocation, queues behave similar to stack implementations–a linked implementation needs an extra `nextnode` field to store the address of the next node, thus increasing the memory overhead.

Dictionaries

A dictionary can be defined as an ordered or unordered list of key-element pairs, where keys (usually unique) are used to locate elements (not necessary unique) in the data structure. For example, a data structure that stores customer information in a retail shop can be considered as a dictionary, where the consumer ID serves as the key for identification of different customers. Dictionaries are also known as associative arrays or maps, as they map keys to values to perform retrieval operations such as addition, removal, and search. Every element of a dictionary consists of a key and an associated element, also known as a key-value pair. This is shown in *Figure 4.11*:

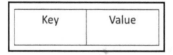

Figure 4.11: Dictionary key-value pair structure

The key in a dictionary is used to differentiate between each key-value pair. It can be any randomly chosen set of values, such as real numbers or strings, with the only restriction that each key is unique, and can be differentiated from the others. The values in the dictionary are also known as vocabulary.

The standard ADT for dictionaries are as follows:

S. No.	Operation	Input	Output
1	Initialization dictionary	Dictionary	Empty dictionary
2	Add an element	Key and value pair	Updated dictionary
3	Delete an element	Key	Updated dictionary
4	Size	None	Size of dictionary
5	Find value based on key	Key	Boolean {TRUE, FALSE}

Table 4.3 Abstract data type for dictionaries

The class for the preceding ADT can be implemented using array-based data structures, as shown in the following code:

```
Adict<-setRefClass(fields = list(
  Alist="list",
  listsize="integer",
  key="integer"
),
methods = list(
  # Re-initialize dictionary
  initialize=function(...){
    listsize<<-0L
    Alist<<-list()
  },

  # Check length of value
  size = function(){},

  # Add following key value pair in Array
  addElement = function(key, val){},

  # remove value with defined
  removeElement = function(key){},

  # remove value with following
  findElement = function(key){},
}
```

The `size` function determines the current size of an array. The `addElement` and `removeElement` functions add and remove elements respectively. The `findElement` function determines the value of the provided key. The dictionary can be implemented in one of the following two ways:

- Ordered
- Unordered

The unordered implementation adds items as they arrive; thus, the `addElement` function takes *O(1)* computational effort. However, the `findElement` and `removeElement` methods take *O(n)* computational effort. Therefore, this implementation is recommended if the number of additions of elements is much larger than that of removal. In the ordered implementation of dictionaries, items are added to the initially empty dictionary in a non-decreasing order of their keys. Thus, the `addElement` function will take *O(n)* computational effort in the worst-case scenario. In the ordered implementation, the `removeElement` function will also take *O(n)* computational effort, as any removal requires gaps created by the operation to be filled. Thus, this implementation is inferior to an unordered dictionary in terms of adding and removing elements. However, the efficiency of the search operation, `findElement`, is considerably improved by using search strategies such as binary search. Thus, in scenarios where the database is static with very little addition or removal of data points and where mostly search operations are required, then ordered implementation is a better choice.

Let's implement an unordered implementation using the list data type from R. The `size` function can be implemented by monitoring the `listsize` variable, as shown in the following code snippet:

```
size = function(){
  return(listsize)
}
```

The `addElement` function can be implemented by passing the key and value to the list data type, and the `removeElement` function utilizes the key to retrieve the element before deleting it from the list:

```
addElement = function(key, val){
  Alist[[key]]<<-val
  listsize<<-listsize+1L
}

removeElement = function(key){
  Alist[[key]]<<-NULL
  listsize<<-listsize-1L
}
```

Finding a value in a dictionary can be performed using a key search. The keys in the list data type in R are stored as names of the list:

```
findElement = function(key){
  return(key%in%names(Alist))
}
```

Finding elements based on a key can be a very simple query just based on ID comparison, and using basic operators such as ==, >=, and <= if the key is an integer. However, if the key is a character, %in% in R could be used to check whether the key is present in the set of keys available in the data structure. Based on the previous functions, let's create an example with characters as keys:

```
> dictvar<-Adict$new()
> dictvar$addElement("key1", 1)
> dictvar$addElement("key2", 1)
> dictvar
Reference class object of class "Adict"
Field "Alist":
$key1
[1] 1
$key2
[1] 1
Field "listsize":
[1] 2
Field "key":
integer(0)
> dictvar$Size()
[1] 2
> dictvar$findElement("key1")
[1] TRUE
> dictvar$removeElement("key1")
```

The preceding implementation can be obtained using other data structures, such as linked list, with minor updates.

Exercises

1. What will be the top value for the following stack operations?

```
PUSH(1)
PUSH(2)
PUSH(6)
PUSH(3)
```

```
POP ()
POP ()
```

2. Assume a stack with the elements {1, 2, 3, 5, 6, 7} in order, with 7 on top. Write the operations required to insert 4 after 3 in the current stack.
3. Explain the difference in the outputs of the following recursion functions:

Output 1	Output 2

`problemfun1<-function(n){`
  `if(n<1) return(1)`
  `problemfun1(n-1)`
  `print(n)`
`}`
	`problemfun1<-function(n){`
	  `if(n<1) return(1)`
	  `print(n)`
	  `problemfun1(n-1)`
	`}`

4. Write a recursive algorithm to evaluate the Fibonacci sequence. (In a Fibonacci sequence, each item is the sum of the previous two.)
5. Write a function to invert the values in a stack.
6. Write a function to implement two stacks using only one array. The routines should not indicate an overflow unless every cell in the array is filled.
7. Create a data structure which supports push, and pop, and finds the maximum values, all in *O(1)* worst-case scenario.
8. Write a class for an array queue implementation using stacks, assuming no other data type is available.

Summary

The current chapter covered the fundamentals of stacks and queues and also introduced implementation using R reference classes. We covered the fundamentals of stacks as a data structure which is based on the LIFO principle. The two types of stack implementation were introduced – array-based and linked list-based stacks along with a comparison of their computational and memory efficiencies. Recursion-based functions utilize stacks inherently, and are covered within the stack functionality. Queues are another very useful data structure that we covered. They follow the FIFO principle in addition and deletion of elements from the data structure. We discussed two types of queues – array-based queue and linked list-based queue implementation. In addition, we learned about dictionaries, an interface ADT for retrieving data from a data structure. The chapter also covered the array-based implementation of dictionaries.

5
Sorting Algorithms

This chapter is intended to cover various sorting algorithms. We perform various kinds of sorts in our everyday lives, such as sorting a pack of cards, ordering a pile of books, comparing multiple bills, and so on. These sorts are primarily based on intuition. Sometimes, sorting can be an essential part of other algorithms which are used for route optimization. In the current chapter, two different types of sorts will be covered. The first is comparison-based sorting, wherein all the key values of the input vector are directly compared with each other prior to ordering. The second type is non-comparison-based sorting, wherein computations are performed on each key value, and then the ordering is performed based on the computed values. Overall, all algorithms primarily follow the principle of divide and conquer. Some of the ways of dividing covered in the chapter are length-based splits (used in merge sort), pivot-based splits (used in quick sort), and digit-based splits (used in radix sort). The initial part of the chapter deals with comparison-based sorts with three simple and intuitive sorting algorithms, which are relatively slow and have an asymptotic complexity of $\theta(n^2)$ in average and worst-case scenarios. Then we'll cover algorithms with better asymptotic performance in worst-case scenarios, such as $\theta(n\log n)$. Finally, non-comparison-based sorts are covered, which show better asymptotic performance in worst-case scenarios, such as $\theta(n)$ under special conditions. The current chapter will cover the following topics:

- Sorting terminology and notation
- Three $\Theta(n^2)$ sorting algorithms
    - Insertion sort
    - Bubble sort
    - Selection sort
    - The cost of exchange sorting
- Shell sort
- Merge sort
- Quick sort

- Heap sort
- Bin sort and radix sort
- An empirical comparison of sorting algorithms
- Lower bounds for sorting

Sorting terminology and notation

In this chapter, the input for any algorithm is a vector of elements (key values) unless stated otherwise. These elements can be of any type: numeric, character, logical, or complex.

Consider an input vector V of elements $i_1, i_2, ..., i_n$. These elements are said to be sorted provided their corresponding values satisfy a particular order. In other words, the elements of vector V are said to be sorted in non-decreasing order provided their values satisfy the condition $i_1 < i_2 <, ..., < i_n$.

All the algorithms presented in this chapter can handle the special case of sorting, that is, duplicate elements in a given input vector; however, only some of them perform it optimally. An algorithm is said to be performing optimally provided it retains the original position of duplicate elements without redundantly ordering them, thereby reducing computation time.

The simplest way to compare performances of two algorithms is by assessing their computational system runtime. *Table 5.2* shows the system runtime of sorting algorithms for comparison purposes. The runtime depends on the following factors:

- Parameters of the input data
    - Number of elements in the input vector
    - Memory size of the elements and their respective keys
    - Allowable range of elements (key values)
    - Original order of the input vector
- Parameters of the algorithm (approach)
    - Number of comparisons between keys
    - Number of swapping or element interchange operations
    - List of vectors that need to be sorted and their frequency of recurrence
    - Asymptotic analysis—functional forms of runtime

Three Θ(n²) sorting algorithms

The following sections deal with three different sorting algorithms, which require $\theta(n^2)$ system runtime to execute both average-and worst-case scenarios. These algorithms are simple to implement, but show poor computational performance.

Insertion sort

Consider a vector V of numeric elements which needs to be sorted in ascending order. The most intuitive way is to iterate through the vector of elements and then perform element insertions at relevant positions within the vector, satisfying the ordering criterion. This kind of ordering based on a series of insertions is termed insertion sorting. The following *Figure 5.1* illustrates the approach for insertion sorting in which each row represents the modified vector for the corresponding *ith* iteration. The sorting operation is indicated by the arrows:

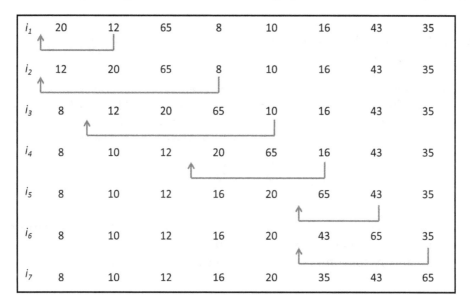

Figure 5.1: Illustration of insertion sort

The following is the code in R which performs insertion sorting to arrange a vector in increasing order:

```
Insertion_Sort <- function(V,n)
{
  if(n==0) stop("No elements to sort")
  for(i in 2:(length(V)))
  {
    val <- V[i]
    j <- i - 1
    while (j >= 1 && val <= V[j])
    {
      V[j+1] <- V[j]
      j <- j-1
    }
    V[j+1] <- val
  }
  return(V)
}
```

Let's analyze the code for best-, worst-, and average-case scenarios using the metric as the number of comparisons (`val < V[j]`).

Worst-case: Assume a vector of *n* elements in decreasing order. The number of comparisons using the first `for` loop is one, second `for` loop is two, and so on till *n-1*. Thus, the total number of comparisons for the complete execution of sorting is given as follows:

$$\sum_{i=2}^{n} i = \frac{(n-1)(n)}{2} \sim \theta(n^2)$$

Best-case: Assume a vector of *n* elements already sorted. The number of comparisons for each of the *n-1* for loops is one, as the `while` condition fails for each iteration. Thus, the total number of comparisons for complete execution of sorting is given as:

$$\sum_{i=2}^{n-1} 1 = n = \theta(n)$$

Average-case: Assume a vector of *n* elements in any order. For the sake of simplicity, consider the first half of the elements to be sorted, and the remaining as unsorted. Then, the first half would require only $\left(\frac{n}{2}-1\right)$ comparisons, while the second half would require $\left(\frac{(n-2)(n)}{8}\right)$ comparisons. Thus, the functional form of system runtime for an average-case scenario is $\theta(n^2)$. So, the average-case scenario is similar to the worst-case scenario asymptotically.

Similar to the number of comparisons, the number of swaps (V[j+1] <- V[j]) within the while loop is also a measure of an algorithm's performance in assessing its computation runtime. The while conditional loop comprises both comparisons and swaps, wherein the number of swaps is one less than the number of comparisons, as the while loop condition fails for every last iteration of comparison. Thus, the total number of swaps is *n-1* less than the total number of comparisons for the complete execution of sorting. Thereby, the functional form of system runtime remains the same for both worst-and average-case scenarios ($\theta(n^2)$), whereas it becomes 0 for the best-case scenario.

Bubble sort

Unlike insertion sort, bubble sort is non-intuitive, tougher to comprehend, and has poor performance even for the best-case scenario. In every iteration, each element within the vector is compared with the rest of the elements, and the smaller (or larger) element amongst all is pushed toward the first (or last) position, just as a water bubble pops out on the water surface; hence, the algorithm is named as bubble sort. It is a step-by-step approach of comparing adjacent elements and swapping key values.

The following is the R code which performs bubble sorting. The code is implemented in an adaptive format, and performs iterations differently. This is explained in detail below the code along with an illustration (*Figure 5.2*):

```
Bubble_Sort <- function(V,n) {
  if(n==0) stop("No elements to sort")
  for(i in 1:length(V)) {
    flag <- 0
    for(j in 1:(length(V)-i)) {
      if ( V[j] > V[j+1] ) {
        val <- V[j]
        V[j] <- V[j+1]
        V[j+1] <- val
        flag <- 1
      }
```

```
        }
    if(!flag) break
    }
    return(V)
}
```

As seen in the preceding code, bubble sort comprises two `for` loops along with a `flag` condition to keep a check on the swapping condition to avoid any redundant iterations. The inner `for` loop is meant to check all adjacent element comparisons and undergo the required swapping operations. If the lower-indexed key value is greater than its higher-indexed key value, then the elements within the vector are swapped. Therefore, the highest key value element is pushed toward the end, and the subsequent lower key value elements are pushed toward the start. As the highest value is pushed right-most, the second iteration of the inner `for` loop does not consider the last key value for comparison with the second-last key value:

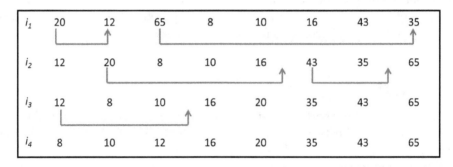

Figure: 5.2: Illustration of bubble sort

Subsequently, iterations are performed using the outer `for` loop, barring each key value one less than the preceding iteration. The `flag` condition helps in avoiding redundant loops once the vector is intermediately sorted, as can be seen in the preceding illustrated example.

Let's analyze the code for best, worst, and average-case scenarios for a number of comparisons ($V[j] > V[j+1]$) without considering the `flag` condition. Then we can observe that for any order of input vector V, the number of comparisons using both the `for` loops increases with a factor of 1 for each iteration. Therefore, the asymptote of system runtime using a number of comparisons as an evaluation metric for all the three cases is $\theta(n^2)$.

Similar to the number of comparisons, the number of swaps can also be considered as an evaluation metric of an algorithm's system runtime. The number of element swaps in a bubble sort depends on the adjacent values within the vector. Assuming half the number of elements to be unsorted for an average-case scenario, the asymptote would be $\theta(n^2)$, estimated using the number of required swaps.

Selection sort

Again, consider a numeric vector which is to be sorted in ascending order. Another intuitive approach for sorting the vector is to first select the smallest element and place it in the first position, then select the second smallest and place it in the second position, and so on. This kind of select and sort approach is termed selection sort. Selection sort follows an **iii** principle, that is, in the ith iteration, select the ith order element from the vector, and place it in the ith position. This approach boils down to a unique feature wherein in the number of swaps required in each iteration is only one unlike what was observed in bubble sort. In other words, for a vector of length n, only n-1 swaps are required for a complete execution of sorting; however, the number of comparisons are similar to the bubble sort algorithm. In selection sort, the position of the smallest element is first remembered, and then swapped accordingly. *Figure 5.3* further illustrates the selection sort for a numeric vector:

i_1	20	12	65	8	10	16	43	35
i_2	8	12	65	20	10	16	43	35
i_3	8	10	65	20	12	16	43	35
i_4	8	10	12	20	65	16	43	35
i_5	8	10	12	16	65	20	43	35
i_6	8	10	12	16	20	65	43	35
i_7	8	10	12	16	20	35	43	65
i_8	8	10	12	16	20	35	43	65

Figure 5.3: Illustration of selection sort

The following R code performs selection sorting. This current raw code is implemented using the `for` loop:

```
Selection_Sort_loop <- function(V,n) {
  if(n==0) stop("No elements to sort")
  keys <- seq_along(V)
  for(i in keys) {
    small_pos <- (i - 1) + which.min(V[i:length(V)])
    temp <- V[i]
    V[i] <- V[small_pos]
    V[small_pos] <-temp
  }
  return(V)
}
```

As the number of comparisons is similar to the bubble sort, the function form of system runtime is $\theta(n^2)$ for all three cases. However, we have seen till now that the swapping operations are much lower. This is advantageous in scenarios where the cost of swaps is higher than the cost of comparisons, such as vectors with large elements or long strings.

Also, selection sort performs very well in vectors with a large number of elements. This is because the swap operations exchange only the position keys (or pointers) instead of position key values (or elements). Thus, additional space is required to store the position keys (or pointers); however, the return of swapping is much faster. The following illustration shows an example of swapping position keys. Consider a numeric vector with four elements. *Fig (a)* in *Figure 5.4* shows the pre-swapped position keys (pointers) along with values, and *Fig (b)* in *Figure 5.4* shows the post-swapped position keys (pointers) along with values:

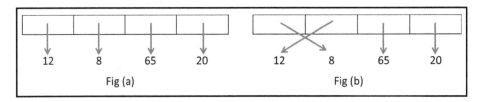

Fig (a)   Fig (b)

Figure 5.4: Example of swapping pointers toward key values

Nevertheless, there is a caveat in the implementation of selection sort. The swapping operation is performed even when the position and order of an element is the same. That is to say, even if the ith order element is present at the ith position, the swapping operation will continue. This can be avoided using a test condition. However, in general, the cost incurred due to the test condition is higher than the cost saved by avoiding swaps. Thus, the functional form of the system runtime based on the number of swaps is $\theta(n)$ for all three cases.

The cost of exchange sorting

Insertion sort, bubble sort, and selection sort are three typical sorting algorithms which are costly to execute for large size vectors and a large number of recurrent vectors. The reasons pertaining to their higher cost of execution are as follows:

- Comparison of only adjacent elements in a vector
- Swapping of adjacent elements (except in selection sort) based on comparisons

The swapping of adjacent elements is called an exchange; hence, these three algorithms are also called exchange sorts. The cost of execution of these exchange sorts is the total number of cell-to-cell movements (also known as number of inversions) by each element before forming into a right-order vector.

Consider a vector of length n. Then, the total number of exchanges or inversions possible is equal to the total number of available pairs, that is, $\frac{n(n-1)}{2}$. On average, the total number of inversions possible is equivalent to $\frac{n(n-1)}{4}$ per vector. Thus, we can comment with certainty that any sorting algorithm performing adjacent pair comparisons (and swaps) will have an associated cost of at least $\frac{n(n-1)}{4} \sim \Omega(n^2)$ for the average-case scenario.

The following *Table 5.1* summarizes the system runtime asymptotes for all the three case scenarios (best, worst, and average) using the number of comparisons and number of swaps for insertion sort, bubble sort, and selection sort algorithms. The system runtime of insertion sort and bubble sort is $\theta(n^2)$ across both average and worst-case scenarios:

		Insertion sort	Bubble sort	Selection sort
Number of Comparisons	Best case	$\Theta(n)$	$\Theta(n^2)$	$\Theta(n^2)$
	Average case	$\Theta(n^2)$	$\Theta(n^2)$	$\Theta(n^2)$
	Worst case	$\Theta(n^2)$	$\Theta(n^2)$	$\Theta(n^2)$
Number of Swaps	Best case	0	0	$\Theta(n)$
	Average case	$\Theta(n^2)$	$\Theta(n^2)$	$\Theta(n)$
	Worst case	$\Theta(n^2)$	$\Theta(n^2)$	$\Theta(n)$

Table 5.1: Comparison of asymptotic complexities using different evaluation metrics

Let's continue with other sorting algorithms, which show considerably better performance as compared to the three exchange-sort algorithms.

Shell sort

Shell sort (also called diminishing increment sort) is a non-intuitive (real-life) and a non-adjacent element comparison (and swap) type of sorting algorithm. It is a derivative of insertion sorting; however, it performs way better in worst-case scenarios. It is based on a methodology adopted by many other algorithms to be covered later: the entire vector (parent) is initially split into multiple subvectors (child), then sorting is performed on each subvector, and later all the subvectors are recombined into their parent vector.

Shell sort, in general, splits each vector into virtual subvectors. These subvectors are disjointed such that each element in a subvector is a fixed number of positions apart. Each subvector is sorted using insertion sort. The process of selecting a subvector and sorting continues till the entire vector is sorted. Let us understand the process in detail using an example and illustration (*Figure 5.5*):

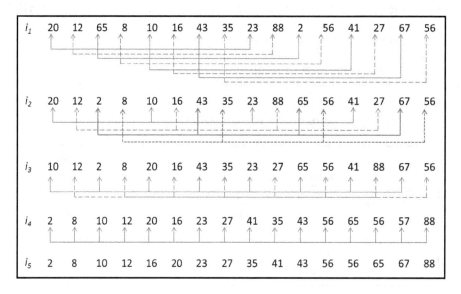

Figure 5.5: Illustration of shell sort

Consider a numeric vector *V* of even length (16 elements) which needs to be sorted in ascending order. Also, let us assume that the subvector split is a multiple of two. Then, the shell sort arrange vector using iterative process as discussed below:

Iteration 1: Split the entire vector *V* into eight subvectors of two elements each such that each element within a subvector is eight positions apart, and the first element of all subvectors are in sequence, as shown in (i_1). Then, perform insertion sorting on each subvector separately.

Iteration 2: Now increase the length of the subvectors by decreasing the splits. Next, split the entire vector *V* into four subvectors of four elements each such that each element within a subvector is four positions apart, and the first element of all subvectors are in sequence, as shown in (i_2).

Similarly, perform iterations till the length of the subvector equals the entire vector, and finally, culminate the sorting with a normal insertion sort of all the elements.

The following R code performs shell sorting on both even and odd length vectors:

```
Shell_Sort <- function(V,n) {
  if(n==0) stop("No elements to sort")
  increment=round(n/2)   ## as.integer
  while(increment>0) {
    for(i in (increment+1):n) {
      temp <- V[i]
      j=i
      while(j >= (increment+1)  && V[j-increment] > temp) {
        V[j] <- V[j-increment]
        j <- j-increment
      }
      V[j] <- temp
    }
    if(increment==2) {
      increment <- 1} else{
        increment <- round(increment/2.2)
    }
  }
  return(V)
}
```

Shell sort is an improvement over the insertion sort, as the sorting is performed initially on subvectors before being performed on the entire vector. All the intermediate iterations nearly sort the entire vector prior to the final iteration. Now, the cost of iterating a nearly sorted vector is relatively much cheaper than performing insertion sorting on the raw input vector.

Another way of further improving shell sort performance is by increasing the length of the subvectors in the initial iteration. For example, in the preceding example, we started the iterations from two elements in each subvector, which can be increased to three. The advantages of increasing the length of the initial subvector are as follows:

- The entire vector would be more nearly sorted for the final iteration
- The number of iterations would reduce

In R, shell short implementation uses gap as $4^k+3.2^{k-1}+1$ (with prefix of *1* and $k \geq 1$) which is a variant from Sedgewick (1986), which has a worst-case scenario of $\theta(n^{4/3})$. The *1* in the prefix is added to ensure sorting yields correct results. Thus, shell sort performs much better than lone insertion sort asymptotically. Shell sort also demonstrates how special properties of other sorting algorithms can be exploited to enhance their existing performance.

Merge sort

Merge sort follows the principle of divide and conquer, wherein the input vector is first divided into two halves, then each half is independently sorted and later merged into a single sorted vector. Its key features are as follows:

- Conceptually simple to understand.
- Asymptotically better performance.
- Empirically lower system runtime.
- Concept of merge – as mentioned earlier, merge is performed on two sorted subvectors (halves). The first element of each subvector is compared, and the smallest is picked up and placed in the first position of the output vector. Subsequently, the picked-up element is removed from its corresponding subvector. This process of first element comparison continues till all the elements in both the subvectors become empty, and are orderly filled in the output vector.
- Requires recursive implementation for effective execution.

The following R code recursively implements merge sort:

```
Merge_Sort <- function(V) {
  if(length(V) == 0) stop("Not enough elements to sort")

  ## Merge function to sort two halves or sub-vectors
  merge_fn <- function(first_half, second_half) {
    result <- c()
    while(length(first_half) > 0 && length(second_half) > 0) {
      if(first_half[1] <= second_half[1]) {
```

```
      result <- c(result, first_half[1])
      first_half <- first_half[-1]
    } else {
      result <- c(result, second_half[1])
      second_half <- second_half[-1]
    }
  }
  if(length(first_half) > 0) result <- c(result, first_half)
  if(length(second_half) > 0) result <- c(result, second_half)
  return(result)
}

## Recursively split the parent vector into two halves (sub-
vectors)
if(length(V) <= 1) V else {
  middle <- length(V) / 2
  first_half <- V[1:floor(middle)]
  second_half <- V[floor(middle+1):length(V)]
  first_half <- Merge_Sort(first_half)
  second_half <- Merge_Sort(second_half)
  if(first_half[length(first_half)] <= second_half[1]) {
    c(first_half, second_half)
  } else {
    merge_fn(first_half, second_half)
  }
}
}
```

The R code comprises two subcodes. One explains how to execute the merge operation (merge_fn), and the other how to operate the main function (Merge_Sort) recursively. The former function executes the merge operation on two input vectors (or two halves of a subvector), whereas the latter function recursively splits the main vector (V) to its lowest possible half (*log n* levels of recursion), and accordingly, performs the merge operation.

Figure 5.6 illustrates the methodology of merge sort in operation:

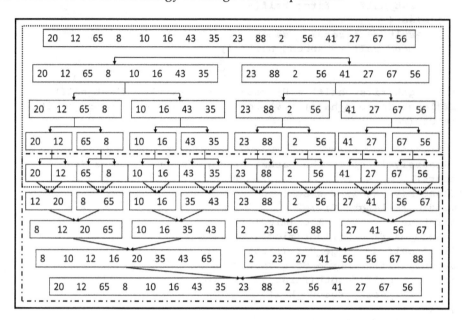

Figure 5.6: Illustration of merge sort

One of the main drawbacks of merge sort is memory management. It requires almost twice the memory required by most of the sorting algorithms. Initially, the main input vector is recursively split into multiple subarrays. These subarrays are again recursively merged into multiple secondary vectors, until a final sorted vector is obtained. Thus, a complete execution requires two sets of supplementary vectors (one while splitting, and the other while merging); a bypass of either step is extremely difficult to implement.

Despite the fact of its recursive implementation, analyzing merge sort asymptotically is not very difficult. The analysis can be divided into two stages:

- **Stage I**: The main input vector (V) with n elements is split recursively into n subvectors, as illustrated in *Figure 5.6*. The vector V is initially divided into two subvectors each with $n/2$ elements, which, in turn, is divided into two with $n/4$ elements each, and so on till all the subvectors have only a single element. Assuming n to be a power of 2, the depth of recursion is $\log n$.

- **Stage II**: The n subvectors are merged iteratively into a final sorted vector, as illustrated in *Figure 5.6*. In the first iteration, each subvector with a single element is merged (along with sort) into $n/2$ subvectors, each with two elements. In the second iteration, merged subvectors are remerged into $n/4$ sub vectors, each with four elements and so on, until a single sorted vector is obtained. Thereby, the asymptote for each iteration is $\theta(n)$, as n steps are required for its completion.

Thus, the functional form of the system runtime of the merge sort algorithm in terms of the number of execution steps is $\theta(n \log n)$, because each $\log n$ level of recursion requires an n number of total merge operation steps. As the cost function is independent of the order of the initial input vector, the asymptote for the best, average, and worst-cases remain the same.

Quick sort

The quick sort algorithm is an updated version of the merge sort algorithm with faster in-memory sorting capability. It is widely used in average-case as against worst-case scenarios. It is also efficient in terms of memory utilization, as it does not require the secondary vector when performing the merge operation. Quick sort can be accessed in R using functions such as sort (base) and quick sort (rje). It is also called partition-exchange sort. Like merge sort, quick sort also requires recursive implementation for effective execution.

The following is the three-step execution methodology of the quick sort algorithm for a given input vector V with n elements:

1. Select the pivot or root element of the given input vector. The pivot element is used to partition the entire vector into two subvectors such that all the elements in the first vector or left vector are less than the pivot, and all the elements in the second vector or right vector are greater than or equal to the pivot. However, the elements within both the partitioned subvectors need not be sorted. Usually, the element with the median value is considered for pivot. However, in our algorithm, we have considered the last element as the pivot for the corresponding vector. The pivot is said to be best when the partitioned subvectors are of the same length, and worst when one of the subvectors is empty.

2. Perform recursive sorting on each of the subvectors (excluding the pivot) obtained after the split.

3. Join the first sorted subvector, the pivot, and the second sorted subvector to obtain the final sorted output.

The following R code implements the recursive form of the quick sort algorithm:

```
Quick_Sort <- function(V,n) {
  if (n <= 1) return(V)
  left <- 0 ##start from left prior first element
  right <- n  ##start from rightmost element
  v <- V[n] ## initialize last element as pivot element

  ## Partition implementation
  repeat {
    while (left < n && V[left+1]  < v) left <- left+1
    while (right > 1 && V[right-1] >= v) right <- right-1
    if (left >= right-1) break
    ## Swap elements
    temp <- V[left+1]
    V[left+1] <- V[right-1]
    V[right-1] <- temp
  }

  ## Recursive implementation of Quick sort
  if (left == 0) return(c(V[n], Quick_Sort(V[1:(n-1)],n=(n-1))))
  if (right == n) return(c(Quick_Sort(V[1:(n-1)],n=(n-1)), V[n]))
  return( c(Quick_Sort(V[1:left],n=left), V[n],
Quick_Sort(V[(left+1):(n-1)],n=(n-left-1))))
}
```

The R code begins with initializing the left and right indices. The left index represents the position of an element prior to the first element in the vector, and the right index represents the position of the last element in the vector. Then, the last element is considered as the pivot element for the corresponding input vector. Consider the following numeric vector with 16 elements:

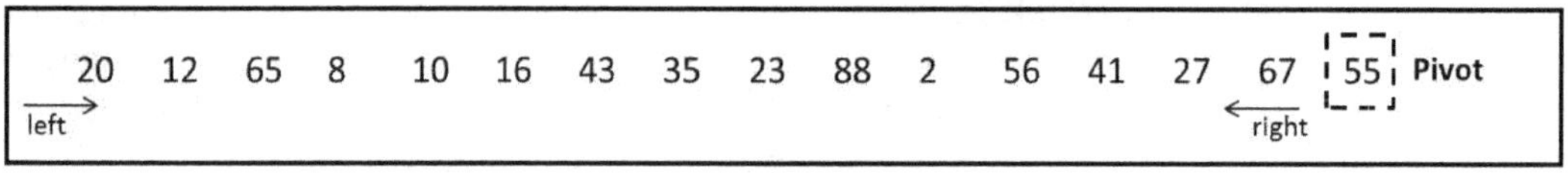

Figure 5.7: An example of a 16-elements numeric vector

Now, the **left** and **right** indices start moving inward under the repeat loop till the indices meet. The inner while loops checks for bounds along with the pivot element prior to updating the **left** and **right** indices. Subsequently, the elements are swapped such that all elements toward the left of the pivot are lower than the pivot element, and all the elements toward the right are higher than the pivot element. However, the elements within the left and right subvectors need not be ordered. *Figure 5.8* illustrates the first swap iterations being performed under the repeat loop:

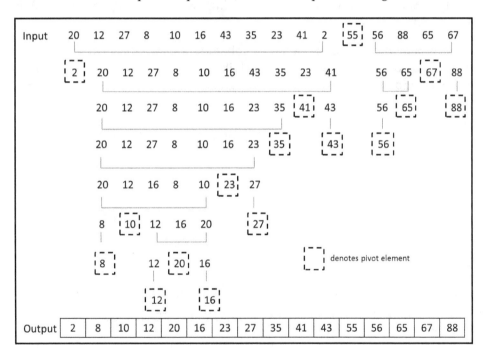

Figure 5.8: Illustration of swap iterations

Once the **left** index meets the **right** index, the `repeat` loop breaks, and the recursive implementation of quick sort begins. Here, the pivot element is correctly positioned, and the remaining elements within the left and right subvectors are subject to recursive sorting. *Figure 5.9* illustrates the complete implementation of the quick sort algorithm:

Figure 5.9: Illustration of quick sort

Let's analyze the asymptote of the quick sort algorithm in detail based on the number of operations performed at each step. Consider an input vector V of length n. A total of n moves are required to complete the traversing of both the left and right indices, till they meet each other. The `repeat` loop can be executed at most n times, and the `while` loop can fail at most n times. Hence, the asymptote of partition based on the pivot element is $\theta(n)$.

Consider a worst-case scenario wherein one of the subvectors has no elements upon partitioning. If this scenario occurs at each partition step, then the asymptote of the algorithm becomes $\theta(n^2)$. In our algorithm, the worst-case scenario is bound to happen only when the input vector possesses all the elements in the descending order. However, this situation can be minimized upon random selection of the pivot value.

Consider a best-case scenario wherein for each iteration (of the `repeat` loop), the pivot value partitions the vector into two equal subvectors. Such a perfect kind of pivot will result in *log n* levels of partitions and n levels of traversing (by the left and right indices), which corresponds to an asymptote of $\theta(nlog\ n)$.

Consider an average-case scenario. Here, the behavior of the partition is between the best and worst-case scenarios, and there is an equal likelihood for any type of subvector partition. The asymptote which satisfies the recurrence relation can be defined as follows:

$$\theta(n) = kn + \frac{1}{n}\sum_{s=0}^{n-1}\Big[\theta(s) + \theta(n-1-s)\Big], where\ k\ is\ a\ constant\ and\ \theta(0) = \theta(1) = k$$

Thus, the closed form solution for the average-case scenario is also $\theta(nlog\ n)$, which is similar to that of the best-case scenario.

Heap sort

Heap sort is an improvised form of selection sort, wherein the algorithm initially splits the input vector into sorted and unsorted vectors, and then iteratively shrinks the unsorted vector by extracting the largest element and placing it in the sorted vector. It is based on the heap data structure which provides a non-quadratic asymptote even for the worst-case scenarios. Heaps are tree-based data structures with the following properties:

- **Shape criterion**: Heaps are primarily complete binary trees with both the left and right child nodes filled with values:

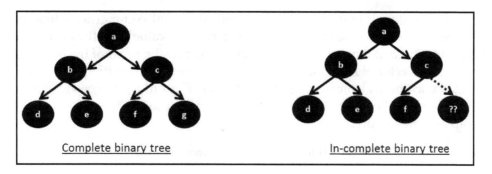

Figure 5.10: Illustration of complete and in-complete binary tree

- **Heap criterion**: The ordering of the tree is unidirectional. In other words, all the parent nodes will be greater than the child nodes (max-heap), or all the child nodes will be greater than the parent nodes (min-heap). Either of the heaps can be used for sorting in any required order. In our example, we will use max-heap to sort the input vector in an ascending order. Also, the values in the nodes are independent of each other. It is possible that all the values of the nodes in a right sub-tree are higher than the values of the nodes in the left sub-tree:

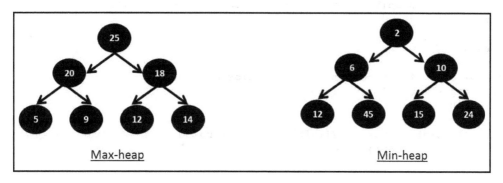

Figure 5.11: Illustration of max-heap and min-heap

The heap sort algorithm possesses some structural advantages which enhance its performance efficiency. It adopts the concept of a complete binary tree wherein the tree is balanced. It requires less in-memory, as the values of the input vector are directly stored in the form of a binary tree. The values need not be explicitly inserted into each of the nodes within the tree. Hence, it is also suitable for large size vectors. The asymptotic performance is also non-quadratic in the best, average, and worst-case scenarios. The functional form of the system runtime is *nlog n*.

The heap sort algorithm is quite easy to implement. The input vector array is first converted into a max-heap (`max_heap` function). Then, the maximum value from the heap is extracted iteratively, and placed at the end of the array, ensuring that the order of the heap remains intact. Consider a vector of length n wherein all the elements are positioned from 1 to n. The first extracted maximum element will be placed in the nth position, the second extracted maximum element will be placed in the $(n-1)^{th}$ position, and so on. The extraction continues till the heap becomes empty.

The following is the R code which implements the recursive form of the heap sort algorithm:

```
Heap_Sort <- function(V)
{
  heapsize <- length(V)    ## Initialize with total vector size
  for (i in floor(length(V)/2):1)
  V <- max_heap(V, i,heapsize)  ## Build initial max-heap
  for (i in length(V):2) {
    temp <- V[i]       ## replace ith with 1st element (maximum)
    V[i] <- V[1]
    V[1] <- temp
    heapsize <- heapsize -1    ##Reduce size of input vector
    V <- max_heap(V, 1,heapsize) ##Re-build max-heap with reduced
input vecto0072
  }
  return(V)
}
## Following function recursively builds max-heap
max_heap <- function(V, i,heapsize) {
  left <- 2*i
  right <- 2*i+1
  if (left<=heapsize && V[left]>V[i]){ ## build left sub-tree
    largest <- left} else{
    largest <- i
    }
  if (right<=heapsize && V[right]>V[largest])
  largest <- right       ## build right sub-tree
  if (largest != i) {
    temp2 <- V[largest]  ##replace largest with ith element
    V[largest] <- V[i]
    V[i] <- temp2
    V <- max_heap(V, largest,heapsize)   ## Recursive run
  }
  return(V)
}
```

Figure 5.12 illustrates the step-by-step implementation of the heap sort algorithm. The first step shows the original vector *V* with 11 elements, which need to be sorted in ascending order. The second step shows the initial max-heap with the largest element in the first node. The third step shows the extraction of the largest element (here, **88**). The extracted element is then placed in the last position of the array. The max-heap tree is again built with the new largest element as its first node. The fourth step shows the extraction of the corresponding largest element (here, **65**). The extracted element is then placed in the second last position of the array. The max-heap tree is rebuilt with a new largest element as its first node:

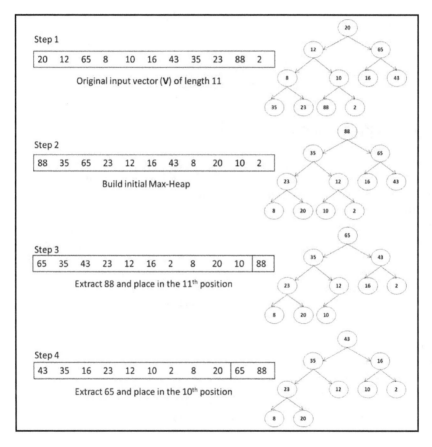

Figure 5.12: Step-by-step illustration of heap sort

These steps continue till all the elements from the max-heap tree are extracted and placed in the relevant positions. The final sorted vector is as follows:

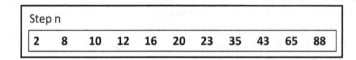

Step n

| 2 | 8 | 10 | 12 | 16 | 20 | 23 | 35 | 43 | 65 | 88 |

Figure 5.13: Final vector positions of heap sort

Now let's analyze the runtime performance of the algorithm assuming a vector of length n. The max-heap recursive function requires $\theta(n)$ runtime, and n extractions of the largest element require $\theta(\log n)$ runtime. Thus, the total runtime of the heap sort algorithm for the best, average, and worst-case scenarios is $\theta(n\log n)$.

Bin sort and radix sort

Bin sort is one of the most efficient algorithms, wherein an input vector is split into multiple bins, and then sorting is performed within each bin. The elements are assigned to the bins based on the computations performed on each element. The bins can be a list of multiple vectors or a linked list. The current execution uses a list of multiple vectors as bins. The following R code performs the bin sort operation on a numeric vector (V) containing n elements. The maxValue variable denotes the element with maximum value within the input vector:

```
Bin_Sort=function(V,n,maxValue){
  bin <-list("binValues"=list(), "nElement"=NA)
  ## create empty bins
  for(i in 1:n){
    bin[["binValues"]][[i]]<-NA
    bin[["nElement"]][i]<-0
  }
  ## add elements into suitable bins
  bin <- addItem(V=V,bin=bin,maxValue=maxValue,n=n)
  ## bind all bins into a single sorted vector
  output <- bindSorted_vec(bin=bin,n=n)
  return(output)
}
```

Initially, an empty bin is created, which contains a list (binValues) and a vector (nElement). The list (binValues) is meant to act as bins to hold elements of the input vector (V), and the vector (nElement) is meant to track the count of elements in each bin.

The functions `addItem` and `insertItem` are meant to allocate each element into bins in a sorted order. The function `insertItem` gets activated when a new element is being inserted into a bin already containing elements. While inserting, the value of the new element is compared with the existing elements. Accordingly, the position is assigned to the new element, ensuring the sorting order (ascending in our case):

```
# add item to bin
addItem=function(V,bin,maxValue,n){
  for(i in 1:n){
    val<-V[i]
    ix<-ceiling((val*n)/maxValue)
    if(is.na(bin[["binValues"]][[ix]][1])){
      bin[["binValues"]][[ix]][1]<-val
      bin[["nElement"]][ix]<-1
    } else
    {
      bin <- insertItem(val=val, ix=ix,bin=bin)
    }
  }
  return(bin)
}

# insert a item into a bin ensuring sorting
insertItem=function(val, ix,bin){
  nElement<-bin[["nElement"]][ix]
  pos<-NULL
  for(i in 1:nElement){
    if(val<bin[["binValues"]][[ix]][i]){
      pos<-i
    }
  }
  if(is.null(pos)){
    bin[["binValues"]][[ix]][nElement+1]<-val
  } else if(pos==1) {
    bin[["binValues"]][[ix]]<-c(val, bin[["binValues"]][[ix]][1])
  } else
  {
    bin[["binValues"]][[ix]]<-c(bin[["binValues"]][[ix]][1:(pos-
    1)], val, bin[["binValues"]][[ix]][pos:nElement])
  }
  bin[["nElement"]][ix]<-nElement+1
  return(bin)
}
```

Some of the key features of the functions `addItem` and `insertItem` are as follows:

- Direct computations are performed on the element values prior to assigning them to each bin. The computation depends on the length of the input vector (n) and the maximum value in the input vector (`maxValue`). This also restricts the input vector to be of integer type rather than numeric.
- The length of the `binValue` list is restricted to n. In other words, the total number of bins is n.
- The vector `nElement` keeps track of the elements in each bin.
- The function `insertItem` intrinsically ensures sorting among the elements within each bin. Whenever a new element needs to be inserted, its position is first determined based on its value, and then inserted accordingly.

Once all the elements of the input vector are allocated to the respective bins, the bins are then bound into a single `output` vector in an order from 1 to *n*. During the bind process, the relative positions of the elements within each bin are maintained. Hence, the output received is a completely sorted vector (ascending order in our case):

```
# bind the list into a sorted vector
bindSorted_vec=function(bin,n){
  output <- c()
  currentIx<-1
  for(i in 1:n){
    if(!is.na(bin[["binValues"]][[i]][1])){
      nElement<-bin[["nElement"]][i]
      for(m in 1:nElement){
        output[currentIx]<-bin[["binValues"]][[i]][m]
        currentIx<-currentIx+1
      }
    }
  }
  return(output)
}
```

The following example shows the working of the bin sort algorithm in R:

```
> V<-c(20,12,65,8,10,16,43,35,23,88,2,56,41,27,67,55)
> n<-16
> maxValue<-88
> Bin_Sort(V=V,n=n,maxValue=maxValue)
[1]  2  8 10 12 16 20 23 27 35 41 43 55 56 65 67 88
```

The performance of the bin sort algorithm is $\theta(n)$ for most of the scenarios. It is evaluated based on the number of operations required to place an element into a bin and then taking out all the elements from the bins into an output vector. However, when the input vector becomes very large, the number of traversing operations required for placement of each element increases considerably, and the performance is drastically affected.

Bucket sort is another representation of the bin sort algorithm, wherein the elements are initially assigned to each bin, and each bin is subjected to a different sorting technique. There is also no initial check on the elements being inserted into non-empty bins. Once all the elements are placed into their respective bins based on a computation criterion, each bin is then exposed to a different sorting algorithm. These individually sorted bins are later bound into a single vector of sorted elements.

Radix sort, on the other hand, is an improvised version of bin sort, wherein the number of bins can be restricted to a smaller number (generally 10 bins), and relative positioning of elements while assigning them into non-empty bins is not required. Consider a vector of *n* elements ranging from 0 to 999 which needs to be sorted in ascending order. Let us also define bins from 1 to 10 such that bin 1 is meant to store elements with the digit 1, bin 2 is meant to store elements with the digit 2, and so on. We can begin assigning elements to each bin based on their units digit. If the units digit of an element is 1, then the element will be placed in bin 1, and if the units digit is 0, the element will be placed in bin 10, and so on. Also, while inserting elements into non-empty bins, the relative positions need not to taken into account as was the case in bin sort. Once all the elements are inserted into the respective bins based on their units digit, all the 10 bins will then be bound into a single vector (without disturbing the overall order of the bins, that is, the first bin follows the second bin, which follows the third bin, and so on) using the `bindSorted_vec` function. Similarly, the process continues for the tens digit and the and hundreds digit. The following R code implements the radix sort algorithm:

```
# add item to bin
addItem=function(V,bin,digLength,n){
  for(i in 1:n){
    val<-V[i]
    ## Extract the required digit from the number
    ix<-floor((val/digLength) %% 10)+1
    ## Assign element to each bin
    bin[["binValues"]][[ix]][bin[["nElement"]][ix]+1]<-val
    ## Track count of elements in each bin
    bin[["nElement"]][ix]<-bin[["nElement"]][ix] + 1
  }
  return(bin)
}

# bind the list into a sorted vector
```

```
bindSorted_vec=function(bin){
  output <- c()
  currentIx<-1
  for(i in 1:10){
    if(!is.na(bin[["binValues"]][[i]][1])){
      nElement<-bin[["nElement"]][i]
      for(m in 1:nElement){
        output[currentIx]<-bin[["binValues"]][[i]][m]
        currentIx<-currentIx+1
      }
    }
  }
  return(output)
}

# radixsort Algorithm
radix_Sort=function(V,n,maxValue,digLength){
  for(digLength in c(10^(0:digLength)))
  {
  bin <-list("binValues"=list(), "nElement"=NA)
  # create empty bins
  for(i in 1:10){
    bin[["binValues"]][[i]]<-NA
    bin[["nElement"]][i]<-0
  }
  bin <- addItem(V=V,bin=bin,digLength=digLength,n=n)
  V <- bindSorted_vec(bin=bin)
  }
  return(V)
}
```

The following example shows the working of the radix sort algorithm in R:

```
> V<-c(67,54,10,988,15,5,16,43,35,23,88,2,103,83)
> n<-14
> maxValue<-988
> digLength <- 2
> radix_Sort(V=V,n=n,maxValue=maxValue,digLength=digLength)
[1]    2    5   10   15   16   23   35   43   54   67   83   88  103  988
```

Figure 5.14, 5.15, and *5.16* illustrate the implementation of the radix sort algorithm. Consider an integer vector (*V*) with 14 elements, with the maximum element as 988, and the length of digits as 2 (one less than the length of the maximum element):

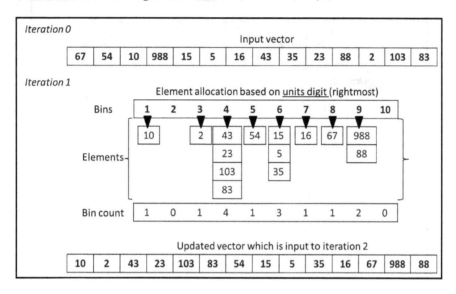

Figure 5.14: Iterations 0 and 1 of radix sort

Iteration 0 in radix sort uses the units digit from rightmost to arrange data in bins. For example, 10 with 0 in right most goes to the first bin and 43 goes to the third bin. Similarly, next iteration will use tens digit as shown in *Figure 5.15*:

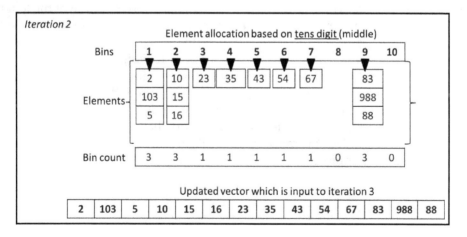

Figure 5.15: Iteration 2 of radix sort

The output from the tens digit is then reallocated using the hundreds digit (leftmost digit) as shown in *Figure 5.16*:

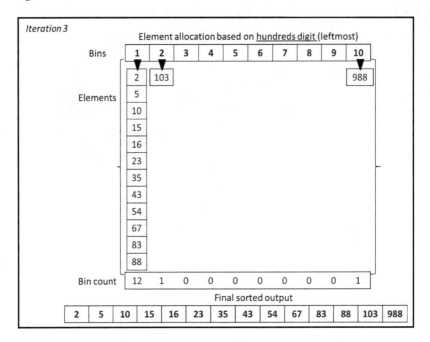

Figure 5.16: Iteration 3 of radix sort

Now, let's analyze the performance of the radix sort algorithm. The asymptote of radix sort is $\theta(n)$ for all types of best, worst, and average-case scenarios irrespective of the length of the input vector. The asymptote primarily depends on the maximum number of digits for a given input vector and the base of the computation. In our algorithm, we have used a base of 10 for performing computations on each element prior to assigning them to the respective bins. The asymptote can be rewritten as $\theta(nk + sk)$, where n represents the total length of the input vector, s represents the base, and k represents the length of the maximum element in the input vector. However, if the length of the input vector is large and most of the values are distinct, then the asymptotic complexity of radix sort changes to $\Omega(nlog\ n)$. Also, if the range of elements is large, then the radix sort algorithm will show its best performance in terms of the $\Omega(nlog\ n)$ asymptote.

Nevertheless, the radix sort algorithm is very difficult to implement efficiently. The implementation requires a number of loop iterations, which affects the runtime performance of the algorithm. The following loops form an integral part of radix sort, which is shown in the preceding three images:

- Loop to initialize the position of the digit (`digLength`) for an element
- Loop to create empty bins
- Loop to perform radix/index computation on each element prior to assigning elements into the respective bins, and to keep a track on the count of elements within each bin
- Loop to extract elements from each bin and assign them to an output vector

Also, radix sort is limited to the integer type of input vectors. Vectors with real numbers and arbitrary element lengths need to be handled with extra care.

An empirical comparison of sorting algorithms

Empirical comparison analysis intends to evaluate the performance of algorithms based on the system runtime. Many algorithms might possess the same asymptote complexity, but their performance might differ based on the size of the input vector. Empirical analysis is performed on the underlying assumption that the system properties and configuration remain the same for all the running algorithms under consideration.

Table 5.2 shows the system runtime for actual implementation of sorting algorithms measured using microbenchmark in R:

Algorithm	10	100	1k	10k	Best case	Worst case
Insertion sort	0.0818	6.831	757.851	77713.30	2.351	1615.53
Bubble sort	0.0866	14.440	1382.405	140627.75	0.772	2224.58
Selection sort	0.0690	6.453	507.285	46800.13	493.901	479.04
Shell sort	0.0914	1.864	28.038	446.30	14.264	33.47
Merge sort	0.0964	2.836	34.649	491.92	16.687	20.06
Quick sort	0.1115	2.211	26.759	907.60	96.938	691.21
Heap sort	0.1986	4.872	67.710	1887.41	70.570	72.84
Bin sort	0.1658	1.592	31.607	1585.52	28.659	28.42
Radix sort	0.4119	3.206	16.881	276.77	16.948	16.725

Table 5.2: Empirical comparison of sorting algorithms using system configuration of 2.8-GHz Intel i7 CPU running Windows. The system runtime is shown in milliseconds

The input used for empirical analysis is a random vector of integers of various lengths ranging from 10, 100, 1,000 to 10,000. The input for the best-case scenario is an increasing sorted vector of length 1,000. Similarly, the input for the worst-case scenario is a decreasing sorted vector of length 1,000. We can observe that the performance of some algorithms is agnostic of the best and worst-case input. The following are some takeaways from the preceding *Table 5.2*:

- Algorithms with asymptotic complexity of $O(n^2)$ perform poorly for large length of input vectors. Shell sort shows superior performance. Bubble sort shows the worst performance unless the input is a best-case (sorted).
- Among the algorithms with asymptote complexity $O(n log n)$, heap sort is the worst performer except in the best-and worst-cases due to overhead of class structure (heaps).
- Overall, radix sort shows a consistently good performance across all lengths of input vectors as compared to other algorithms.

Lower bounds for sorting

So far, we have covered performance assessment of algorithms based on their time complexity (number of operations). Empirical analysis shows the performance based on actual system runtime, while asymptotic analysis evaluates the performance based on the number of operations (or comparisons). However, for non-comparison-based sorts, such as bin sort and radix sort, the asymptotic complexity is evaluated using the number of iterations based on the value of specific digits as against the whole element itself. *Table 5.3* summarizes the asymptotes of sorting algorithms based on the best, average, and worst-case scenarios depending on their type of sort:

Algorithm	Type of sort	Best case	Average case	Worst case
Insertion sort	Comparison sort	$O(n)$	$O(n^2)$	$O(n^2)$
Bubble sort	Comparison sort	$O(n)$	$O(n^2)$	$O(n^2)$
Selection sort	Comparison sort	$O(n^2)$	$O(n^2)$	$O(n^2)$
Shell sort	Comparison sort	$O(n log n)$	$O(n^{4/3})$	$O(n log^2 n)$
Merge sort	Comparison sort	$O(n log n)$	$O(n log n)$	$O(n log n)$
Quick sort	Comparison sort	$O(n log n)$	$O(n log n)$	$O(n^2)$
Heap sort	Comparison sort	$O(n log n)$	$O(n log n)$	$O(n log n)$
Bin sort	Non-comparison sort	-	$O(n)$	$O(n^2)$
Radix sort	Non-comparison sort	-	$O(n)$	$O(n)$

Table 5.3: Asymptotic complexities of various assorting algorithms

Now, let's analyze the complexity induced by the problem (of sorting) itself. The upper bound of the sorting problem is the asymptotic complexity of the fastest known algorithm, whereas the lower bound is the best possible efficiency that can be achieved using any sorting algorithm (also includes algorithms which are not invented yet). Once the lower and upper bounds meet using an algorithm, then we can safely assume that no other algorithm can beat this in terms of efficiency.

The best possible bounds of the current sorting algorithms for a given size of input vector are $\Omega(n)$ and $O(nlog\ n)$. This is because of the following reasons:

- Every algorithm takes at least n iterations to read the input vector and write n elements to attain the output vector
- Also, every element needs to be scanned before recognizing whether the input vector is sorted or not

To date, no one has ever devised an algorithm which can perform better than the $O(nlog\ n)$ asymptote in both average and worst-case scenarios owing to the previously mentioned reasons. Thus, for a given worst-case scenario, we can comfortably presume that any sorting algorithm which requires $\Omega(nlog\ n)$ comparisons also requires $\Omega(nlog\ n)$ system runtime, which, in turn, shows that the problem of sorting also requires $\Omega(nlog\ n)$ system runtime. Hence, we can conclude that no comparison-based sorting algorithm with asymptotic complexity of $\theta(nlog\ n)$ can improve more than a constant factor.

Exercises

1. Write a bin sort and radix sort algorithm using linked lists. Compare their runtime with algorithms implemented using lists.
2. Rewrite the original selection sort algorithm such that redundant swaps (of the same elements) are removed, and also compare its system runtime with the original algorithm.

3. Out of the following, which algorithm preserves the original ordering of duplicate elements in the input vector? Can you suggest modifications which can prevent redundant swaps from occurring?

   - Insertion sort
   - Bubble sort
   - Selection sort
   - Shell sort
   - Merge sort
   - Quick sort
   - Heap sort
   - Bin sort
   - Radix sort

4. Can you prove why comparison-based sorting algorithms require a minimum asymptotic complexity of $O(n\log n)$ for worst-case scenarios?

5. Compare the empirical performance of merge sort using vector-based and linked list based implementation.

Summary

The current chapter builds the fundamental of sorting algorithm. The chapter introduced two kinds of sorting algorithm – comparison-based and non-comparison-based. The chapter introduced fundamentals of insertion sort, bubble sort, and selection sort, which are comparison-based algorithms and cover its implementation in R. The second half of the chapter focused on non-comparison-based sorting algorithms such as shell sort, merge sort, quick sort, heap sort, bin sort, and radix sort. The chapter also provided empirical comparison of various sorting algorithms.

6
Exploring Search Options

Searching is a widely used process in computer applications, primarily to determine whether an element with a particular value is present in a vector or list of elements or not. It acts as a substitute in case of deletions, as without searching an element of a particular value, deletion operations cannot take place. A search can be an evaluation of finding an element (exact match) in a set of given elements, or finding a group of elements (range match) which falls under a certain range of values. In a search operation, the location of the element is also determined. The location can be used later in deletion operations. A search is said to be successful if the element of a particular key value is found in the given vector (or list), and is said to be unsuccessful if the element of a particular key value is not found in the given vector (or list). This chapter shall cover concepts of sequential search operations and direct access by key value (hashing) search operations.

This chapter deals with search operations carried on both vectors and lists (including linked lists). The topics covered are as follows:

- Searching unsorted and sorted vectors
- Self-organizing lists
- Hashing

The approaches discussed in the first two sections are more effective in implementation while using an in-memory-(single node) based system, and the third approach discussed is more effective in implementation while using either in-memory-(single node) or disks (multiple nodes) based systems.

Searching unsorted and sorted vectors

Vectors are simple and widely used data structures used to perform search operations in R. The simplest form of search operation performed on vectors is a linear search or sequential search. In a linear search, each element is compared sequentially within the vector, and then suitable insertions or deletions are performed. Consider an element, S which is to be searched in an unsorted vector, V of length n (indexed from 1 to n). If the element S is not present in vector V, then a minimum of n comparisons are performed, and if it is present in V at position i, then a minimum of i comparisons are performed. In both scenarios, the number of comparisons is linear, resulting in *O(n)* as the functional form of system runtime for sequential search in the worst case scenario. The following R code performs a linear search of element S in a vector V of length n:

```
Sequential_search <- function(V,S,n)
{
  i=1
  present = FALSE
  while(i <= n & present==FALSE)
  {
    if(V[i] == S)
    present=TRUE else i = i+1
  }
  return(list(present=present,key=i))
}
```

Figure 6.1 illustrates two different sequential operations. **Part (a)** represents the situation wherein the element S is not present, and **Part (b)** represents the presence of element S. Each step corresponds to a comparison, regardless of whether the current element in the vector is equal to S or not:

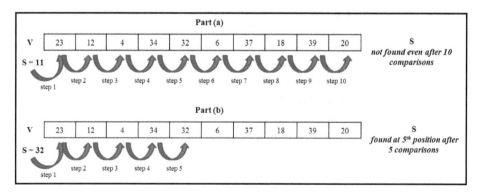

Figure 6.1: Sequential or linear search

Sequential search becomes a bottleneck when n is a very large value. One way to deal with large vectors is to pre-process them using multiple sorting techniques learned previously, and then perform a sequential search. If the current element in vector V is larger than the element S, then the search operation can be terminated early. This reduces the system runtime; however, the asymptote of the search operation does not improve beyond $O(n)$ for the worst-case scenario. The following R code performs a sequential search on an ordered vector V of length n:

```
Seq_ord_search <- function(V,S,n)
{
    i=1
    present = FALSE
    while(i <= n & present==FALSE )
    {
        if(V[i] == S)
        present=TRUE else if(V[i] > S)
        stop("element S not found") else i=i+1
    }
    return(present)
}
```

Figure 6.2 illustrates a sequential search operation being performed on an ordered vector in which the element S is not present. Here, each step corresponds to two comparisons: One, whether the current element is equal to S or not, and the other, whether the current element is greater than S or not (provided S is not equal):

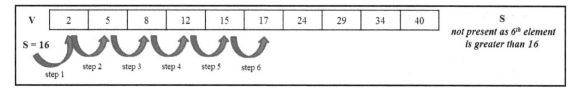

Figure 6.2: Sequential or linear search performed on an ordered vector

Now, consider a situation in which the element S is directly compared with the element in the third position and is found to be greater; then, it becomes imperative that element S is greater than the elements in the first and second position, without even comparing explicitly. This kind of comparison performed on intermittent elements (best possible jumps) rather than on each element of the vector is a key feature of the jump search algorithm.

A jump search algorithm is an improvisation on the current sequential search algorithm performed on sorted vectors. Here, the element S is initially compared with elements of the vector V positioned at regular intervals, i. In other words, the element S is initially compared with V[i], V[2i], V[3i], and so on, till the condition of S being lower is met. Once the position wherein the element in that position (key value) is greater than the element S is determined, then the sequential search is performed on its previous *i-1* elements. That is, if the element S is lesser than the element V[3i], then the sequential search is performed on elements between V[2i] and V[3i]. This dividing of the vector into sub-vectors and then performing search operations is similar to the concept of divide and conquer discussed in the *Merge sort* section in Chapter 5, *Sorting Algorithms*. The best possible i for a vector of length n is $\sqrt{n}$. The following R code performs a jump search algorithm on a sorted vector V of length n. The jumps are performed at an interval of $\sqrt{n}$:

```
Jump_search <- function(V,S,n)
{
  jump <- floor(sqrt(n))
  present = FALSE
  i=1
  while(jump < n & V[jump] < S)
  {
    i=jump
    jump = jump+floor(sqrt(n))
    if(jump>=n)
    stop("element S not found")
  }
  while(V[i] < S & i <= jump)
  i = i+1
  if(V[i]==S)
  present=TRUE
  return(present)
}
```

Figure 6.3 illustrates the working of a jump search algorithm. Initially, jumps are performed till the current value of the jumped position is greater than the element s, and then linear search is performed within the sub-vector (here, elements in positions **4**, **5**, and **6**):

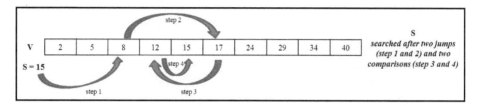

Figure 6.3: Jump search algorithm

The jump search algorithm can also be modified such that the jumps are performed at two stages, and sequential search is performed at the third stage. In a sense, a sub-vector is first determined based on a certain jump; then, within that sub-vector, smaller jumps are performed to determine a sub-sub-vector within which the sequential search is performed. This can be generalized using recursive implementation of generating sub-vectors till a single element in the vector V is left out for comparison. This generalized jump search implementation is equivalent to a binary search algorithm. The approach of binary search is to jump directly toward the element in the middle of the vector, and then compare s with it. If the value of s is greater than the middle element, then jump backward, otherwise, jump forward. The jump is always performed toward the middle element of any sub-portion of the vector in consideration. The asymptote of a binary search algorithm for an average case scenario is *O(log n)*.

A binary search algorithm can be implemented recursively or iteratively. However, recursive implementation can sometimes be risky. Following is the R code implementation of the binary search algorithm:

- Recursive implementation (returns the position of the element S if found in V):

```
Bin_search_recursive <- function(V,S,l,h) {
  if ( h < l ) {
    stop("h should be more than l")
  } else {
      m <- floor((l + h) / 2)
      if ( V[m] > S )
      Bin_search_recursive(V, S,l,m-1)
      else if ( V[m] < S )
      Bin_search_recursive(V, S, m+1, h)
      else
      return(m)
  }
}
```

- Iterative implementation (returns whether element S is present in the vector V or not):

```
Bin_search_iterative <- function(V, S,n) {
  l=1
  h=n
  i = 0
  while ( l <= h ) {
    m <- floor((l + h)/2)
    if ( V[m] > S )
    h <- m - 1
    else if ( V[m] < S )
    l <- m + 1
    else if(V[m]==S)
    return(TRUE)
  }
  return(FALSE)
}
```

Figure 6.4 illustrates the implementation of binary search on a sorted vector V:

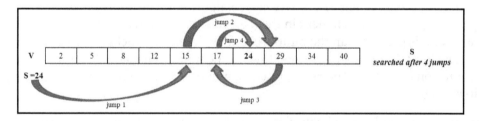

Figure 6.4: Binary search algorithm

In any of the algorithms covered so far, the distribution of key values (elements of the vector) has not been considered for search operations. Suppose you need to search a word algorithm in a dictionary. The first step will be to look for all the words which begin with the letter a, and then, within those, search for words which begin with al, and so on, till the word algorithm is found. In other words, the distribution of the word is taken into account before computing the next steps of where to search in the dictionary. This form of search, in which the knowledge of element S is considered before computing the next search steps, is called dictionary search or interpolation search. The first search position (*p*) for the element *S* in the sorted vector *V* is computed as follows:

$$p = \frac{S - V[1]}{V[n] - V[1]}$$

Upon computing the primary search position p, the element S is compared with $V[p]$. If S equals $V[p]$, then the search operation is terminated; otherwise, the position p is used to split the vector into two sub-vectors. Based on the value of S with respect to $V[p]$, the search continues in either of the sub-vectors, as illustrated in *Figure 6.5*. The split at position p is similar to the split in the binary search algorithm. Again, the new position of the sub-vector is computed based on the distribution of elements within it, and the search operation continues till the element S is found or the vector is narrowed until no elements are left. The system runtime reduces considerably, which follows an asymptote of $O(log\ log\ n)$ for average case scenarios.

The following R code performs an interpolation search of element S in the sorted vector V of length n:

```
Interpolation_search <- function(V,S,n)
{
  i=1; j=n; l=V[1]; h=V[j];
  if(S<l | S>h) return(FALSE)
  while(i < j)
  {
    k = floor(i+((j-i)*(S-l))/(h-l))
    split = V[k]
    if(S>split){
      i=k+1; l=split
    }else if(S < split){
      j=k-1; h=split
    }else if(V[k]==S){
      return(TRUE) }
  }
  return(FALSE)
}
```

Figure 6.5 illustrates the working of an interpolation search:

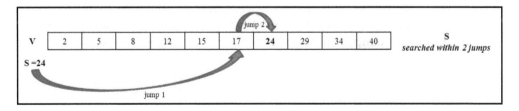

Figure 6.5: Interpolation or dictionary search algorithm

Self-organizing lists

So far, we have learned that the performance of search can be enhanced by sorting the vectors based on their key values prior to the search operations. However, there seems to be an another approach for sorting vectors, which is not based on key values but on the expected frequency of accessing the key values for comparison purposes. This kind of sorting based on expected frequency of access can sometimes be cheaper compared to sorting based on key values, thereby increasing the performance of search operations.

Consider a vector v sorted based on the frequency of access of key values, but not on the value of its elements. In other words, the elements with a higher probability (p_i) of getting compared with the search element s is placed first, followed by the element with the second highest probability, and so on. The search for element s is performed sequentially on all the sorted elements in the vector. Upon multiple search iterations, the expected number of comparisons required for one search is given as follows:

$$C'n = 1p_1 + 2p_2 + \ldots + np_n$$

Here, the cost to access the first element is *1* (only a single element to compare with s), and the probability of access of this first element is p_1. Similarly, the cost to access the second element is *2* (as the first and second elements need to be compared with, and its probability of access is p_2, and so on. Assuming the possibility of search on each of the elements in the vector, the sum of all the probabilities from p_1 to p_n is infinity.

This approach of sorting based on the frequency of comparisons has some disadvantages. Primarily, it is very difficult to determine the probabilities of access in advance if the corresponding vector has not been iterated over a bunch of search elements. Moreover, the records which had a higher frequency of access initially may not continue to stay for long time. Thus, the probability of access for some elements might change over time. These constraints led to the concept of self-organizing lists, wherein the pattern of element access is also taken into account along with their frequency of access. These self-organizing vectors are based on heuristics, examples of some heuristics for self-organizing vectors are as follows:

- **Count**: This is the most basic heuristic of self-organizing vectors. Here, the count refers to the number of comparisons or accesses being made with the elements of the vectors. The count of each key value is stored, which is used in ordering of the vector. In parallel, the elements are also moved toward the left of the vector as its count starts increasing more than the elements preceding it. The main drawback of this heuristic is that the ordering is very hostile to the change in frequency of access over time. In other words, once the element gets a higher count, it nearly always remains toward the left of the vector regardless of further changes to other elements' counts. Also, this method requires additional memory to store the count information.

- **Move-to-front**: In this heuristic, once the element S is found, the corresponding element in the vector is moved toward the first position, and all the other elements are pushed back by one positon. This kind of heuristic is called move-to-front. This is easy to implement in linked lists against vectors. In vectors, bringing a near-end element toward the front of the vector requires the displacement of a large number of preceding elements. The cost of move-to-front is almost twice the cost required by the count heuristic, wherein n searches are performed on the vector and the elements are, accordingly, order based on the frequency of access. It performs better in scenarios where the elements are accessed frequently for a brief period of time, as these elements will be near the front of the vector during this period of access. However, it performs poorly when elements are processed repeatedly in a sequential order.

- **Transpose**: The heuristic of swapping adjacent elements based on their frequency of access is termed as transpose. It performs well in both linked lists and vectors. The transpose will inherently move the most frequently accessed elements to the front of the vector. The elements which were initially accessed frequently and moved to the front will start to slowly drift backward once they are no longer accessed frequently. Thus, it performs well for scenarios where there is change in the frequency of access. In some situations, it performs poorly. Assume a sequence of search operations wherein the last and second-last elements are accessed alternately. Then these elements will get swapped for each iteration, but neither of them will move toward the front of the vector. However, these kinds of situations are rare. This can be resolved if the accessed elements are moved forward by some fixed number of positions instead of swapping with their adjacent preceding element.

Now let's understand each heuristic using an example. Consider a numeric vector, V of eight elements arranged in an order of key values, as shown in the following diagram:

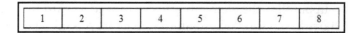

Figure 6.6: Example of numeric vector arranged in order of key values

Now, let's perform a series of 12 search operations in the following order of elements (S):

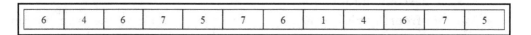

Figure 6.7: Vector of search operations to be performed

Heuristic 1 – Count

In count based heuristic, the frequency of access of the elements start moving forward. After the first three searches, the element **6** will be first, followed by **4**, and so on. The total cost of all these accesses will be 45 comparisons. The following R code implements self-organizing lists, and returns a sorted vector based on sequential search. The input is a vector V, the sequence of search elements is S, the number of elements to be searched (that is, length of S) is n_search, and the number of elements in the input vector (that is, the length of V) is n:

```
SOL_count <- function(V,S,n_search,n)
{
  if(is.null(V)) stop("NO elements in input vector")
  if(is.null(S)) stop("NO elemens to search")
  i=1
  count <- as.list(sapply(1:n,function(x) 0))
  names(count) <- V
  cl <- class(V)
  while(i<=n_search)
  {
    if(Sequential_search(V,S[i],n)$present){
      key <- Sequential_search(V,S[i],n)$key
      count[key][[1]] <- count[key][[1]] + 1
      count <- count[order(-unlist(count))]
      V <- as.numeric(names(count))
    }
    i=i+1
  }
  return(V)
}
```

The final sorted vector based on count is as follows:

6	7	4	5	1	2	3	8

Figure 6.8: Output from Heuristic 1 – Count

Heuristic 2 – Move-to-front

Here, upon finding the element S, the element is moved toward the front of the vector. The following R code implements the move-to-search heuristic of self-organizing lists, and returns a sorted vector. The input is a vector V, the sequence of search elements is S, the number of elements to be searched (that is-length of S: n_search) and number of elements in the input vector (that is, the length of V: n):

```r
SOL_move <- function(V,S,n_search,n)
{
  if(is.null(V)) stop("NO elements in input vector")
  if(is.null(S)) stop("NO elemens to search")
  i=1
  while(i<=n_search)
  {
    if(Sequential_search(V,S[i],n)$present){
      if(Sequential_search(V,S[i],n)$key !=1){
        key <- Sequential_search(V,S[i],n)$key
        temp <- V[key]
        V <- V[-key]
        V <- c(temp,V)
      }
    }
    i <- i+1
  }
  return(V)
}
```

The total cost of these accesses will be 54 comparisons, and the final sorted vector is as follows:

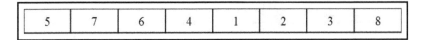

| 5 | 7 | 6 | 4 | 1 | 2 | 3 | 8 |

Figure 6.9: Output from Heuristic 2 – Move-to-front

Heuristic 3 – Transpose

Here, the elements, once found, are transposed with the adjacent element till it moves toward the front. The following R code implements the transpose heuristic of self-organizing lists, and returns the sorted vector. The input is a vector V, the sequence of search elements is S, the number of elements to be searched (that is, the length S) is n_search, and the number of elements in the input vector (that is, the length of V) is n:

```r
SOL_transpose <- function(V,S,n_search,n)
{
  if(is.null(V)) stop("NO elements in input vector")
  if(is.null(S)) stop("NO elemens to search")
  i=1
  while(i<=n_search)
  {
    if(Sequential_search(V,S[i],n)$present){
      if(Sequential_search(V,S[i],n)$key !=1){
        key <- Sequential_search(V,S[i],n)$key
        temp <- V[key-1]
        V[key-1] <- V[key]
        V[key] <- temp
      }
    }
    i <- i+1
  }
  return(V)
}
```

The total cost of these accesses will be 62 comparisons, and the final sorted vector is as follows:

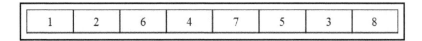

| 1 | 2 | 6 | 4 | 7 | 5 | 3 | 8 |

Figure 6.10: Output from Heuristic 3 – Transpose

The asymptote of self-organizing lists based on system runtime is $O(log\ n)$, which is similar to binary search trees; however, the former performs better in many scenarios. The main advantage of self-organizing lists is the non-requirement of a pre-sorted vector, as sorting itself requires a certain cost. Also, the cost to insert a new element is also low, as its position need not be determined, which is compulsory in the case of insertion in a sorted vector. Self-organizing lists are simple to implement, and show better performance even for smaller vectors (or lists). Thus, with a minor change in the algorithm, the performance of a sequential search can be enhanced using self-organizing lists without any prerequisite for a sorted vector.

Hashing

Hashing is a different type of search technique, wherein the key values of the vector are directly accessed. It is a process of searching the element using some computation to map its key value to a position in the vector. The values of the vector can be placed in any order satisfying certain calculations rather than being based on any key value or their frequency of access. The function which performs the computation to map the key values to positions in a vector is termed a hash function, also denoted by h. The vector which holds the elements after the necessary calculations is termed a hash table (also denoted by HT), and its positions (or keys) are termed slots. The number of slots in a hash table is denoted by m, and each slot is numbered between 1 and m. The key objective of hashing is to arrange the elements in a hash table HT such that for any key value K and some hash function h, the slot in the hash table is defined as $i = h(K)$, where i lies between 1 to m and the element in $HT[i]$ is K. The concept of hashing can be explained using ISBN book codes. In a library, each book is assigned a unique ISBN code, which is used for searching for books. The books form the raw elements (key values) of the vector, and the library is its hash table. The hash function is used to allocate the ISBN code for each book, and the codes serve as slots of the hash table.

The key purpose of hashing is to determine whether an element belongs to a particular vector or not. It is not suitable for situations where multiple elements have the same key value. It does not support searching elements falling in a certain range, or searching for an element with a maximum or minimum key value. It does not even allow access to the elements in the order of the keys. Hashing supports both in-memory and disk-based searching, and it is one of the widely used approaches for organizing large databases stored on disks.

Let's begin with a simple scenario, with each record being assigned to each unique key value upon hashing. Although it is very rare, here, the hash table *HT* can be generated directly using the key values as its slots. In other words, the element *k* is assigned to *HT[k]* using a simple hash function $h(k) = k$.

Now, let's consider scenarios that occur more often. The scenario in which two elements k_1 and k_2 are assigned to the same slot α using the hash function *h*, that is–$h(k_1) = h(k_2) = \alpha$, is termed collision. This is generally avoided by using different forms of hash functions and increasing the slots in the hash table. Suppose the number of slots is increased much higher compared to the number of elements that need to assigned. In this case, there is a risk of skewed distribution. Also, the hash table will be left with many empty slots, thus requiring a lower number of slots in the hash table sufficient to handle all the elements without any skewed distribution.

Following is a two-step procedure devised to find the element *K* in a hash table *HT* generated using a hash function *h*:

1. Compute the slot in the hash table using the hash function $h(K)$
2. Search for the element with value *K* starting from the slot $h(K)$ such that the likelihood of collision is minimized

Hash functions

Technically, any function which is used for distributing the elements (key values) of a vector (or a list) into a hash table is termed a hash function. These functions perform direct mathematical operations on the elements, and the corresponding output is then used for assigning the elements to the respective slots in the hash table. Quite often, the elements belong to a much larger numeric range compared to the range of slots in the table. Due to this kind of reduction, the possibility of the elements being assigned to a single slot increases, leading toward collision. Consider a group of 50 employees in an organization. Now, what is the probability that two employees will have the same birthday?

One of the key objectives of hash functions is to minimize the number of collisions. Hashing with zero collisions is termed perfect hashing. In perfect hashing, no two elements are assigned to a single slot of the hash table. This can be made possible if we have all the elements of the input vector prior to selecting the hash function. Once the hash table is generated using this hash function, the elements can be accessed directly without any further search required within each slot. Selecting this kind of perfect hash function can be very expensive, but it can be a trade-off toward achieving extremely efficient search performances.

Along with minimizing collisions, hash functions should also account for minimizing the number of slots in the hash table. It is advisable not to have many empty slots in the hash table, as it occupies unnecessary memory. However, it is highly unlikely to achieve zero collisions with all elements (key values) assigned to all the slots of the generated hash table.

In a nutshell, a hash function can assign all elements to a single slot of the hash table, or generate a unique number of slots for each corresponding element. It is always desirable to select the hash function in such a way that each slot of the hash table has equal probability of getting filled with any key value of the input vector. But it is implausible to have control over the key values of the input vector. The efficiency of the hash function depends on how it distributes the key values within the allowable range of slots (or keys) of the hash table. If the key values of the input vector are a random selection of numbers uniformly distributed within a key range, then any hash function that generates slots within this key range with equal probability of elements being assigned to it will also uniformly distribute the input key values in the hash table. In such scenarios, the input key values are well distributed across the hash table. However, in most scenarios, the input key values are highly skewed toward a smaller range or poorly distributed across the key range. This makes it more difficult to devise the hash function which can uniformly distribute these skewed key values into a hash table. This can sometimes be minimized if the distribution of input key values is known in advance.

The following are some reasons for non-uniformity observed among the input key values:

- If the input key values are a natural frequency of occurrences, then they are highly likely to follow a Poisson distribution. In other words, only a few key values occur more often, and many others occur relatively rarely. For example, consider the number of Internet connections across the country. The number of connections in urban areas is quite high compared to the number of connections in rural areas. Also, the number of rural areas is quite high compared to the number of urban areas. Therefore, the distribution of Internet connections is highly skewed toward a lesser number of areas (urban) across the country.
- Sometimes, data collection can be skewed due to improper adoption of sampling techniques.

Thus, the distribution of input key values plays a vital role in designing the hash functions. If the distribution of input key values is unknown, then select the hash function appropriately such that the key values are distributed across the hash table, avoiding any undue skewedness. If the distribution of input key values is known, then select the hash functions based on its distribution, thereby avoiding any undue skewedness.

The following hash function performs hashing of integers into a hash table of size 18:

```
hash_int <- function(K)
{
   return (K %% 18)
}
```

The following hash function performs hashing on strings of characters using the folding approach:

```
hash_string <- function(K,n,M)
{
   hashValue <- 0
   for(i in 1:n){
      hashValue <- hashValue+as.numeric(charToRaw(substr(K,i,i)))
   }
   return(hashValue %% M)
}
```

In this preceding function, the ASCII values of each character in a string are added, which is then used to derive a slot key of hash table. Thereby, the order of characters in a string plays no role in deciding the value of slot keys. Generally, a hash table of smaller size tends to perform better as all the characters within a string are given equal weights (irrespective of their order), and this, in turn, helps ensure a uniform distribution of strings across the slots in the hash table. Similarly, this can also be adopted for the hashing of integers (by adding the digits of integers). However, an underlying assumption is that there are no integers that can skew the results considerably (such as 14, 41, 50, 5, 23, 32; and they each will be assigned to the slot key of value 5), and generate hash keys much larger than the size of the hash table (M). As a final step, the modulus operation is performed on the summed up values to obtain values of the slot keys in the range of 0 to $M-1$. A good distribution of slots primarily depends on the range of expected summations of each string. For example, the summation range of strings of length 5 (all uppercase) will be in the range of 325 to 450, as the ASCII value of A is 65 and Z is 90. As the range is not very spread out, larger hash tables tend to show more skewed distributions, and the key values are not evenly distributed across slots.

In most practical scenarios, collision remains to haunt the implementation of hashing. These collisions can be minimized using certain resolution techniques, such as the following:

- **Open hashing or separate chaining**: The collisions are stored outside the hash table
- **Closed hashing or open addressing**: The collisions are stored within the hash table such that one of the colliding key values is stored in another slot of the hash table

Open hashing

In open hashing, slots in the hash table are defined as heads of a linked list, and colliding values are assigned to each slot of the hash table. *Figure 6.11* illustrates the working of open hashing. Consider a vector of values 484, 253, 697, 467, 865, 823, 963, and 651, which are hashed into a table with keys 0 to 9 using the hash function: *h(K) = K mod 10*. The numbers are inserted into the hash table in the aforementioned order. Collisions are observed at two slots: key 3 and key 7, and the key values within these slots are linked with each other using pointers. Other slots have only single key values.

Once the slot is identified using the hash function, the search operation begins within that corresponding slot. The key values within each slot can be ordered using multiple techniques such as insertion order, key-value order, frequency-of-access order, move-to-front order, or transpose order. In the case of key-value order, the search operation can be efficient, as it culminates once it encounters a key value greater than the search element. Whereas, if the elements within the slot are unordered or ordered using self-organizing techniques, then all the elements within each slot need to be accessed before culminating the search operation for the worst-case scenario (that is, the search element is not present in the slot):

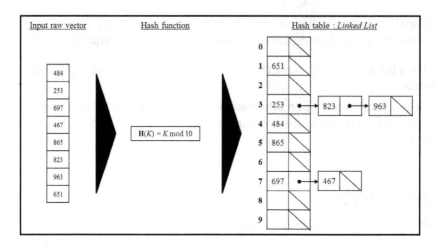

Figure 6.11: Open hashing

Suppose the number of input key values is higher than the number of available slots in the hash table, then an ideal hash function is one which distributes all the input key values uniformly among all the available slots. On the other hand, if the number of input key values is less than the number of available slots in the hash table, then an ideal function will distribute in such a way that only one key value is assigned to each slot, avoiding any collision. In the former scenario, the search operation continues post evaluating the slot in the hash table, whereas, in the latter, the search operation culminates once the slot is identified. Thus, the average cost of system runtime for the latter scenario is $\theta(1)$, which is lower than the average cost of the former.

The hash tables can be generated both in-memory (single-node cluster) or on disks (multiple-node cluster), where different slots of the hash table (or linked lists) can be assigned to different node clusters. In the single-node cluster format, all the elements are accessed seamlessly within the same node, whereas in the multiple-node cluster format, different disks need to be accessed before completing the search operation. Open hashing is more suitable for in-memory-based hash tables than disk-based hash tables, as a multi-node cluster defeats the very purpose of hashing, which is to provide seamless access to search particular key values.

One can observe similarities between open hashing and the binsort algorithm. Some of them are listed next:

- In a binsort algorithm, the elements of the input vector are initially assigned to multiple bins, and each bin can have multiple elements. Similarly, in open hashing, the input elements are initially assigned to multiple slots of the hash table, and each slot can have multiple elements.

- In binsort, the number of elements in each bin is a smaller number and sorting is performed individually on each bin. Similarly, in open hashing, the number of elements assigned to each slot is a smaller number; thereby, fewer accesses are required to complete the search operation.

Closed hashing

In closed hashing, all the input key values are stored within the hash table itself. If any collision arises, a collision resolution policy is adopted. Initially, hashing is performed on each element based on its key value, and its corresponding home slots are identified. While assigning each element to its corresponding home slot, if a new element collides with an already assigned element for a given home slot, then the new element is assigned to another empty surrogate slot based on a collision resolution policy.

This resolution policy is also adopted during search operations, because not all elements are assigned to their respective home slots, and other elements which are assigned to empty surrogate slots can also be recovered to complete the search.

Bucket hashing

Bucket hashing is one of the variants of closed hashing. In bucket hashing, the slots of the hash table are initially grouped into a relatively smaller number of buckets. Suppose there are M slots in a hash table, and there are B buckets, then M/B number of slots are assigned to each bucket. The hash functions are now directly linked to the bucket keys. Initially, the hash function starts assigning key values to the first empty slot in the bucket. In case of a collision, the slots in the bucket are sequentially searched till an empty slot is found. In the worst case, where the bucket gets filled, the elements are assigned to empty slots in an overflow bucket of infinite capacity. The overflow bucket is shared by all the buckets. A good implementation is one where most of the key values are filled in the respective buckets, and very few (kind of outliers) are assigned to the overflow bucket. *Figure. 6.12* illustrates the implementation of bucket hashing. Consider a vector of values 484, 253, 697, 467, 865, 823, 963, and 651, which are hashed into a table with buckets 0 to 4 using the hash function $h(K) = K \bmod 5$. Each bucket has two slots along with an overflow bucket, in case the existing bucket gets filled. Upon sequential hashing of the given vector, zero elements are assigned to bucket 1, one element is assigned to bucket 5, two elements are assigned to buckets 1 and 2, and three elements are assigned to bucket 3.

As bucket 3 has only two slots, the third element is assigned to the common overflow bucket:

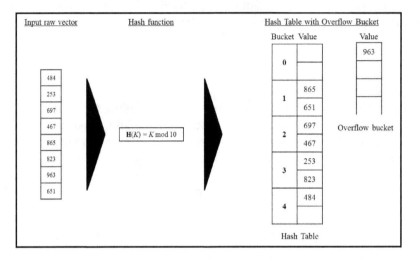

Figure 6.12: Bucket hashing

In case of a search operation, the first step is to determine which bucket the search element can be attributed to, using the hash function *h*. Then, the elements within this bucket are searched. If the search element is not found inside the bucket and the bucket is not full, then the search operation culminates. In case the bucket is full, the overflow bucket is then searched until the search element is found or all the elements within the overflow bucket have been searched. The search operation can sometimes be time consuming if the overflow bucket is too large.

So far, the key values are hashed to a given bucket with some number of slots. Consider a scenario wherein the key values are hashed to a slot which, in turn, belongs to a bucket. In short, the buckets are indirectly related to the hash function, and the slots in each bucket play a pivotal role. Here, the key values are initially assigned to their respective home slots, which belong to a certain bucket. In case the home slot gets filled up, the slots in the respective bucket are scanned sequentially, and then filled accordingly. Consider a bucket of six slots marked from 0 to 5, with the third slot already filled. Suppose a new element is again assigned to the third slot of the given bucket, then the collision resolution process will begin. In this process, initially the fourth and fifth slots are scanned for any vacancy, followed by the first and second slots. In case all the slots are full, the new element is assigned to an empty slot in the overflow bucket (which has the capacity to hold infinite slots). This approach is advantageous over the former approach, as here, any slot in a bucket can act as a home slot, whereas in the former approach, only the first element of the bucket can act as a home slot. Thereby, the number of collisions is also reduced.

Figure 6.13 illustrates the working of modified bucket hashing:

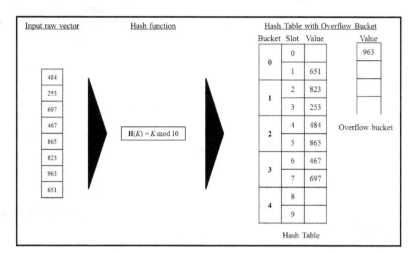

Figure 6.13: Modified bucket hashing

Unlike open hashing, bucket hashing is good to implement on multiple disks or nodes. The size of the buckets can be used to determine the size of each node cluster. Whenever a new search or insertion happens, the corresponding bucket is called into memory and all the search/insertion operations occur seamlessly as there is only one node to access. In case the bucket is full, the overflow bucket is pulled into the given node. It is highly recommended to keep the overflow bucket small enough to prevent any unnecessary node accesses.

Linear probing

Linear probing is one of the widely used closed hashing techniques which is devoid of bucketing, and has the potential to access any slot of the hash table using the updated collision resolution policy.

The primary objective of the collision resolution policy is to obtain the free slot in the hash table when any collision occurs, that is, when the home slot of any key value is already filled. The collision resolution approach can be updated such that it generates a sequence of slots which can be orderly filled upon collisions. The first slot of the sequence acts as a home slot, and subsequent slots act as surrogates. In case of a collision, the slots are sequentially scanned till an empty slot is obtained. This sequence of slots is termed a probe sequence, which is generated using a probe function represented p.

Similarly, also during the search operation, the same probe function is used to retrieve all the relevant key values which were earlier inserted for a given home slot. One of the key assumptions of the probe sequence generated using the probe function is that at least one of its slots for every key is kept empty.

This is to prevent infinite looping of unsuccessful search operations. Thus, the count of filled slots for every key's probe sequence needs to be tracked such that no further insertion takes place once the respective probe sequence is left with only one empty slot.

So far, we have covered a simple form of collision-resolution policy, wherein once the home slot is filled with a key value, the subsequent key values occupy the empty slots, which are found while traversing toward the bottom of the bucket. This kind of probing for empty slots in a linear sequence is termed linear probing, which is defined as follows: $p(K,i) = i$.

In the preceding statement, i represents the slot, which is offset by i steps down the hash table. Once the probe sequence reaches the bottom of the hash table, linear probing wraps around to start tracing from the beginning of the hash table. Thus, all the slots in the hash table are available for filling with key values before the probe sequence reaches the home slot.

Linear probing is one of the most primitive options for the resolution of collisions. However, it is one of the worst collision-resolution approaches. The main problem with linear probing is that the slot's probability of getting filled with a key value changes drastically upon insertion of every new key value into the hash table. This can be explained in detail using an illustration, as depicted in *Figure 6.15*. Consider a hash table with 0 to 9 slots (or keys), whose hash function is $K \bmod 10$. Consider five elements, which need to be inserted into the hash table in the given order: 453, 362, 396, 156, and 957. Initially, assume that each slot has an equal chance (1/10) of being a home slot, and the slot next to it has an equal chance of getting filled (due to linear probing) once its previous slot (home) gets filled. As a first step, the third slot is filled with 453, as its hash key (slot) is 3. Now, the chances of slot 4 getting filled increases to 2/10, as it can be filled either with a key value whose hash key is 3 (linear probing) or 4 (home slot). Upon second insertion, which is at slot 2, the chances of slot 4 getting filled further increases to 3/10, as now it can be filled with key values ending with 2 (linear probing), 3 (linear probing), and 4 (home slot). The chance of the remaining slots (that is, 0, 1, 5, 6, 7, 8, and 9) is still 1/10. Upon insertion of the third element, (396), at slot 6 (as home slot), the chance of slot 7 getting filled increases to 2/10, leaving other probabilities unaffected. Now, upon insertion of the fourth element (156) at slot 7 (due to linear probing), the chance of slot 8 getting filled increases to 3/10, leaving other slots' probabilities unaffected. Finally, upon insertion of the fifth element (957) at slot 8 (due to linear probing), the chance of slot 9 getting filled increases to 4/10.

Thus, the following are the resultant probabilities upon completion of all five insertions:

Slot No.	0	1	2	3	4	5	6	7	8	9
Chances	1/10	1/10	0	0	3/10	1/10	0	0	0	4/10

Figure 6.14: Probabilities obtained after insertion

Such kind of linear probing, where the slots are clustered based on their tendency to get filled up, is called primary clustering. These small clusters (at slots 4 and 9) tend to increase into a big cluster, which can further increase the discrepancy of probing:

Step 0			Step 1			Step 2			Step 3			Step 4			Step5		
Slot No.	Key Values	Probab ility	Slot No.	Key Values	Probab ility	Slot No.	Key Values	Probab ility	Slot No.	Key Values	Probab ility	Slot No.	Key Values	Probab ility	Slot No.	Key Values	Probab ility
0		1/10	0		1/10	0		1/10	0		1/10	0		1/10	0		1/10
1		1/10	1		1/10	1		1/10	1		1/10	1		1/10	1		1/10
2		1/10	2		1/10	2	362	0	2	362	0	2	362	0	2	362	0
3		1/10	3	453	0	3	453	0	3	453	0	3	453	0	3	453	0
4		1/10	4		2/10	4		3/10	4		3/10	4		3/10	4		3/10
5		1/10	5		1/10	5		1/10	5		1/10	5		1/10	5		1/10
6		1/10	6		1/10	6		1/10	6	396	0	6	396	0	6	396	0
7		1/10	7		1/10	7		1/10	7		2/10	7	156	0	7	156	0
8		1/10	8		1/10	8		1/10	8		1/10	8		3/10	8	957	0
9		1/10	9		1/10	9		1/10	9		1/10	9		1/10	9		4/10

Figure 6.15: Linear probing

One quick way of preventing primary clustering is to skip slots by a constant c instead of linearly probing by a single slot. This would modify the earlier probe function into the following: $P(K,i) = ci$. In the preceding function, c is a constant with a value less than the number of slots in the hash table.

The prime advantage of the former probe function is that the probe sequence traverses through all the slots of the hash table before reaching the home slot, which is not the case with the latter. Here, the traversing across slots is governed by the constant c. If $c=2$, then the probe function would divide the sequence into two mutually exclusive sequences; one being an even sequence and the other odd. If the hash function returns an even home slot, and is already filled, then the traversing occurs only across all even-numbered slots before the probe sequence returns to the home slot.

The case when the hash function returns an odd home slot is similar. In an ideal scenario, if both the sections have a similar number of input key values, then this kind of probing has little significance.

However, if the number of input key values is different in both the sections, then the section with the higher number of key values will have more collisions and show poorer performance, whereas the other section, with fewer key values, will have a good distribution and show better performance. Overall, the performance of the probe function decreases as the section with the higher number of collisions might dominate the declining performance.

If the constant c is relatively prime to the number of slots of the hash table, then the probe sequence will cover all the slots before it culminates at the home slot. As an example, for a table of size 10, the constant c can take the values 1, 3, 7, or 9. Similarly, for a table of size seven, any constant c lying between 1 and 6 would generate a probe sequence covering all the slots in the hash table.

Though the constant c should be able to address the issue of primary clustering, it is not in a position to completely control it. For example, when constant c assumes the value 2, the probabilities of the slots in the even and odd sequences tend to change drastically. If $h(K)=4$, then the probe sequence would continue along slots 6, 8, 10, and so on. Similarly, when $h(K)=6$, the probe sequence would continue along slots 8, 10, and so on. thereby directly affecting the likelihood of the next slot getting filled. This kind of high fluctuation observed in the probabilities because of interlinking between slots makes it more complex to address the issue of primary clustering.

This leads to a new form of probe sequence in which the untraced slots are randomly checked for availability. This would ensure no interlinking among slots, which is the main reason for primary clustering. Here the probe sequence should randomly select the slots for traversing. However, it is recommended to implement random slot selection, as duplication of the same probe sequence is not possible, which is inevitable for search operations. Nevertheless, pseudo-random probing can be implemented which has both the options: pseudo random selection and traceability for search. Here, the jth slot of the probe sequence is defined as $(h(K) + r_j) \bmod M$, where M is the size of the hash table, and r_j is the jth slot of the random permutation of numbers between 1 and $M\text{-}1$. These random permutations of numbers are stored in a vector and used for both insertion and search purposes. The probe function is written as $p(K,i) = Perm[i\text{-}1]$, where *Perm* is a vector of random numbers between 1 and $M\text{-}1$.

Another form of probe function is quadratic probing, which also controls primary clustering. The probe function defining quadratic probing is as follows: $P(K,i) = c_1 i^2 + c_2 i + c_3$.

In the preceding function, c_1, c_2, and c_3 are constants.

Quadratic probing comes with a serious disadvantage which is not applicable for many probing functions: not all the slots become a part of the probing sequence. For example, if the size of the hash table is 10, then only slots 0, 1, 4, and 9 are accessible for the quadratic function $p(K,i) = i^2$. Even if the other slots are empty, they cannot be filled up as they do not become a part of probing sequence. This becomes a grave issue when some key values are left out (not inserted) of the hash table, even though some slots are empty, as those slots do not fall under the probe sequence.

In a nutshell, the right combination of hash table size and probe function will enhance the performance of insertion and search operations. If the size of the hash table is a prime number and the probe function is i^2, then at least half of the slots in the hash table become a part of the probe sequence. Alternatively, if the size of the hash table is a power of two and the probe function is $(i^2+1)/2$, then all the slots become a part of the probe sequence.

Although pseudo-random probing and quadratic probing can control primary clustering, they induce a new form of clustering known as secondary clustering. As the probe function of these methods depends only on the home slot key (i) instead of the key value (K), the probability of the slots getting filled in a probe sequence depends solely on the home slot key. If two key values are directed toward the same home slot, then the probability of only those slots which are part of the home slot's probing sequence is affected. This kind of clustering confined to a particular home slot's probing sequence, defined using a pseudo-random probe function or a quadratic probe function, is termed secondary clustering. This can be controlled if the probe function factors in the original key value (K) along with the home slot's key (i). This can be achieved using the linear probe function in which the probe sequence consists of slots separated by a constant c, and the value c is determined using a different hash function, h_2. As a result, the modified linear probe function becomes $P(K,i) = i*h_2(K)$. This kind of two-step hashing is called double hashing. Double hashing tends to perform well when all the constants of the probe function are relatively prime to the size of the hash table (M). This can be achieved in two cases.

These are, when the size of the hash table (M) is a prime number, and the hash function h_2 returns a constant value between 1 and $M-1$:

- When the size of the hash table (M) is a power of two (2^m), and the hash function h_2 returns an odd number which lies between 1 and 2^m, where m is any real number.

Analysis of closed hashing

This section primarily deals with the analysis of hashing. The performance of hashing mainly depends on the number of accesses made before completing an operation. The operation can be an insertion, search, or deletion. Deletion can only be implemented once the element is found in the hash table. As finding an element is a part of the search operation, the number of accesses made for a search operation is equal to the number of accesses made for a deletion operation. Similarly, to perform an insertion, the slots within a probe sequence are traversed till an empty slot is found. Also, if the key value is already present in the hash table, then it is not inserted, as it causes redundancy in the hash table. Thus, a successful search (element found in the hash table) is required for a deletion, and an unsuccessful search (element not found in the hash table) is required for an insertion.

To begin with, consider an empty hash table. Then, with only one single access, insertion of the first element in its respective home slot occurs. Also, the search operation and delete operation would require only a single element access if all the elements are inserted in their respective home slots of the hash table. As the hash table starts getting filled, the probability of a new key value occupying its home slot decreases. If the new key value is hashed to an already filled home slot, then the collision resolution policy begins to search for another empty slot confined to the home slot's probe sequence. This increases the number of element accesses for performing any insertion, search, or deletion. Thus, the cost of any operation depends on the number of slots occupied within the hash table.

Let's define load factor (α) as the ratio of the number of slots currently filled (N) and the total number of slots in the hash table (size of hash table denoted as M):

$$\alpha = \frac{N}{M}$$

This load factor can be used analytically to obtain the cost function for an insertion operation, assuming that the probe sequence is generated using random permutation of slots. Thereby, we can safely assume that each empty slot has an equal probability of being assigned to a new key value as its home slot, and the load factor can be considered analogous to the probability of an empty slot being occupied by a new key value as its home slot. Thus, the probability of finding a home slot occupied with subsequent i probing slots, also occupied, can be defined as follows:

$$\frac{N(N-1)\ldots(N-i-1)}{M(M-1)\ldots(M-i-1)}$$

For larger values of N and M, the probability approximates to $(N/M)^i$. The expected number of slots in the probing sequence can be approximated as follows:

$$1 + \sum_{i=1}^{\infty} (N/M)^i \approx \frac{1}{1-\alpha}$$

Thereby, the average cost of insertion is calculated as follows:

$$\frac{1}{\alpha} \int_{0}^{\alpha} \frac{1}{1-x} dx = \frac{1}{\alpha} \log_e \frac{1}{1-\alpha}$$

So far, the average cost of insertion is based on an assumption that the probe sequence is generated using random permutation of slots in the hash table. But this assumption is not always valid. Hence, the aforementioned cost represents the lower bound of the average insertion cost. Following are the true cost estimates of insertion and deletion operations using linear probing:

- Insertion or unsuccessful search: $\frac{1}{2}\left(1 + \frac{1}{(1+\alpha)^2}\right)$

- Deletion or successful search: $\frac{1}{2}\left(1 + \frac{1}{(1-\alpha)}\right)$

Thus, the growth of cost in case of insertion or unsuccessful search is faster than the growth of cost in case of deletion of a successful search. The cost defines the expected number of accesses to perform a particular operation using a hash table. On similar lines, the growth of cost in the case of linear probing is faster than the growth of cost in the case of random probing.

Deletion

An element from the hash table can only be deleted if it is successfully found during the search operation. These deletions satisfy some considerations, such as the following:

- The deleted element's slot is again reusable for insertion purposes.

- The deleted element's slot does not hamper any sequential search operation. In other words, consider a probe sequence of four filled slots in which the element positioned in the second slot is deleted. The empty second slot does not intermittently culminate any search operation, and all the subsequent slots (third and fourth) of the probe sequence will be searched.
- No duplicate key values will be inserted into the deleted element's slot.

To satisfy these considerations, the deleted element's slot is specially marked, and is termed **tombstone**. The key features of tombstone are as follows:

- It behaves as an indication of an element's deletion.
- It allows search to continue as per slots in the probe sequence without any interference, if it is encountered prior to the completion of the search.
- It allows for insertion of new elements if it is encountered during the insertion operation. However, prior to an insertion of a new element, the search operation is performed on the entire probe sequence (devoid of the tombstone slot) to ensure that no duplicate record is inserted. In case of multiple tombstones, the new element is inserted in the first encountered tombstone. Thus, tombstone ensures reusability.

Generally, a hash table is initially created using a set of key values, and later deletions and insertions take place, which gives rise to a set of tombstones. During the initial phase of deletions, the average length of the probe sequence increases due to tombstones, which inherently increases the distance among the elements. Upon new insertions, the count of the tombstones decreases, thereby decreasing the average distance among elements within the probe sequence. However, the decrease may not be relatively substantial. This can be explained using an example. Let us assume that the initial average path distance without any tombstones is 1.3. In other words, an average of 0.3 slots is accessed for every search operation beyond the home slot. After some deletions and insertions, the average path distances increase to 1.6 due to some tombstones. The value 1.6 may seem to be reasonable, but the relative increment of two times might seem to be a problem. This can be resolved using the following solutions:

- Upon deletion, reorganization of slots within the probe sequence might help in reducing the average path distance. One crude way of performing this is to move the intermediate tombstone toward the end of the probe sequence. This can be done by simply swapping the elements (beyond the tombstone) with their previous slot such that the tombstone moves toward the end. However, this may not work for all kinds of collision resolution policies or certain probe functions.

- A periodic rehashing of elements into a new hash table after a set of deletions and insertions will ensure a lower average path distance. Due to rehashing, the tombstones are removed, and the frequently accessed elements are given an opportunity to get placed in their respective home slots.

Exercises

- In a jump search algorithm, the optimum number of jumps required to attain the minimum cost of comparisons is $\sqrt{n}$, where n is the length of the input vector. Can you derive it? Also, what is the cost of comparison for the worst case, when the number of jumps is $\sqrt{n}$.
- Evaluate the cost of searching an unsorted and a sorted (sorting based on frequency) vector, where each element has an equal probability of being accessed during the search operation, under the following conditions:
    - $p_i = 1/n$, where i is the element in the given vector
    - $p_i = 1/n^2$, where i is the element in the given vector
    - $p_i = 1/2^n$, where i is the element in the given vector
- Implement the hash function in R using the mid-square method for four-and six-digit integers.
- Implement the dictionary ADT using a hash table.

Summary

The current chapter builds foundation for search arrays and hash functions. It also covers searching on sorted and un-sorted arrays. The approach utilizes vector sorting for search operations using key-value pairs. The chapter also introduces approaches such as self-organizing lists which do not utilize key values for searching rather uses expected frequency of accessing the key values for comparison purposes. The chapter also introduces hashing concepts and covers various approaches for hashing, such as hash functions, open hashing, and closed hashing. Analysis on the computation required with the deletion operation is also covered in the final part of chapter. The next chapter will introduce tree based indexing data structures such as 2-3 trees, B-tree and B+ tree.

7
Indexing

In this chapter, we will introduce indexing concepts, which are essential in file structuring to organize large data on disk. Indexing also helps in attaining efficiency in data access, data search, and memory allocation. This chapter will build the foundation of indexing, and cover various type of indexing, such as linear indexing, **Indexed Sequential Access Method (ISAM)**, and tree-based indexing. The chapter introduces linear indexing and ISAM concepts (which are an improvement over linear indexing) using R. The current chapter will also cover advanced tree-based indexing data structures. The following is the list of topics that will be covered in detail:

- 2-3 trees
- B-trees
- B+ trees

Linear indexing

Indexing is defined as the process of associating a key with data location. The basic field of a data index includes a search key and a pointer. The search key is set of attributes that is used to look up records from a file and the pointer stores the address of the data stored in memory. The index file consists of records, also known as index entries, of the form shown in *Figure. 7.1*:

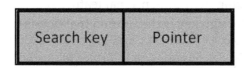

Figure 7.1: Example of index entries

Indexing helps in organizing a large dataset. A database has the following generic properties:

- The records are in a structured tabular format
- Records are searched using single or a combination of keys
- Aggregation queries such as sum, min, max, and average are used to summarize the dataset

Indexing in databases is used to enforce a uniqueness into records, which helps in speedy access of data. A database can have several filesystems associated with it by using indexing. This is shown in *Figure 7.2* using a store database example. The store database consists of three tables: the `Customer` table, which stores all customer-related information, the `Order` table, which stores transactional level information for all orders placed by customers, and the `Employee` table, which stores all employee-related information:

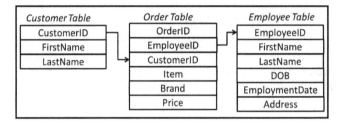

Figure 7.2: Example of store database

All tables in the store database can be mapped together using primary, secondary, or foreign keys. The columns in the database can be classified as follows:

- **Primary key**: The primary key is the column which uniquely identifies each row in the table. For example, `CustomerID`, `OrderID`, and `EmployeeID` act as primary keys in the tables `Customer`, `Order`, and `Employee` respectively.
- **Secondary key**: The secondary keys are one or more columns which do not have a unique sequence. For example, `FirstName` and `LastName` in the `Employee` table are not able to uniquely represent each row of the table, and a second field will be required to make this column act as the primary key. Secondary keys can be used for indexing in M-dimensional feature space.
- **Foreign key**: A foreign key is the column that points to the primary key in other tables. For example, `CustomerID` and `EmployeeID` in the table `Order` act as foreign keys. This key provides an interface for a smooth interaction with other tables in the database.

In linear indexing, the keys are stored in a sorted order, and the value of the key can point to the following:

- A record stored in the filesystem
- Primary key of the dataset
- Values of the primary key

The indexes can be stored in the main memory or storage disk depending on the size of data and the keys required to map it. For example, a linear index generated based on sequence is shown in *Figure 7.3*:

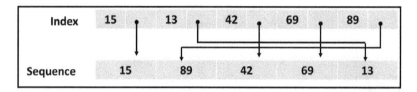

Figure 7.3: Example of linear indexing on sequence

A linear index contains the key field, and each key field has an associated pointer which links it with the actual dataset position. The sorting of the index allows an efficient search query using binary search. Binary search locates the pointers to the disk blocks or records in the file with specific key indices. As data size increases, storing the index in the main memory would not be feasible. To deal with the issue, one solution is to store the index in the hard disk. However, this would make search an expensive process, making the current indexing approach inefficient. The current issue could be addressed by using a multi-level linear index. Multi-level indexes utilize the sorted index property and computation property of binary search to minimize computation time. The computational property of binary search requires $log_2 bi$ block accesses to search for an index with b_i block. Each step performed during binary search reduces the search part of the index file by a factor of 2.

Multi-level indexing utilizes this property to reduce the part of the index to be searched by a larger blocking factor, also known as fan-out (*fo*, where *fo* is greater than 2), thus improving the search to $log_{fo} bi$. For *fo* equal to 2, there is no computational improvement due to multi-level indexing. An example of second-level linear indexing is shown in *Figure 7.4*.

Figure 7.4 demonstrates a second-level linear indexing in which the first base level is the usual-ordered primary index with a distinct value for each key. Similarly, the second base level is a primary index for the first level. The second level is the block anchor, that is, it has a one entry for each block in the first level:

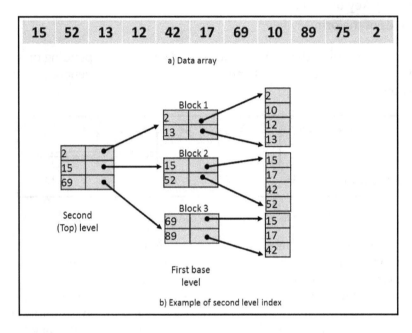

Figure 7.4: Example of a second-level linear index

The blocking factor or fan-out parameter for all levels is kept the same during indexing. Thus, if the first level has n_1 entries, then the blocking factor is bf, which is also the fan-out factor fo; so, the first level needs (n_1/fo) blocks, which is also the number of entries needed for the second level. Thus, with each addition of a level, the number of blocks is reduced by the fan-out factor. This approach can be repeated as many times to create a multi-level indexing, and is repeated until only one block is needed to fit all the indexes. Multi-level linear indexing can be used on any type of index, such as primary, secondary, or clustering, until the first-level index is represented with distinct keys. Linear indexing is quite efficient in structuring datasets. However, the main drawback is that any insertion or deletion operation would require a big change in the linear index, which would affect the computation effort significantly.

ISAM

ISAM, promoted by IBM and Ingres DBMS, also uses the linear indexing philosophy of primary key sorting. In ISAM, files on disk are divided into cylinders on disk. The cylinders are tracks readable from a particular placement of the head on a multiple platter of disk drive. ISAM addresses the limitation of linear indexing of insertion or deletion to some extent due to its static structure, but it is only suitable for small changes. Thus, ISAM is usually applied in databases which are not frequently updated. Static index allocation makes frequent insertion and deletion an expensive process. However, it helps with concurrent access of records, which helps to scale the efficiency of the current data structure. The drawbacks of ISAM with regard to insertion/deletion was later addressed by B-tree based indexing. The ISAM approach was used before the adoption of tree-based indexing:

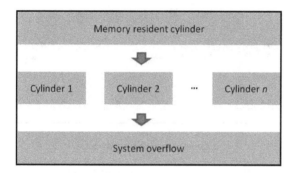

Figure 7.5: Illustration of ISAM structure

The ISAM data structure consists of a memory-resident cylinder index, cylinder index, and system overflow as illustrated in *Figure 7.5*. The memory-resident cylinder keeps the highest-value key from each cylinder. Similarly, each cylinder index keeps the highest-value key for each block. Each cylinder in ISAM consists of the following:

- **Cylinder index**: Each cylinder in ISAM contains an index that keeps updated the highest-valued key for each block.
- **Records**: Data block which stores the records.
- **Overflow**: Overflows are kept in cylinders to allow insertion of records. Based on the cylinder index, the correct overflow is identified for insertion of new records.

The system overflow in the ISAM structure is used if the cylinder overflow is completely utilized by insertion. This could drastically increase the search time:

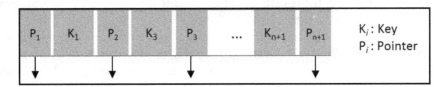

Figure 7.6: ISAM node structure

The node structure of ISAM consists of *n* keys, which are associated with *n+1* pointers, as shown in *Figure 7.6*. An example of a node structure is shown in the following diagram:

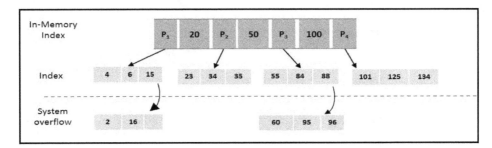

Figure 7.7: Example of ISAM indexing

As records in system overflow increase due to insertion, the performance of ISAM decreases. This is usually handled by database reorganization of records by minimizing the imbalance in records by updating the memory-resident cylinder index. The more efficient structure of ISAM is utilized in tree-based structures, as discussed in the next section.

Tree-based indexing

Linear indexing is efficient on static databases, that is, records from the database are rarely inserted or deleted. ISAM improves the performance of linear indexing, and can be used for limited updates of the database. As ISAM uses a two-level linear indexing schema, it would break down for a database where the top-level index is already too big to fit into the memory. Thus, as databases become large, we require better organization methods. One approach proposed in `Chapter 6`, *Exploring Search Options*, is that a binary search tree could potentially be utilized for indexing to store the primary and secondary keys. The binary search tree provides an efficient structure to store duplicates, and to perform operations such as deletion and insertion given that sufficient memory is available. However, the only disadvantage with a binary search tree is that it could become unbalanced.

Unbalancing becomes an issue, especially in a scenario when the tree is stored in the disk, as any operation requires data to be loaded from the disk to the memory on the path to leaf node. Thus, to minimize operation time such as insertion or search, it is recommended to store each subtree in the same block, as shown in *Figure 7.8*:

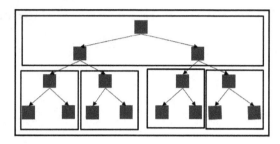

Figure 7.8: Example of breaking BST into blocks

In *Figure 7.8*, the subtree in block is loaded; thus, in the current scenario, any operation requires two block load. The R script for the BST node structure is as follows:

```
bstnode <- function(key, value) {
  node <- new.env(hash = FALSE, parent = emptyenv())
  node$key <- key          # Node key
  node$value <- value      # Node Value
  node$left <- NULL         # left children key
  node$right <- NULL        # Right children key
  class(node) <- "bstnode"
  return(node)
}
```

The load requirement could drastically increase if the tree is unbalanced, as shown in *Figure 7.9*, unless the whole tree resides in the main memory, which will keep operation time restricted to *O(log n)*, where *n* is the tree depth:

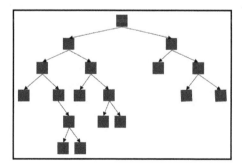

Figure 7.9: Example of unbalanced tree

The two major challenges to be addressed in tree-based indexing are the following:

- How to keep the tree balanced
- How to minimize the path from the root node to the leaf node

Balancing the tree in BST is quite expensive as, usually, balancing requires reorganization of data. A *2-3 tree*, discussed in next section, is an initial framework to balance a tree by keeping the leaves at the same level. The 2-3 trees are further extended to B-trees, which will be discussed later in the *B-trees* section.

2-3 trees

A 2-3 tree is a type of tree-based indexing where each internal node in the tree has either two nodes with one key or three nodes with two keys thus, it is classified as a balanced tree. Also, all the nodes in a 2-3 tree are at the same level of tree height. An example of a two-node structure is shown in *Figure 7.10:*

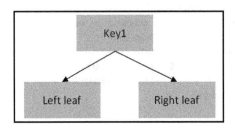

Figure 7.10: Example of a two-node tree structure

A two-node structure consists of one key and two children/subtrees. All the keys on the left side are smaller, and all the keys on the right subtree are bigger than the key. Similarly, three-node structure has two keys with three children/subtrees, as shown in *Figure 7.11:*

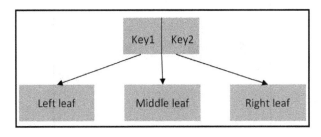

Figure 7.11: Example of a three-node tree structure

In the three-node structure, the keys are arranged in a sorted order, the first key being the smallest. All keys on the left of the subtree are smaller than the first key. All the keys in the middle of the subtree are greater than the first key and smaller than the second key. All the keys on the right of the subtree are greater than the second key. The node structure for a 2-3 tree can be represented as follows:

```
tttnode <- function(lkey=NULL, lvalue=NULL, rkey=NULL, rvalue=NULL) {
    node <- new.env(hash = FALSE, parent = emptyenv())
    node$lkey <- lkey               # left Node key
    node$lvalue <- lvalue           # Node Value
    node$rkey <- rkey               # right Node key
    node$rvalue <- rvalue           # right Node Value
    node$left <- NULL               # left children key
    node$center <- NULL             # left children key
    node$right <- NULL              # Right children key
    class(node) <- "tttnode"
    return(node)
}
```

The node structure for a 2-3 tree consists of two keys and a value pair with three children. The insertion in 2-3 nodes can be performed using steps listed next:

- If the tree is empty, create a new node otherwise find a leaf where the value belongs. For example, let's try to add **70** to a new tree:

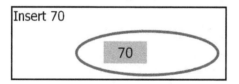

Figure 7.12(a): Insert a value into an empty tree

The insertion, as shown in the preceding image, can be obtained by creating a node using `tttnode`, with the following line of code:

```
extttree <- tttnode(70, 70)
```

- If another value is to be inserted, it checks whether the root node has space for insertion, else finds the leaf node where the value is to be inserted. For example, adding a new value to `extttree` will check whether it's vacant, and add the element accordingly:

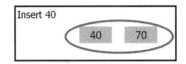

Figure 7.12(b): Insert second value to extttree

- The empty tree can be checked by evaluating both key values, and if there is empty space, then the value will be inserted in the leaf. Before insertion, the value may need to be sorted:

```
# Function to check if node is empty
check_empty<-function(node){
   ifelse((is.null(node$lkey) & is.null(node$rkey)), T, F)
}
```

The insertion script at the root is as follows:

```
# Function to insert if the node has empty space
leaf_insert<-function(node, key, val){
   if(check_empty(node)) return(tttnode(lkey=key, lvalue=val))
   if(is.null(node$rkey)){
     if(key>node$lkey){
        node$rkey<-key
        node$rvalue<-val
     } else
     {
        node$rkey<-node$lkey
        node$rvalue<-node$lvalue
        node$lkey<-key
        node$lvalue<-val
     }
   } else
   {
      node$left<-tttnode(key, val)
   }
   return(node)
}
```

- If there are three elements in the node, then the median of the node is promoted. For example, if element **80** is added to extttree, then the tree is updated as shown in *Figure 7.12(c)*:

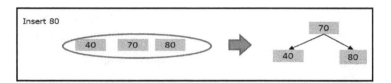

Figure 7.12(c): Insert element 80 to extttree

The preceding step will be repeated to generate the tree. The generalized pseudocode for element insertion in a 2-3 tree is as follows:

```
ttinsert<-function(node=NULL, key, val){
  if(check_empty(node)) return(tttnode(lkey=key, lvalue=val))
  if(is.null(node$left)) node<-leaf_insert(node, key, val)
  ## Add element to internal nodes
  if(key<node$lkey){
    subtree = ttinsert(node$left, key, val)
    if (identical(subtree, node$left))
    {
      return(node);
    } else
    {
      assign("left", subtree, envir = node)
      return(node)
    }
  } else if(ifelse(is.null(node$rkey), T,      key<node$rkey)){
    subtree = ttinsert(node$center, key, val)
    if(identical(subtree, node$center))
    {
      return(node)
    } else
    {
      assign("center", subtree, envir = node)
      return(node)
    }
  } else
  {
    subtree = ttinsert(node$right, key, val)
    if(identical(subtree, node$right)) {
      return(node)
    } else
    {
      assign("right", subtree, envir = node)
```

```
        return(node)
    }
  }
}
```

The implementation involves recursively determining the location where the insertion has to be made. There are two major parts to the process of insertion:

- Inserting the key and value in the root node
- Inserting the key and value in the internal node; the node is the current tree or subtree where insertion will be performed, and `key` and `val` are keys and the values/records to be inserted to the tree respectively

- The aforementioned insertion process is repeated, and nodes are splitted and promoted as required. For example, let's try and add the values **95** and **99** in two steps. The tree will be updated as shown in *Figure 7.12(d)* and *Figure 7.12(e)*:

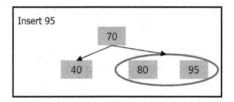

Figure 7.12(d): Insert element 95 to exttree

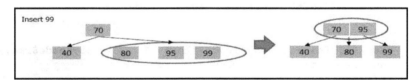

Figure 7.12(e): Insert element 99 to exttree

- Another critical aspect is searching for values using the key in a 2-3 tree. The search pseudocode within a 2-3 tree is shown as the following R function:

```
search_keys<-function(node, key){
  if (is.null(node)) return(NULL) # empty node
  if (node$lkey== key) return(node$lvalue)
  if(!is.null(node$rkey) & node$rkey==key) return(node$rvalue)
  if(key<node$lkey) {
    sort_keys(node$left, key)
  } else if(is.null(node$rkey)){
    sort_keys(node$center, key)
  } else if(key<node$rkey) {
```

```
        sort_keys(node$center, key)
    } else
    {
        sort_keys(node$right, key)
    }
}
```

Another important aspect is deletion. Deleting a key in 2-3 tree (pretty much in all tree-based data structures) requires deleting the key only in the leaf; thus, the easiest scenario for deletion is when the leaf only contains two keys. However, if deletion is required in an internal node, then deletion occurs at the leaf, and then the deletion effect is possibly propagated up the tree. The details of deletion in tree-based data structure will be covered in Chapter 8, *Graphs*, while discussing the generalization of B-trees.

The B-tree is the other most widely used data structure within databases. B-trees are a generalization of the 2-3 trees which address the data retrieval issue from storage devices, as discussed in the next section.

B-trees

Memory efficiency is an important aspect to be considered while designing data structure and algorithms. Memory can be broadly classified into two types:

- Main memory (RAM)
- External storage such as hard disk, CD ROM, tape, and so on

Data stored in main memory (RAM) has minimal access time thus preferred by most of the algorithms, whereas, if the data is stored in external drives then access times become critical, as it usually takes much longer to access data from external storage. Also, as the data size increases, retrieval become an issue. To deal with this issue data is stored in chunks as pages, blocks, or allocation units in external storage devices and indexing is used to retrieve these blocks efficiently. B-trees are one of the popular data structures used for accessing data from external storage devices. B-trees are proposed by R. Bayer and E. M. McCreight in 1972 and are better than binary search trees, especially if the data is stored in external memory.

B-trees are self-balancing (or height-balanced) search trees, where each node corresponds to a block on an external device. Each node of a B-tree stores data items and the address of successors blocks. The properties of B-trees include the following:

- The tree will have a single root node and each node may have one record and two children, if the tree is empty

- Non-leaf nodes of B-tree will have values between *d/2* and *d-1* sorted records with *d/2 +1* and *d* children, where *d* is ordered
- Keys in the ith subtree of a B-tree node are less than the $(i+1)^{th}$ key and greater than the $(i-1)^{th}$ key (if they exist)
- B-trees are self-balancing, that is, all leaf nodes are at the same level

B-trees address all the issues related to data access from external memory, which include the following:

- B-trees minimize the number of operations required while performing read/write access from external devices
- B-trees keep similar keys on the same page, thus minimizing the access required
- B-trees also maximize space utilization by distributing data efficiently
- B-trees are self-balancing, that is, all leaf nodes are at the same level

An example of a B-tree with order four is shown in *Figure 7.13*, where the order of the tree is defined by the maximum number of children that each non-leaf node supports:

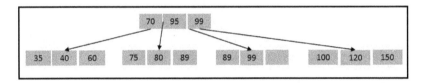

Figure 7.13: Example of a fourth-order B-tree

A B-tree of the fourth order will have three keys, and internal nodes can have up to four children. A B-tree is a generalization of the 2-3 tree at the dth order, where the order is decided to fill the disk block. The search in a B-tree is a generalization of the 2-3 search strategy by using binary search on the nodes to find whether the key is present. Similarly, B-tree insertion is a generalization of 2-3 insertion by just checking whether a node can be inserted at the key. If there is space for insertion, then the key is inserted, as the node needs to be split. The insertion requires finding an appropriate leaf node where insertion will be performed – if there is space in the leaf node, then it is straightforward and the value is inserted in the leaf node. In cases where the current leaf is already full, then it must be split into two leaves with one storing the current value. The parents are updated to store the new key and the child pointer. If the parents are full, then a ripple effect takes place, and updates are performed till the B-tree properties are satisfied. The ripple effect can go up to root node at the most. In cases where the root node is also full, a new root is created and the current root node is split into two.

An example of insertion in a B-tree is shown in the following diagram:

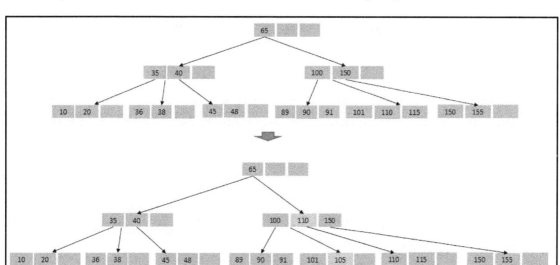

Figure 7.14: Example of insertion order B-tree (element 105 is inserted in leaf node in a B-tree which propagated the update in non-leaf node as leaf node is completely filled)

Similarly, deletion in a B-tree can be performed as shown in *Figure 7.15*. The deletion makes the tree unbalanced at one node where the number of elements is less than $d/2$; thus, readjustment is performed to balance the tree.

The generalization provided by a B-tree makes it a stronger data structure than 2-3, and most of the databases currently use B-tree or its variants. Since the development of B-tree, many variants have been proposed. The two most-used variants are B* tree and B+ tree. The B* tree variant of B-tree ensures that every node is at least two-thirds full (instead of half full); thus, in an overflow situation during insertion, B* tree applies a local redistribution scheme which delays splitting until the nearby nodes are also filled. It usually splits into three nodes instead of two. The other major variation of B-tree is B+ tree, which is the most utilized variant of B-tree, and will be discussed in detail in the next section:

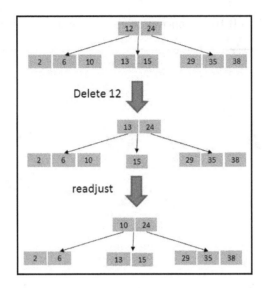

Figure 7.15: Example of deletion in B-tree

B+ trees

Queries are executed quickly if the data is stored in a sorted order as a linear indexing strategy. Thus, they are very good for static data. However, when it comes to adding operations such as insertion and deletion, they are not good, as it requires rewriting the whole data. When it comes to dealing with stored datasets, B-trees are good in indexing data in external storage devices as they read data in blocks, although any insertion and deletion could potentially lead to a lot of empty space. B+ trees generalize the B-trees to address this issue by keeping all the values in the leaf and the internal nodes only contain the keys. All the leaves which store values are linked, and the internal nodes only help to guide the operations on the leaves. A B+ tree stores up to *d* references to children and up to *d-1* keys. An example of a B+ tree is shown in *Figure 7.16*:

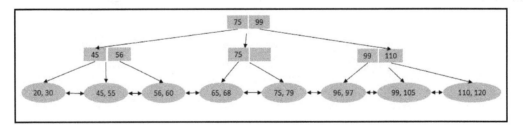

Figure 7.16: Example of B+ tree

The B+ tree requires all leaves to be equidistant from the root node. Thus, in the example shown in *Figure 7.16*, searching for any value will require three nodes to be loaded from the disk – root node, second-level, and a leaf. In practice, depth *d* will be a number as large as it takes to fill the block in the disk. For example, if a block size is 6 KB, our block is an 8-byte integer, and each reference is a 4-byte offset, then *d* is selected as the maximum value by using the equation $8(d-1) + 4d \leq 8192$, which comes out to be 682. The following properties need to be maintained in a B+ tree:

- If a node has more than one reference, then it has keys.
- All leaves are at the same distance from the root node.
- Every N^{th} non-leaf node has *k* number of keys. All keys in the first child's subtree are less than *N*'s first key, and all keys in the ith child's subtree $(2 \leq i \leq k)$ are between the $(i – 1)^{th}$ key of *n* and the ith key of *n*.
- The root has a minimum of two children.
- Every non-leaf, non-root node has children between *floor(d/2)* and *d*.
- Each leaf contains at least *floor(d/2)* keys.
- Every key from the table appears in a leaf in a left-to-right sorted order.

The pseudocode for a B+ tree node using R is shown as follows:

```
bplusnode<-function(node=NULL, key, val){
  node <- new.env(hash = FALSE, parent = emptyenv())
  node$keys<-keys
  node$child<-NULL
  node$isleaf<-NULL
  node$d<-NULL
  class(node) <- "bplustree"
  return(node)
}
```

The child node is of type doubly linked list to have a connection as shown in *Figure 7.11*:

```
dlinkchildNode <- function(val, prevnode=NULL, node=NULL) {
  llist <- new.env(parent=create_emptyenv())
  llist$prevnode <- prevnode
  llist$element <- val
  llist$nextnode <- node
  class(llist) <- " dlinkchildNode"
  llist
}
```

The above function can be utilized to create a doubly linked list. In the case of a new object, a new environment is created as shown below while adding a value 1 to a new doubly linked list:

```
> dlinkchildNode(1)
<environment: 0x000000000d034c88>
attr(,"class")
[1] " dlinkchildNode"
```

The B+ tree uses the copy-up and push-up approach for insertion. Let's take an example: Initially, B+ tree will have a single node during tree creation, and as the node overflows, the B+ tree will split the node into two. The new node is generated as the new root. The first key in the right node is copied up to the new root, as shown in *Figure 7.17*:

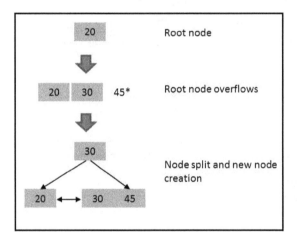

Figure 7.17: Example of B+ tree creation

The preceding example can be used to set up the insertion process for a B+ tree, which follows a schema very similar to the 2-3 tree insertion, and is stated in the following steps:

- Insert a key at the root if the node is empty
- If the node is full, then split the node into two, distributing the keys evenly between the two nodes
- For the leaf node, copy the minimum value in the second of these two nodes, and recursively repeat this to insert it into the parent node
- For the internal node, exclude the middle value during the split, and repeat the insertion algorithm to insert this excluded value in the parent node

Similar to the B-tree, the B+ tree supports exact match queries, that is, it finds the value for the given key. Furthermore, B+ trees are also very efficient for range queries, that is, finding all the values within a defined range. For an exact match query, the B+ tree follows a single path from the root node to leaf node, as depicted in *Figure 7.18*, which shows the search path for key **56**:

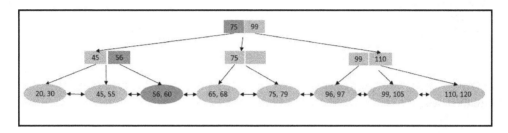

Figure 7.18: Exact query match example in B+ tree

B+ trees also very efficiently support range queries, that is, finding all the objects within a defined range. This is due to the fact that all the leaf nodes are sorted and linked together. If we want to search for all objects lying within a defined range of values, this can be achieved by performing an exact match for the lower-value key, and then following the sibling leaf using connection. An example of a range query is shown in *Figure 7.19*:

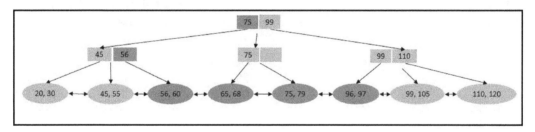

Figure 7.19: Range query example in B+ tree

The preceding diagram shows an example of a range query for all objects between [56, 97]. The B+ tree first locates the lowest value within the tree, and then transverses through the nodes to find all the values till 97. The pseudo script in R for a range query is written as follows:

```
### Function for range queries
querry_search<-function(node, key1, Key2){
  ## Function to get values within leaf node using link list
  search_range<-function(child, key1, key2, val=NULL){
    if(child$element>key1 & child$key2){
      val<-c(val, child$element)
      search_range(child$nextnode, key1, key2, val)
```

```
    } else
    {
      return(val)
    }
}

if(key1>key2){
   temp<-Key2
   key2<-key1
   key1<-temp
}
child<-search_lower_key(node, key1)    # search lower leaf
rangeVal<-search_range(child, key1, key2)   # Return Range
return(rangeVal)
}
```

The `search_lower_key` function uses a structure similar to the `search_key` function in 2-3 node. Once the leaf with the lower key is identified, the `search_range` function transverses through the interconnected leaves to find all the values till the higher limit is hit.

To delete an object from a B+ tree, the path from the root to the leaf is identified, and then the object is removed from the leaf. After removal, if the leaf is more than half-full, then nothing needs to be done. However, if, after removal, the leaf size decreases to less than half, then the algorithm redistributes values from the neighbors to underflowing nodes. In cases where redistribution is not possible, the underflowing node is merged with a neighbor. An example of deletion is shown in *Figure 7.20*:

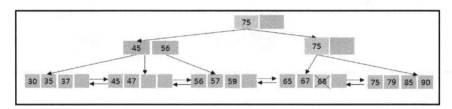

Figure 7.20: Deletion in B+ tree when leaf has sufficient number of objects after deletion

In *Figure 7.19*, the deletion of key **68** has not unbalanced the tree. However, if another element **67** is deleted from the tree, the tree readjusts as shown in *Figure 7.21*, and **79** is pushed up the node:

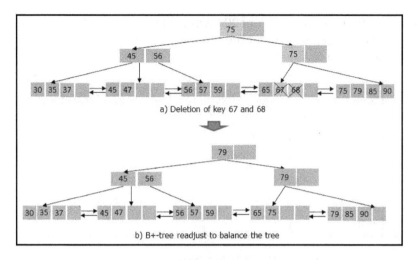

a) Deletion of key 67 and 68

b) B+-tree readjust to balance the tree

Figure 7.21: Deletion in B+ tree when leaf has an insufficient number of objects after deletion

In cases where neighboring nodes are not able to satisfy, then the nodes are merged and readjusted accordingly.

The B+ tree also supports standard of aggregation queries due to its efficiency with range queries such as count, sum, min, max, average, and so on. One approach to performing aggregation queries using a B+ tree is to keep a temporary aggregate value; starting with an initial default value, the aggregator keeps updating with every value found in the tree. On completion of the search, the aggregator's final value is returned. However, this approach is not efficient as it will require a computational effort of $O(log_b n + t/b)$, where t is number of keys and b is the tree average branching factor. The approach is also not suitable for large queries, as it requires a lot of disk pages to be accessed while aggregation. Another way to implement the B+ tree with reduced computation while aggregation is to store the aggregated values of the subtrees. Thus, when any query is executed, the local aggregates are used, and it avoids browsing the whole subtree.

B-tree analysis

B+ trees have received a lot of attention, and have been used widely in databases for indexing. Before we get into an analysis of the B+ tree, let's introduce some of its practical aspects. The minimum number of occupancy in B+ tree is 100. Thus, the fan-out parameter for a B+ tree will be between 100 and 200. From a practical perspective, an average page capacity in a B+ tree is around 66.7%.

Thus, a page with a fan-out parameter of 200 will contain *200*0.667 = 133* elements. Thus, the relationship between the height and the number of objects that a typical B+ tree can hold can be evaluated as shown in *Table 7.1*:

Depth	Average number of object	# of leaf nodes
$d=0$	133	1
$d=1$	$133^2=17,689$	133
$d=2$	$133^3=2,352,637$	17,689
$d=3$	$133^4=312,900,721$	2,352,637
...	...	...
$d=n$	133^n	133^{n-1}

Table 7.1: Deletion in B+ tree when leaf has an insufficient number of objects after deletion

The initial levels of a B+ tree have very few number of pages. For example, if a disk page is 4 KB large, then the first two levels will hold *4*134=536 KB* space on the disk, which is small enough to be stored in-memory, and need to be scanned to go down the leaf while searching.

In B-trees and B+ trees, operations are asymptotic with I/O cost of $O(log_b\ n)$, where n is the total number of records in the tree and base b is the tree average branching factor. The operation time for insertion, deletion, and search is the same in both B-trees and B+ trees as both data structures follow the path from the root to the leaf for an operation. Let's assume that the time spent on each node is $O(d)$ in the main memory. As B-tree ensures every node is at least half-full, the average branching factor will be $d/2$ where d is the order. Thus, operations in a B+ tree are asymptotic with $O(log_{d/2}\ n)$. The search, insert, and delete operations will take $O(d\ log_{d/2}\ n)$ time. To further reduce the computation, especially while inserting a lot of records, the B+ tree uses bulk load approaches, which sorts in the input, and fills the leaf nodes in a sequential order in block of page size. If the keys are sorted, then the bulk load method reduces the insertion time by $O(n/S)$, where $2S$ is the number of keys stored in a leaf.

Exercises

1. Consider that a secondary-level index with 10,400 blocks needs to be represented using multi-level linear indexing. The blocking factor is 52 entries per block, which is also the fan-out factor for multi-level indexing:

    - How many levels are required for indexing?
    - How many blocks are required at the second level?
    - What would be the minimum blocking factor to fit the dataset using a second-level linear index?

2. Write the code for deletion of an element from a 2-3 tree. Also, prove that the number of leaf nodes in a 2-3 tree with height h will be between 2^{h-1} and 3^{h-1}.

3. Assume a computer system with disk blocks of 8,192, and that you want to store records with 16-byte keys and 64-byte fields. What will be the greatest number of records that can be stored in a file if a linear index of size 4 MB is used? Assume the records are sorted and packaged sequentially into the disk file.

4. In the balanced binary tree given in the figure that follows, how many nodes will become unbalanced when inserted as a child of the node **g**?

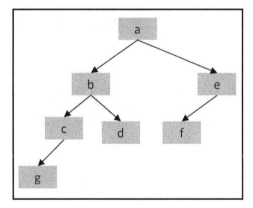

Figure 7.22: Balanced binary tree

5. Illustrate what the insertion of 1, 3, 6, 2, 7, 9, 10 (in same order) into a B+ tree will look like.

6. Suppose *N* is an interior node whose capacity is *m* keys and *m+1* leaves. Let *m* be assigned the *m+2* leaf because of leaf splitting below which leads to the creation of a new node *m* which will be siblings to immediately to its right of *m*.

7. Write a program to create and manage a B+ tree. The program should implement the following operations: creation, insertion, deletion, and tree display.

Summary

The current chapter covered the fundamentals of indexing. The chapter built on the fundamentals of linear indexing, and extended it to ISAM. The linear indexing method is a good approach for static datasets which do not change over time; however, if any updates are required, they come at a very high computation cost. To address this issue, the ISAM indexing approach has been introduced, which tries to address the updating issue of databases. But it is still suitable for a few updates only.

The chapter also covered tree-based indexing structures which utilize the binary search tree-based structure to minimize search and updates. Multiple tree-based indexing approaches were also covered. The most primitive version is a 2-3 tree which uses the two-key and three-child strategy. The 2-3 tree indexing approach is a good starting point for tree-based indexing approaches, but retrieval of data from disk-based storage is slow.

The approach is further generalized as a B-tree which ensures that the tree is balanced, and is a suitable indexing structure for disk storage as well. The B+ tree, an enhanced version of B-tree which stores data only in the leaf (B+ tree) is discussed in later part of the chapter. The B+ tree stores data only in leaves, and all leaves are interconnected, which allows multiple types of aggregation queries to be efficiently executed. The next chapter will introduce graph-based data structures, which are highly useful in understanding relationships between objects.

8
Graphs

A graph is a type of data structure capable of handling networks. Graphs are widely used across various domains such as the following:

- **Transportation**: To find the shortest routes to travel between two places
- **Communication-signaling networks**: To optimize the network of inter-connected computers and systems
- **Understanding relationships**: To build relationship trees across families or organizations
- **Hydrology**: To perform flow regime simulation analysis of various fluids

This current chapter will build fundamentals for graphs and the following topics will be covered:

- Terminology and representations
- Graph implementations
- Graph traversals
    - Depth-first search
    - Breadth-first search
    - Topological sort
- Shortest-paths problems
    - Single-source shortest paths
- Minimum-cost spanning trees
    - Prim's algorithm
    - Kruskal's algorithm

Terminology and representations

A graph (G) is a network of vertices (V) interconnected using a set of edges (E). Let $|V|$ represent the count of vertices and $|E|$ represent the count of edges. The value of $|E|$ lies in the range of 0 to $|V|^2 - |V|$. Based on the directional edges, the graphs are classified as directed or undirected. In **directed graphs**, the edges are directed from one vertex towards the other, whereas in undirected graphs, each vertex has an equal probability of being directionally connected with the others. An **undirected graph** is said to be connected if all the vertices are connected with at least one edge. If the vertices are indexed, then it is said to be a labeled graph, and if the edges are associated with some value (cost or weights), then it is said to be a weighted graph. Adjacent vertices (P and Q) connected by an edge are termed as neighbors (P, Q), and the connecting edge is termed as an incident. *Figure 8.1* represents undirected, directed, and labeled (with weights) graphs.

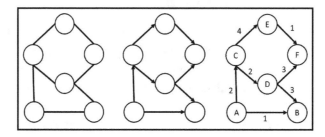

Figure 8.1: Representation of an undirected graph, directed graph, and labeled (directed) graph (from left to right)

Consider a graph with *n* vertices. A sequence of interconnected vertices $(v_1, v_2, v_3 \ldots v_n)$ is termed as a path, and the path is said to be simple if all the vertices of the path are unique. The length of the path is the number of edges, which is one less than the number of vertices (*n-1*). In case the vertices of a given path are not unique and the length of the path is greater than two, then the path becomes a cycle. A cycle is simple if all the intermediate vertices are unique and only the first and last vertices are same. An undirected graph with no cycles is called an acyclic graph, and a directed graph with no cycles is called a **directed acyclic graph** (**DAG**).

A graph can be further split into multiple subgraphs (S) as shown in *Figure 8.2*.

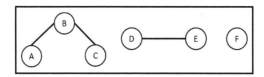

Figure 8.2: A graph split into three sub-graphs. Even a single vertex forms a graph

A free tree is a form of a connected undirected graph with no cycles in simple form. It has $|V|$-*1* number of edges.

Consider a graph (G) with n number of vertices, which can be represented in two forms. These forms can be directly used to perform mathematical computations:

- **Adjacency matrix**: The adjacency matrix is an $n \times n$ array, with rows representing the **from** vertices and columns representing **to** vertices. The numbers in the matrix can either denote the presence of a directed connection between two vertices, or can indicate the weight (or distance) associated with the edge connecting the two vertices. As each position in the adjacency matrix can take in a numeric value, it requires one bit of memory. Thus, the asymptote of total memory requirement is $\theta(|V|^2)$.

- **Adjacency list**: As the name suggests, the adjacency list is an array of linked lists of length n. Each position in the array stores the pointers connecting linked lists of its adjacent connected vertices, and each linked list stores the value of its connecting edge. Unlike an adjacency matrix, the memory requirement of adjacency lists depends on both, the number of vertices ($|V|$) and the number of edges ($|E|$). The array takes into account vertex memory requirement, and the list takes in the account of edge memory requirement. Thus, the asymptote of total memory requirement is $\theta(|V| + |E|)$.

The aforementioned two forms of representation can be used to transform and store both directed and undirected graphs. Also, based on the number of interconnecting edges, the graphs can be termed as sparse or dense. A graph with a relatively less number of edges is termed as sparse, whereas a graph with a relatively large number of edges is termed as dense. Also, in case of all interconnected vertices, the graph is termed as complete (special case of a dense graph).

Assume two vertices, P and Q. If P and Q belong to a directed graph with P pointed towards Q, then in case of an adjacency matrix, only the position of P (in row) and Q (in column) would be filled with the edge value, and the position of Q (in row) and P (in column) would be left blank. Similarly, in case of adjacency lists, the array will have both the vertices P and Q, but the edge value will be assigned only to the linked list of P, which stores a pointer towards Q. If P and Q belong to an undirected graph, then both the positions of P and Q will be filled with the edge value in case of an adjacency matrix, and both the edge values will be assigned to both the linked lists of P and Q in case of adjacency lists. *Figure 8.3* elucidates both directed and undirected graphs along with their respective adjacency matrices and adjacency lists.

In an adjacency matrix, one denotes the presence of a directed connection (from row to column) and zero represents no connection.

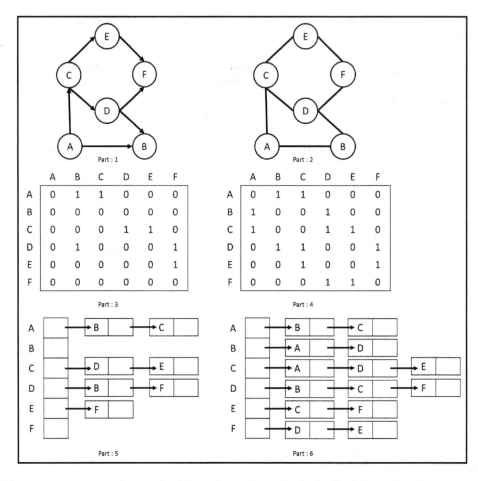

	A	B	C	D	E	F
A	0	1	1	0	0	0
B	0	0	0	0	0	0
C	0	0	0	1	1	0
D	0	1	0	0	0	1
E	0	0	0	0	0	1
F	0	0	0	0	0	0

Part : 3

	A	B	C	D	E	F
A	0	1	1	0	0	0
B	1	0	0	1	0	0
C	1	0	0	1	1	0
D	0	1	1	0	0	1
E	0	0	1	0	0	1
F	0	0	0	1	1	0

Part : 4

Figure 8.3: Representation of graphs using an adjacency matrix and adjacency lists. Part 1 shows a directed graph and Part 2 shows an undirected graph. Part 3 and 5 shows an adjacency matrix and adjacency list for directed graph. Parts 4 and 6 shows an adjacency matrix and adjacency list for an undirected graph.

Now let us analyze the memory efficiency of an adjacency matrix and adjacency list. The first differentiating factor is the number of edges in the graph. The matrix formulation of the adjacency matrix requires memory for each possible edge irrespective of its existence, whereas the linked list formulation of adjacency lists stores only those edges that are present in the graph. On the contrary, adjacency lists require additional memory for storing pointers, which can sometimes be relatively costlier. The cost primarily depends on the value of the edge (costlier in case of a binary flag indicating the mere existence of a connection). Thus, an adjacency matrix is relatively more efficient in case of denser graphs, as it has more number of edges (thereby more edge values), and an adjacency list is relatively more efficient in case of sparse graphs, as it has less number of edges (thereby less pointers to be stored).

The second differentiating factor is the number of computations required to complete a single iteration. Asymptotically, an adjacency matrix is relatively costlier than adjacency lists. In case of an adjacency matrix, all the positions within the matrix need to be scanned prior to the completion of the iteration, whereas in case of adjacency lists, only the linked connections (using pointers) are scanned, thereby reducing unnecessary lookups. Thus, the system runtime of an adjacency matrix is $\theta(|V|^2)$ and that of adjacency lists is $\theta(|V| + |E|)$. Thus, the performance of an adjacency matrix is relatively poorer in case of sparse graphs, and is almost comparable to adjacency lists in case of dense graphs.

Graph implementations

Let us create an ADT (Graph_ADT) for the implementation of functions on a given graph. The key features of ADT for a given graph analysis are the following:

- Fixed number of vertices
- Provision for addition and deletion of edges
- Provision to support a mark array, which can assist algorithms in traversing along the graph

The vertices are denoted using non-zero integer values, and can additionally store vertex names or some kind of application-based predetermined values.

The following are some ADT functions that are widely used for implementing graph functions:

- `num_vert`: This function returns the number of vertices for a given graph.
- `num_edge`: This function returns the number of edges for a given graph.
- `weightEdge`: This function returns the weight of an edge connecting two adjacent vertices. Its input is a pair of two connected vertices and its output is a numeric value indicating its weight.
- `assignEdge`: This function is used to assign weight to a given edge of a graph. The input is a pair of vertices. It can take in only a non-zero positive value, as a zero value means no connection (thereby no assignment required) and a negative value can skew the computational results.
- `deleteEdge`: This function is used to delete the weight of a given edge. The input is a pair of vertices, which has a connected edge.
- `firstVertex`: This function returns the index of the first edge vertex based on a sorted list of vertices, which are connected to a given vertex. The input is a vertex for a given graph.
- `nextVertex`: This function returns the subsequent index of vertices for a given pair of connected vertices such that the returned vertex will have an edge connecting to the first vertex. Assume that V1 is connected with V2 and V3 such that the index values of V2 are less than V3. Then, the `firstVertex` function will return the edge vertex of V1 as V2 (as the index value of V2 is less than V3), and the `nextVertex` function will return V3, as it is a subsequent connected vertex index of V1 for a given V2.
- `isEdge`: This function returns a Boolean number, where 1 represents the presence of an edge, and 0 represents the absence of an edge.
- `getMark`: This function returns the mark of a given vertex from an array `mark`.
- `initMark`: This function marks the unmarked vertex in an array `mark`.

Each graph algorithm needs to traverse every vertex before it can culminate its execution. The functions `firstEdge` and `nextVertex` facilitate such kind of traversing across the graph. It is generally implemented using loops, wherein each vertex searches for all its linked vertices and then obtains their corresponding edge weights.

The following R code implements graph ADT. It takes a number of vertices *n* as input:

```
Graph_ADT <- setRefClass(Class = "adjacency_Matrix",
  fields = list(n = "integer"),
  methods = list(
    ## Initialise a graph of n vertices
    Initialize = function(n){},
```

```
   ## Return number of vertices and edges
   num_vert = function(){},
   num_edges = function(){},
   ## Return weight of an edge for a pair of vertices v1 and v2
   weightEdge = function(v1,v2){},

   ## Assign weight(wt) of an edge for a pair of vertices v1 and
   v2
   assignEdge = function(v1,v2,wt){},

   ## Delete weight of an edge for a pair of vertices v1 and v2
   deleteEdge = function(v1,v2){},

   ## Return first connecting vertex for a given vertex v
   firstVertex = function(v){},

   # Return next vertex for a given v and its neighbor w
   nextVertex = function(v,w){},

   ## Check for presence of an edge for a pair of vertices v1 and
   v2
   isEdge = function(v1,v2){}
))
```

The `GraphADT` function can be implemented using either adjacency matrix or adjacency list representations. In this chapter, a sample implementation of graph ADT is shown using both an adjacency list and adjacency matrix; however, the creation of a graph object has not been addressed. In lieu of the graph object, the `assignEdge` function can be used to build graphs based on edges.

In the adjacency matrix implementation, a list, `mark`, stores the output of the `setMark` function, and the `getMark` function can be used to extract the `mark` of a given vertex. The edge matrix `mat` is an $n \times n$-dimensional array of integers, which store the weights of edges. The rows represent the **from** vertices, and the columns represent the **to** vertices. In case of no connection between two vertices, their edge weight is stored as zero:

```
adjacencyMatrix <-
setRefClass( Class = "adjacencyMatrix",
  fields = list(n = "integer"),
  methods = list(
    ## Initialise the graph of n vertices
    Initialize <- function(n){
      numVertices <<- as.integer(n)   ## with n vertices
      numEdges <<- 0L       ## with no connected edges
      mark <<- list()         ## initialize mark list

      ## initialize the mark of all vertices to 0 (unvisited)
```

```
        for(i in 1:numVertices)
        mark[[i]] <<- 0L

        ## generate a new nxn matrix with initial weights as 0
        mat <- matrix()
        for(i in 1:numVertices)
        for(j in 1:numVertices)
        mat[i,j] <<- 0L
    },

    ## get number of vertices
    num_vert <- function() return(numVertices),

    ## get number of edges
    num_edges <- function() return(numEdges),

    ## return the first adjacent neighbor of vertex index v
    firstVertex <- function(v){ },

    ## return next adjacent vertices of index v after
    ## getting index w using firstVertex
    nextVertex <- function(v,w){ },

    ## Assign weight to each connected edge of indices v1 and v2
    assignEdge <- function(v1,v2,wt){ },

    ## Delete a connected edge between indices v1 and v2
    deleteEdge <- function(v1,v2){ },

    ## Check whether an edge exists between indices v1 and v2
    isEdge <- function(v1,v2){
        return(mat[v1,v2] != 0) },

    ## Get weight of the connected edge between indices v1 and v2
    weightEdge <- function(v1,v2){
        return(mat[v1,v2]) },

    ## Get the mark of a vertex of index v1
    getMark <- function(v1){
        return(mark[[v1]]) },

    ## initialise the mark of a vertex of index v1 with 1
    initMark <- function(v1,val){
        mark[[v]] <<- val}
))
```

For a given vertex V, the `firstVertex` function scans through the row V of the matrix mat to locate the first edge and its corresponding **to** vertex. If the function fails to find the first vertex, it returns the value *n+1*. The `nextVertex` function is used to find the subsequent connected edge for the vertex V. If the edge is found, the `nextVertex` function will return the index value of the connected vertex, or else it will return the value *n+1*. The following R snippet can be used to get `firstVertex` and `nextVertex`:

```
## return the first adjacent neighbor of vertex index v
firstVertex <- function(v){
  for(i in 1:numVertices)
  if(mat[v,i] != 0)
  return(i)
  return(numVertices+1)
},

## return next adjacent vertices of index v after
## getting index w using firstVertex
nextVertex <- function(v,w){
  for(i in (w+1):numVertices)
  if(mat[v,i] != 0)
  return(i)
  return(numVertices+1)
},
```

The `assignEdge` function is used to append the edges of a graph in the array, and `deleteEdge` is used to delete the edge from the array. The `weightEdge` function is used to return the edge value of the given **from** and **to** vertices. The following R code implements the adjacency matrix representation of graphs. It takes in a number of vertices *n* as an input. The R script for `assignEdge` and `deleteEdge` is shown as follows:

```
## Assign weight (wt) to each connected edge of indices v1 and v2
assignEdge <- function(v1,v2,wt){
  if(wt<0) stop(""Weight should be positive"")
  ## increase the count of edges as the weights are assigned
  if(mat[v1,v2] == 0) numEdges <<- numEdges + 1L
  ## replace 0 with the wt
  mat[v1,v2] <<- wt
},
## Delete a connected edge between indices v1 and v2
deleteEdge <- function(v1,v2){
  if(mat[v1,v2] != 0) numEdges <<- numEdges - 1L
  mat[v1,v2] <<- 0
}
```

In case of adjacency lists, the data structure is not as simple as in the case of an adjacency matrix. Here, a list `vertex` of length n is initialized, and each element in the list is assigned to its edges using the linked lists form of data structure. These lists store the index value of connected vertices along with their edge weights. It takes in a number of vertices n as input:

```
adjacencyList <-
setRefClass( Class = "adjacencyList",
  fields = list(n = "integer"),
  methods = list(
    ## Initialise the graph of n vertices
    Initialize <- function(n) {
      numVertices <<- n # with n vertices
      numEdges <<- 0L # with no connected edges
      mark <<- list() # initialise mark list

      ## initialize the mark of all vertices to 0 (unvisited)
      for(i in 1:numVertices)
      mark[[i]] <<- 0L

      ## generate a list of edges each for
      ## each vertex in the list
      vertex <- list()
      for(i in 1:numVertices)
      vertex[[i]] <<- llistofEdges()
    },

    ## get number of vertices
    num_vert <- function() return(numVertices),

    ## get number of edges
    num_edges <- function() return(numEdges),

    ## return the first adjacent neighbout of vertex index v
    firstVertex <- function(v) { },
    ## return next adjacent vertices of index v after
    ## getting index w using firstVertex
    nextVertex <- function(v,w) { },
    ## Assign weight to each connected edge of indices v1 and v2
    assignEdge <- function(v1,v2,wt) { },
    ## Delete a connected edge between indices v1 and v2
    deleteEdge <- function(v1,v2) { },
    ## Check whether an edge exists between indices v1 and v2
    isEdge <- function(v1,v2) {
      pos <- currentPos(vertex[[v1]], firstAdjVert(vertex[[v1]]))
      while(pos < length(vertex[[v1]])) {
        adjVert <- nextAdjVertex(vertex[[v1]],vertex[[v1]][pos])
        if(adjVert == v2) {
```

```
          return(TRUE) } else {pos = pos+1 }
       }
    },

    ## Get weight of the connected edge between indices v1 and
    v2
    weightEdge <- function(v1,v2){
      if(isEdge(v1,v2)){
        adjEdge <- getValue(vertex[[v1]],v2)
        return(adjEdge)
      } else {return (0)}
    },

    ## Get the mark of a vertex of index v1
    getMark <- function(v1){
      return(mark[[v1]])
    },

    ## initialise the mark of a vertex of index v1 with 1
    initMark <- function(v1,val){
      mark[[v]] <<- val
    } ))
```

The functions `firstVertex` and `nextVertex` scan through the list to determine adjacent vertices using the R function as follows:

```
## return the first adjacent neighbour of vertex index v
firstVertex <- function(v){
  if(length(vertex[[v]]) == 0)
  ## indicates no adjacent neighbour
  return(numVertices+1)
  ## Move to the first adjacent vertex
  adjVert <<- firstAdjVert(vertex[[v]])
  ## get the current position of AdjVert
  pos <<- currentPos(vertex[[v]],adjVert)
  ## get value of connecting edge
  adjEdge <<- getValue(vertex[[v]],adjVert)
  return(adjVert)
},

## return next adjacent vertices of index v after
## getting index w using firstVertex
nextVertex <- function(v,w){
  if(isEdge(v,w)){
    if(pos+1 > length(vertex[[v]])){
      ## move the next adjacent vertex of w
      adjVert <<- nextAdjVertex(vertex[[v]],w)
      ## get the current position of adjcent vertex
```

```
        pos <<- currentPos(vertex[[v]],adjVert)
        ## get value of connecting edge
        adjEdge <<- getValue(vertex[[v]],adjVert)
        return(adjVert)
    }
    ## no connecting edge
  } else return(numVertices+1)
},
```

The functions `assignEdge` and `deleteEdge` traverse across the linked lists of a given vertex. The following R code implements the adjacency list representation of graphs:

```
## Assign weight (wt) to each connected edge of indices v1 and v2
assignEdge <- function(v1,v2,wt){
  if(wt<0) stop("Weight should be positive")
  ##check whether edge exists between v1 and v2
  if(isEdge(v1,v2)){
    ## insert vertex v2 along with edge weight wt
    insertVertex(vertex[[v1]],v2,wt)
  }
},

## Delete a connected edge between indices v1 and v2
deleteEdge <- function(v1,v2){
  if(isEdge(v1,v2)){
    removeEdge(v1,v2)
    numEdges <<- numEdges - 1L
  }
},
```

Graph traversals

The concept of traversing across various nodes (or vertices) in a graph along connected edges is termed as graph traversal. The traversing across nodes is typically organized, but can sometimes be random. However, in both the scenarios, traversing begins from a specified start node and ends at a specified final node. Usually, the start and final nodes are not directly connected. In order to establish an indirect connection, a selective organized search is instantiated across the various connected paths. Graph traversal algorithms are generally designed to begin at a given start node and then search for subsequent connected nodes before terminating at the given final node.

Additionally, these traversing algorithms also need to factor in some plausible issues such as the following:

- **Infinite looping**: Traversing can end in an infinite loop provided the graph contain cycles
- **Disconnected graph**: Traversing (from a specified start node) sometimes can culminate without reaching all the nodes, as they are not connected with the traversed path

These issues are typically addressed by keeping track of the nodes encountered along the paths traversed. The nodes once marked are generally not visited again, unless otherwise specified. Thus, infinite looping can be prevented from happening. In addition, if all the nodes are not visited in a traverse, then a new traversal is initiated from an unmarked node, which continues until all the nodes are visited at least once.

The following R code shows the structure of a graph traverse algorithm. It takes in `Graph_ADT`, number of vertices n, and a vector of `vertices` as inputs:

```
graph_Traverse <- function(Graph_ADT, n, vertices)
{
  ## Initialise marks to zero
  verticesMarks <- list()
  for( i in 1:n)
  verticesMarks[[i]] <- Graph_ADT$initMark(vertices[i],0) ## 0 means
  not visited

  ## Initiate traversing upon checking for unmarked nodes
  for(i in 1:n)
  if(Graph_ADT$getMark(vertices[i])==0)
  initTraverse(verticesMarks, vertices[i])
}
```

The following are some approaches to implement graph traversal algorithms (the `initTraverse` function):

- Depth-first search (DFS)
- Breadth-first search (BFS)
- Topological sort

Depth-first search

DFS is a recursive implementation of the graph traversal algorithm, applicable to both directed and undirected graphs. At each step during the traverse, DFS recursively checks and visits all the unvisited nodes, which are directly connected with the node under consideration. Simultaneously, all the visited nodes along the path are pushed into a stack in the order of the traverse. During the traverse, if nodes with no unvisited nodes directly connected to them are encountered, then such nodes are popped out of the stack leaving behind the ones with directly connected unvisited nodes. This keeps track of those nodes that determine the forward traverse path such that all the nodes are visited prior to culmination. The following R code implements the DFS algorithm with three inputs. The inputs are `Graph_ADT`, n (number of nodes in the graph), and v (node under consideration to perform DFS):

```
DepthFirstSearch <- function(Graph_ADT, n, v)
{
  ## Ensure all nodes are visited and processed prior node v
  preVisit(v)

  ## mark the node v under consideration as 1 (i.e. visited)
  VerticesMarks <- list()
  VerticesMarks[[v]] <- Graph_ADT$initMark(v,1)

  ## Recursively visit all connected nodes of v till all are      marked
  as 1
  ## get the first vertex
  node <- Graph_ADT$firstVertex(v)
  ## check node belongs to neighboring nodes using conVert      function
  while(node %in% conVert(v)){
    ## check if the node is unvisited
    if(Graph_ADT$getMark(VerticesMarks[[node]] == 0))
    ## recursively run DFS
    DepthFirstSearch(Graph_ADT,n, node)
    ## assign next neighbouring vertex
    node <- Graph_ADT$nextVertex(v,node)
  }

  ## Run post processing remaining un-visited nodes
  postVisit(v)
}
```

An example of a DFS algorithm on an undirected graph is shown in *Figure 8.4*.

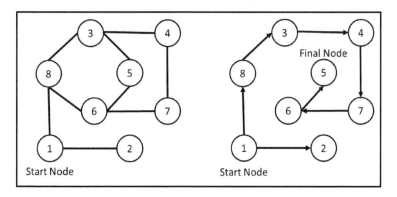

Figure 8.4: Represents an undirected graph (left) along with its final search path (right) using a DFS algorithm

Figure 8.4 illustrates an initial undirected graph and its corresponding final search path obtained using the DFS algorithm. *Figure 8.5* illustrates the working of DFS in detail using stacks. The sub-function `nextVertex` selects the node with the lowest index value among all the directly connected unvisited nodes. As the graph is undirected, the DFS algorithm can move in either of the directions as against the directed graph, where the DFS algorithm can move only in a single direction.

The asymptote of the DFS algorithm is $\theta(|E|+|V|)$. $|E|$ represents a visit to each node (traversing all edges only once) and $|V|$ represents visiting each node (only once).

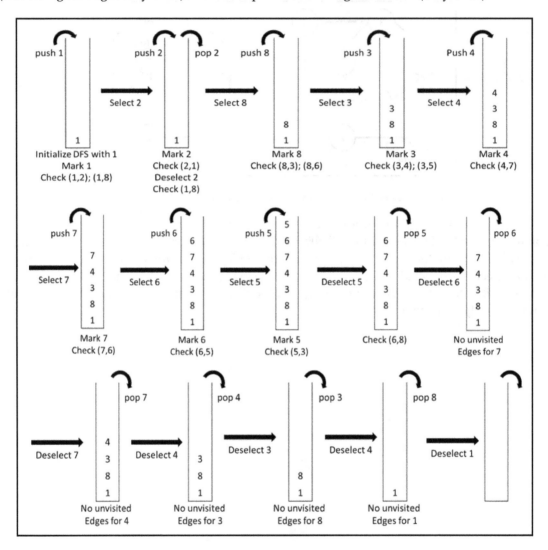

Fig 8.5: Illustration of recursive processing using the DFS algorithm and using A as a start vertex

Breadth-first search

BFS works on a principle similar to the DFS algorithm except the following:

- BFS is not a recursive implementation unlike DFS
- To keep track of the marked nodes, BFS uses queues as against the stacks used in DFS
- Prior to moving to the next node, BFS ensures visits to all of its directly unmarked connected nodes unlike DFS, wherein only one of the unmarked connected nodes is visited at each iteration

The following R code implements the BFS algorithm using four inputs. The inputs are Graph_ADT, startVertex (starting nodes of the graph to begin the traverse), queue (an empty queue to keep track of connected nodes in the order of visit), and n (total number of nodes in the graph):

```
BreadthFirstSearch <- function(Graph_ADT,startVertex, queue, n)
{
  ## initialise an empty queue with a start vertex
  queue <- initQueue(startVertex)

  ## Initialise first vertex by marking it as 1 (visited)
  VerticesMarks <- list()
  VerticesMarks[[v]] <- Graph_ADT$initMark(v,1)

  ## Subsequently start processing in queues
  while(length(queue) != 0){
    ## extract first element in the queue
    v <- extQueue(queue)

    ## Pre-Process all directly connected nodes of v
    preVisit(v)

    ## Mark visited nodes with 1 and accordingly queue the nodes
    node <- firstVertex(v)
    while(node %in% conVert(v)){
      if(getMark(graph[node] == 0)){
        graph <- Graph_ADT$initMark(node,1)
        queue <- initQueue(node)
      }
      node <- Graph_ADT$nextVertex(startVertex,node)
    }
  }
}
```

Figure 8.6 illustrates an initial undirected graph and its corresponding final search path obtained using the BFS algorithm.

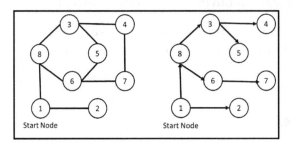

Figure 8.6 : Represents an undirected graph (left) along with its final search path (right) using the BFS algorithm

Application of the BFS algorithm on queues is illustrated in *Figure 8.7.*

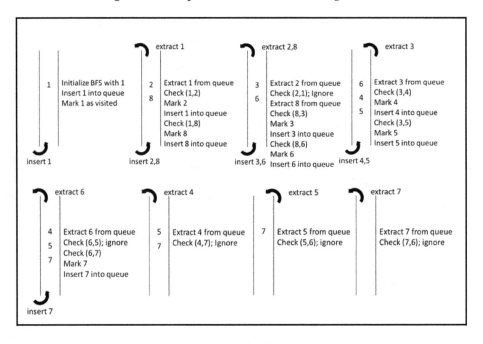

Figure 8.7 : Illustration of processing using the BFS algorithm and using 1 as a start vertex

Topological sort

The topological sort algorithm is primarily used in scenarios where nodes are conditionally dependent on previous nodes. In other words, the graph traversal can only happen if all its predecessor-connected nodes are visited (or processed). It is generally used in jobs where each stage is scheduled one after the other. For example, during construction of a tower, the columns cannot be raised till the foundation is complete, and roofing cannot be done till the columns are erected. Here, laying the foundation is followed by the erection of columns, which is followed by laying of the roof.

DAG form the basis of topological sort algorithms. In DAG, all the nodes are directionally connected, which takes care of order, and none of the nodes form a cycle, which ensures no conflict with any predecessor nodes (already visited and marked). Thus, DAG safeguards the linearity order among interconnected nodes, thereby being suitable for implementation of the topological sort algorithm. *Figure 8.8* illustrates an example of a DAG acceptable for implementing the topological sort algorithm. The topological sort of this graph is 1, 2, 3, 4, 5, 6, 7, 8.

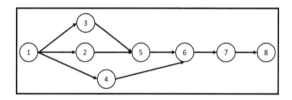

Figure 8.8: An example graph to perform topological sort

The topological sort algorithm is performed using both the DFS and BFS algorithm on DAGs.

In the case of a DFS approach, when a node is visited, no pre-processing is performed (using the `preVisit` function), whereas during recursive implementation, if the same node is revisited, then that node is returned as an output (using the `postVisit` function). Thus, the order of output-returned nodes is a reverse sort. The output for the preceding example DAG using the DFS algorithm is 8, 7, 6, 4, 5, 2, 3, 1. Thus, the topological sort is reverse of the output, that is–1, 3, 2, 5, 4, 6, 7, 8. This is also called In-order search (pre-order and post-order). Also, in-order search leads to a sorted output.

The following R code implements a topological sort using the recursive DFS algorithm. The inputs are `Graph_ADT`, n (total number of nodes in the graph), and `vertices` (a vector of vertices of the graph):

```
## Main function to perform topological sort
Topological_DFS_sort <- function(Graph_ADT, n, vertices)
{
  ## initialise all nodes with 0 (unvisited)
  verticesMarks <- list()
  for(i in 1:n)
   verticesMarks[[i]] <<- Graph_ADT$initMark(vertices[i],0)
  ## Process all nodes by recursive traversing
  for(i in 1:n)
   if(Graph_ADT$getMark(vertices[i]) == 0)
    topological_secondary(Graph_ADT,i)
}

## recursive secondary function to help main function
topological_secondary <- function(Graph_ADT,i)
{
  ## Mark the node as 1 (visited)
  verticesMarks[[i]] <<- Graph_ADT$initMark(vertices[i], 1)

  ## Perform traversing across connected nodes
  v <- Graph_ADT$firstVertex(vertices[i])
  while(v %in% conVert(vertices[i])){
    if(Graph_ADT$getMark(vertices[i] == 0))
    topological_secondary(vertices,v)
    v <- Graph_ADT$nextVertex(vertices[i],v)
  }
  return(v)
}
```

In the case of the BFS approach, the topological sort algorithm is implemented using queuing logic. Here, the nodes are inserted into the queue, not only purely based on their index value (as described in the previous section), but also taking the account of each node's pre-requisites. One of the widely used pre-requisites is the count of inward edges for each node. These counts determine the constraints for each node. Once each node is assigned its respective counts, the nodes with zero count are considered as starting nodes, and are placed in the queue in a predefined order (for example, based on their index value). Then the queuing process begins, where each node is pushed out of the queue, and all its relevant connected nodes are pushed into the queue. Once a node is pushed out, the counts of its directly connected nodes are decreased by a value of one, and the nodes, which have their current count reduced to zero, are pushed into the queue. The order in which the nodes are pushed out of the queue determines the output of the topological sort. Sometimes, the queue becomes empty and not all the nodes are visited.

These situations arise because of some cyclicity present in the graph or on violation of any of the node's prerequisites. The output of the preceding example using the BFS algorithm in topological sort is 1, 2, 3, 4, 5, 6, 7, 8, 9.

The following R code shows an implementation of BFS in topological sort. The inputs are `Graph_ADT`, x (total number of nodes in the graph), `vertices` (a vector of vertices of the graph), and `queue` (an empty queue to keep track of connected nodes in the order of visit):

```
Topological_BFS_sort <- function(Graph_ADT, queue, n, vertices)
{
  ## Initialise a list to track count of inwards edges for each node
  countEdge <- list()

  ## initialise count of each node to 0
  for (i in vertices)
   countEdge[[i]] <- 0

  ## Assign count (inward nodes) prerequisite to each node
  for(i in vertices){
    v <- Graph_ADT$firstVertex(vertices[i])
    while(v %in% conVert(vertices[i])){
      countEdge[[v]] <- countEdge[[v]] + 1
      v <- Graph_ADT$nextVertex(vertices[[i]],v)
    }
  }

  ## Initialize queue with nodes which have zero count of inward
  edges
  for(i in vertices)
   if(countEdge[[i]] == 0)
    queue <-  Graph_ADT$initQueue(i)

  ## Process the nodes which are in the queue
  while(length(queue) != 0){
    v <- extQueue(queue)
    print(v)
    w <- Graph_ADT$firstVertex(v)
    while(w %in% conVert(vertices[v])){
      ## Decrease the count prerequisite by 1
      countEdge[[w]] <- countEdge[[w]] - 1
      if(countEdge[[w]] == 0) ## no prerequisites
      queue <- initQueue(w)
      w <- Graph_ADT$nextVertex(vertices[v],w)
    }
  }
}
```

Shortest path problems

Consider a city with a large number of roads interconnecting all its core areas, and you need to drive from an area P to an area Q. As the network of road is dense, you can have multiple options to reach area Q; nonetheless, you would desire to take the shortest route. However, the shortest route can have higher traffic; hence, you may now desire to take a new route, which minimizes travel time with a trade-off with distance. Adding further constraints, not all the routes allow bi-directional traffic. In other words, the shortest route needs to satisfy multiple constraints, and then, suggest the best possible route. Analogously, in a graph, each node corresponds to a city, and the edges correspond to the interconnecting roads. The weights of the edges can either be compared to distance or to travel time (based on traffic). These graphs can also be directed or un-directed based on whether a lane allows traffic in a single direction or both. Hence, it is not trivial to deduce the shortest path satisfying all the constraints. The graph in *Figure 8.9* illustrates a network of roads with respective distances and directions.

Assume that you need to travel from node A to node F. Then, there are five possible routes connecting node A to node F. Each path comprises of a set of intermediate nodes (except one direct connection), and each edge connecting these nodes contributes for the calculation of distance from node A to node F. The distance of travel from A to E to F is 33, whereas the distance from A to C to F is only 19. In addition, the distance from A to B to F is 26, from A to B to D to F is 18, and A directly to F is 25. Thus, the shortest distance from A to F is 18. Now, this brings out some interesting nuances such as the following:

- Not all direct connections have a minimal cost. Here, the shortest distance from A to F is not a direct connection.
- Paths with less intermediate nodes need not have a lower cost. Here, the shortest path has the maximum number of intermediate nodes (that is–2).
- Unconnected nodes assume an infinite distance between them, such as the distance of the edge directly connecting C and D.
- All the distances (or costs / weights) assume to take in positive values. Negative values imply a reverse direction in case of directed graphs and zero value (disconnect) in case of undirected graphs.

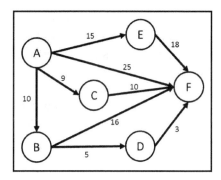

Figure 8.9 : Example of a road network connecting six nodes (A to F)

Single-source shortest paths

This section deals with the analysis of all possible shortest paths for a given single source (that is–a start vertex V) in a graph G. The shortest paths are determined between the start vertex V and all other vertices in the graph. In other words, the computation of the shortest distance between a start vertex V and an end vertex W would involve finding all possible shortest paths from start vertex V to all other intermediate vertices (worst-case scenario). It is widely used in computer routing networks, which involve transfer of data from one start source to multiple sources across the network. The time taken to transfer data or the edge network connectivity governs the cost parameter of the graph network.

As studied earlier, graphs can be broadly classified based on direction and edge weights. In case of undirected and unweighted (or equal weighted) graphs, the BFS algorithm is widely used to estimate single-source shortest paths. Once the edges are assigned with different weights, Dijkstra's algorithm is widely used to estimate single-source shortest paths regardless of their directions. The key features of Dijkstra's algorithm are as follows:

- It maintains a track of the shortest possible distance between the source vertex and all other vertices of the graph
- It also keeps a track of the path that outlines the shortest possible route from the source vertex to all other vertices of the graph

Initially, an infinite value is assigned to each vertex of the graph. The value here represents the distance from the given source vertex. To begin with, the value of the source vertex is decreased to zero, and all its adjacent neighbors are processed with the updated distance values. Then, the vertex with the least value is extracted, and the values of all its adjacent unmarked vertices are updated accordingly. This process continues until all the vertices are extracted and all the values processed. In the end, the algorithm returns two key outputs. One output displays the shortest possible distances to each vertex from the source vertex V, while the second output shows the linkage of each vertex with its parent vertex. The second output is used to deduce the shortest path to any vertex from the given source vertex V.

In the current implementation of Dijkstra's algorithm, all the vertices and their distance values are initially stored in a priority queue. The priority queue is used for insertion (push) and extraction (extractMinVertex) of key-value pairs. The Push function is used in insertion of a new key-value pair to the priority queue, and the extractMinVertex function is used in extraction of a key-value pair with the least value. The value represents the distance of the key (vertex) from the source vertex. The vertices are subsequently extracted, processed, and stored in two different hash maps. One hash map stores the shortest distances from the source vertex, and the other stores parent vertices to keep track of the shortest path from the source vertex.

The current implementation of the priority queue function uses R5 classes. The R code is as follows:

```
PriorityQueueInit <-
  setRefClass("PriorityQueueInit",
  fields = list(keys = "integer", values = "integer"),
  methods = list(
   push = function(key,value) {
     keys <<- append(keys, key)
     values <<- append(values, value)
   },
   extractMinVertex = function() {
     minPos <- which(values==min(values))
     key <- keys[[minPos]]
     value <- values[[minPos]]
     return(list(key=key,value=value))
   }
))
```

Using the preceding priority function and two hash maps (from the `cran` package hashmap), the following R code implements Dijkstra's algorithm. The four inputs to this function are `Graph_ADT`, a `sourceVertex`, a vector of all the vertices of the graph, and the number of vertices, n:

```
DijkstraShortestPath <- function(graph,sourceVertex,vertices,n) {
 library(hashmap)  ## To create new hashmap instance
 ## Initiate a new priority queue
 priorityQueue <- PriorityQueueInit$new()
 # Initiate a hashmap to store shortest distance from
 # source vertex to every vertex
 distanceMap <- hashmap(keys=vertices, values = rep(0,n))
 # Initiate another hashmap to store the parent vertex to keep a
 # track of shortest path from source vertex to every vertex
 parentMap <- hashmap(keys = sourceVertex, values = "NULL")
 # initialize priority queue with value of all vertices to infinity
 for( i in vertices) priorityQueue$push(vertices[i],Inf)
 ## Set the distance of sourceVertex as zero
 priorityQueue$values[which(priorityQueue$keys==sourceVertex)] <- 0
 ## Begin iteration till the all the vertices from
 ## priorityQueue becomes empty
 while(length(priorityQueue$keys) != 0){
 ## Extract vertex with minimum value from priority queue
   headVertex <- priorityQueue$extractMinVertex()
   ## Assign the key of the head vertex as current vertex
   currentVertex <- headVertex$key
   ## Append distancemap with current key and its value
   distanceMap[[currentVertex]] <- headVertex$value
   ## Check for all directly connected vertices for current vertex
   for(conVert in getConVertex(graph,currentvertex)){
     ## get all the corresponding edge value
     edgeValue <- getEdgeValue(graph,currentvertex,conVert)
     ## Check priority queue contains the adjacent connected
     ## vertex (conVert) or not
     if(!priorityQueue$keys %in% conVert){ next }
     ## Now evaluate the distance of the adjacent vertex (conVert)
     updDistance <- distanceMap[[currentVertex]] + edgeValue

     ## Updated parentmap using value of the adjacent vertex
     ## in priorityQueue
     if(priorityQueue$values[which(priorityQueue$keys==conVert)]
     > updDistance){
       priorityQueue$values[which(priorityQueue$keys==conVert)] <-
       updDistance
       parentmap[[conVert]]  <- currentVertex
     }
   }
 }
```

```
        }
    }
```

The time complexity of the current implementation is $\theta(|E|\ log(V))$, as during the worst case scenario, the size of the priority queue will be $|V|$, and the number of push and extract operations will be $|E|$. However, memory complexity of the current implementation is $\theta(|E| + |V|)$, because during the worst case scenario, the size of the priority queue and distance map will be $|V|$, and the size of the parent map will be $|E|$.

Let us understand the working of Dijkstra's algorithm based on the graph given in *Figure 8.9*. Initialize vertex A as the source vertex with value zero and rest of the vertices with value infinity. Then extract A, as it has the minimum value, and check for all its adjacent connected vertices. Update vertices B, C, E, and F with the respective distance values of edges (from source vertex A). Then, extract vertex C, as it has the least value among the remaining lot of vertices. Now, search for its connected vertices, which is F. The current value of F is 25, based on edge (A, F); however, based on the edge connection from C, the distance of F from A is the sum of edge distances (A, C) and (C, F), which comes out to be 19 (lesser than 25). Hence, update the value of F with 19, and assign C as a parent of F. Now, based on the updated vertex values, select the unmarked/unvisited vertex with the least distance, and continue updating the adjacent vertices. *Table 8.10* shows the updated vertex values at the end of every extraction.

	A	B	C	D	E	F
Initialise	0	∞	∞	∞	∞	∞
Extract A	0	10	9	∞	15	25
Extract C	0	10	9	∞	15	19
Extract B	0	10	9	15	15	19
Extract D	0	10	9	15	15	18
Extract E	0	10	9	15	15	18

Table 8.10: Illustration of updated vertices values at the end of each extraction using Dijkstra's algorithm

Minimum-cost spanning tree

A **Minimum Spanning Tree** (**MST**) works on graphs with directed and weighted (non-negative costs) edges. Consider a graph G with *n* vertices. The spanning tree is a subgraph of graph G with all its *n* vertices connected to each other using *n-1* edges. Thus, there is no possibility of a cycle with the subgraph. If the spanning tree does have a cycle, then it is advisable to remove any one edge, probably the one with the highest cost. The spanning tree with the least sum of edge weights is termed as a MST. It is widely used in applications such as laying of power cables across the city, connecting all houses using the least length of power cables. Here, the weight of each edge is the length of the cable, and the vertices are houses in the city. The most common algorithms to find the minimum cost spanning tree are Prim's algorithm and Kruskal's algorithm. *Figure 8.11* shows the minimum cost spanning tree for an undirected-weighted graph.

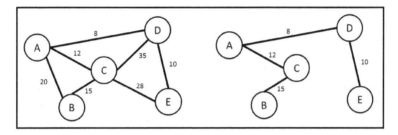

Figure 8.11: Illustration of an undirected graph (left) and its minimum-cost spanning tree (right)

Prim's algorithm

Prim's algorithm works on lines similar to Dijkstra's algorithm to find the least cost edges connecting all the vertices in the graph. In case of Dijkstra's algorithm, the selection of least cost edges depends primarily on the source vertex, whereas in case of Prim's algorithm, the least cost edge does not depend on any source vertex. Now let us understand the working of Prim's algorithm in detail. Consider a graph G with *n* vertices, all edges weighted with non-negative costs. Initially, select any vertex V from the graph to begin the traverse. Then, look for all its connected edges, and select the one with the least cost. Let us assume the next selected vertex based on least cost is W. Now, again look for all connected edges of V and W, and select the edge with the least cost. Now, add this new vertex with the V and W. Continue searching for least cost edges until all the vertices are traversed across the graph. The selected edges will then form a MST of the graph such that one can traverse from any vertex to any other vertex. Prim's algorithm works greedily, because at each step, the algorithm tries to select the new (unmarked) vertex, which has the least edge cost compared to all the edges connected to a certain marked vertex.

The algorithm's key purpose is to select least cost edges, but it does not care whether the selected vertices form a minimum-cost spanning tree or not. This trickles down to a question of whether the output of Prim's algorithm is actually a minimum-cost spanning tree? The proof for the output being a MST is an exercise question for the readers.

Now, let us understand the working of Prim's algorithm with an example graph shown in *Figure 8.12*. Initialize the algorithm with vertex A, and scan for all its connected edges. It leads to vertex D, as the connecting edge (A, D) has the least cost, 8. Now, assign edge (A, D) to MST, and scan for all other edges connected to vertices A and D. It leads to vertex E, as the connected edge (D, E) has the least cost, 10. Now, assign edge (D, E) to MST, and scan for all other edges connected to vertices A, D, and E. This leads to vertex C, as the connecting edge (A, C) has the least cost, 12. Now, assign edge (A, C) to MST, and scan for all other edges connected to vertices A, C, D, and E. This leads to vertex B, as the connecting edge (C, B) has the least cost, 15. Now, assign edge (C, B) to MST. Thus, a minimum-cost spanning tree is obtained with all the vertices connected using least cost edges.

The key difference in the implementation of Prim's algorithm and Dijkstra's algorithm is in the way the value of a vertex is updated over an extraction. In Dijkstra's algorithm, the distance value of each vertex is updated based on the value of the current vertex and the connecting edge value with the current vertex. However, in case of Prim's algorithm, the distance value of each vertex depends only on the edge value of the current connecting vertex. In the former approach, each vertex seeks closeness towards the source vertex, whereas in the latter approach, each vertex can seek closeness towards any vertex in the graph.

The following R code implements Prim's algorithm. It uses the same priority queue as that of Dijkstra's algorithm:

```
primMST <- function(Graph_ADT,vertices,n)
{
  library(hashmap)   ## To create new hashmap instances
  ## Initiate a new priority queue
  priorityQueue <- PriorityQueueInit$new()
  ## Initiate a hashmap to store shortest distance from source
  ## vertex to every vertex
  distanceMap <- hashmap(keys=vertices, values = rep(0,n))
  ## Initialise a list to store final MST result
  MSTResult <- list()
  # initialize priority queue with value of all vertices to infinity
  for( i in vertices) priorityQueue$push(vertices[i],Inf)
  ## begin with a random vertex
  startVertex <<- vertices[sample(1:n, 1)]
  ## Set the distance of startVertex as zero
  priorityQueue$values[which(priorityQueue$keys==startVertex)] <- 0
  ## Begin iteration till the all the vertices from priorityQueue
```

```
## becomes empty
while(length(priorityQueue$keys) != 0){
  ## Extract vertex with minimum value from priority queue along
  ## with its value
  headVertex <- priorityQueue$extractMinVertex()
  ## Assign the key of the head vertex as current vertex
  currentVertex <- headVertex$key
  ## Append distancemap with current key and its value
  distanceMap[[currentVertex]] <- headVertex$value
  # Check for all directly connected vertices for current vertex
  for(conVert in getConVertex(graph,currentvertex)){
    ## get all the corresponding edge value
    edgeValue <- getEdgeValue(graph,currentvertex,conVert)
    ## Check priority queue contains the adjacent connected vertex
    ## (conVert) or not
    if(!priorityQueue$keys %in% conVert){ next }
    ## Update the distance with the edge value
    updDistance <- edgeValue
    ## Check whether the value of the adjacent vertex
    if(priorityQueue$values[which(priorityQueue$keys==conVert)]
                                              > updDistance){
      priorityQueue$values[which(priorityQueue$keys==conVert)]
                                              <- updDistance
      MSTResult[[currentVertex]] <- conVert
    }
  }
}
}
```

Kruskal's algorithm

Similar to Prim's algorithm, Kruskal's algorithm is also a greedy algorithm in which the algorithm greedily selects edges based on edge value to generate a MST. Initially, partition all the vertices into an equivalent number of |V| sets, each with an individual vertex. Then, select an edge with the least cost and combine the equivalent sets of the **from** and **to** vertices into a single set. Also add the edge into the MST. Continue the process of selecting the minimum edge until all the vertices combine into a single set. In case of combining two inequivalent sets, first find the sets containing the **from** and **to** vertices, and accordingly merge those two sets. If both, **from** and **to** vertices for a particular edge, lie in the same set, then ignore the edge and proceed ahead.

Let us understand the implementation of Kruskal's algorithm for the graph in *Figure 8.9*. First, split the five vertices into five different sets. Then, select edge (A, D), as it has the least weight among all the other edges. As A and D are in two different sets, combine them into a single set, and add the edge (A, D) into MST. Then, select edge (D, E), as it has the second least edge weight. As D and E are in two different sets, combine them into a single set, and add edge (D, E) into MST. Then, select edge (A, C), as it has the third least edge weight. As A and C are in two different sets, combine them into a single set, and add edge (A, C) into MST. Then, select edge (C, B), as it has the fourth least edge weight. As C and B are in two different sets, combine them into a single set, and add edge (C, B) into MST. Thus, all the vertices, A, B, C, D, and E, are present in a single set and the selected edges form a MST. *Figure 8.12* illustrates the steps involved in Kruskal's algorithm for the graph in *Figure 8.9*.

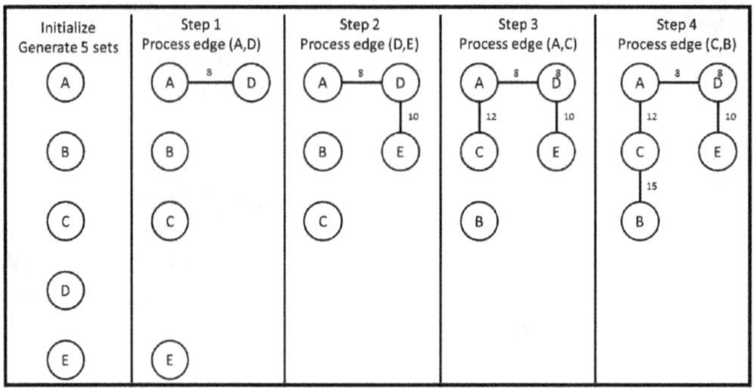

Figure 8.12: Illustration of Kruskal's algorithm on an example graph

The edges are processed in the order of edge weights using a priority queue reference class (kruskalArray). Here, pre-sorting of edge weights is not required, hence it reduces system runtime. In the kruskalArray reference class, the edges, along with their **from** and **to** vertices can be appended using the push function, and the edge with minimum weight can be extracted using the extractMinEdge function. Once the edge is extracted out, it is then removed from the array. The kruskalArray function is implemented using the R5 class, and it is as follows:

```
kruskalArray <- setRefClass("kruskalArray",
   fields = list(fromVertex = "numeric",
   toVertex = "numeric",
   weight = "numeric"),
   methods = list(
      ## insert new from and to vertices along with edge
      push = function(f, t, w){
         fromVertex <<- append(fromVertex, f)
         toVertex <<- append(toVertex, t)
         weight <<- append(weight, w)
      },
```

```
    ## extract from and to vertices having minimum edge value
    ## also remove from, to and edge value from the array
    extractMinEdge = function() {
      minPos <- which(weight==min(weight))
      from <- fromVertex[[minPos]]
      to <- toVertex[[minPos]]
      fromVertex <<- fromVertex[[-minPos]]
      toVertex <<- toVertex[[-minPos]]
      weight <<- weight[[-minPos]]
      return(list(from=from,to=to))
    }
))
```

Using the `disjoinSetPointer` function, the operations of `union`, `differ`, and `find` are undertaken. Two different sets of vertices are combined using the `union` operation, and the `differ` operation is used to check whether two sets are disjoint or not. In case of a set with more than one vertex, the `find` operation is used to check whether a vertex belongs to that set or not. The `disjoinSetPointer` function is implemented using the R5 class, and it is given as follows:

```
disjoinSetPointer <- setRefClass("disjoinSetPointer",
  fields = list(vertex = "vector",
  set1 = "vector",
  set2 = "vector",
  currentVertex = "integer"),
  methods = list(
    ## merge two sets
    union = function(set1,set2){
      return(c(set1,set2))
    },
    ## check whether set1 and set 2 are disjoint
    ## return TRUE if they are disjoint
    differ = function(set1,set2){
    if(sum(set1 %in% set1) ==0){
      return(TRUE)} else(return(FALSE))
    },
    ## Find whether a vertex is in a set or not
    ## returns root of the currentVertex
    ## function ROOT returns root of the vector
    find = function(currentVertex){
      return(ROOT(vertex[currentvertex]))
    }
))
```

The following R code implements Kruskal's algorithm using the preceding two reference classes. The inputs are `Graph_ADT`, the number of vertices, `n`, and the number of edges, `e`, in the graph:

```
kruskalMST <- function(Graph_ADT,n,e)
{
  ## initialize reference classes disjoinSetPointer and      kruskalArray
  vertexArray <- disjoinSetPointer$new()
  edgeArray <- kruskalArray$new()

  ## Initialise a list to store final MST result
  MSTResult <- list()

  ##  Put all the edges in the edgeArray
  for(i in 1:n){
    j <- firstVertex(i)
    while(i <= n){
      edgeArray$push(i,j, Graph_ADT$weightEdge(i,j))
    }
  }

  ## Initialise n equivalent sets
  numMST <- n

  ## Iteratively combine equivalent sets based on edge weights
  ## edges are extracted based on their value. Smallest edges are
  extracted first
  for(i in 1:e){
    while(numMST >= 1){
      # get the from and to vertices having minimum edge value
      temp <- edgeArray$extractMinEdge()
      fromVertex <- temp$from
      toVertex <- temp$to

      ## Check whether two vertices are in different sets
      if(vertexArray$differ(fromvertex,toVertex)){
        ## if yes, then combine from and to vertices into one set
        vertexArray$union(fromvertex,toVertex)
        ## add this edge to MST
        MSTResult[[i]] <- c(fromVertex,toVertex)
        ## decrease the sets by 1
        numMST <- numMST - 1
      }
    }
  }
  return(MSTResult)
}
```

The asymptote of Kruskal's algorithm, based on system runtime in a worst-case scenario is $\theta(|E| \log|E|)$, as all the edges need to be processed before the completion of generating a minimum-cost spanning tree. However, quite often, the number of minimum-value edge extractions is equivalent to the number of vertices in the graph (as shown in the preceding example). This makes the algorithm have a system runtime asymptote of $\theta(|V| \log|E|)$, generally observed in average-and best-case scenarios.

Exercises

1. Generate an adjacency matrix and an adjacency list for the following graph:

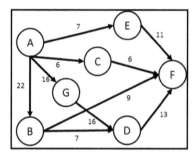

2. Generate a DFS and BFS tree for the preceding graph.
3. Prove the following hypothesis: An acyclic undirected graph with n nodes has no more than n-1 edges.
4. Find the MST for the graph given in *Figure 8.13* using Prim's and Kruskal's algorithm. Do they give the same MSTs? If no, in what type of situations do they give different MSTs?
5. Starting from vertex B, can you obtain single-source shortest paths using Dijkstra's algorithm? Do the edges obtained in question 4 of *Exercises* overlap with the edges obtained using Dijkstra's algorithm? If yes, explain the logic behind the overlap.

Summary

This current chapter covers the fundamentals of graphs and introduces terminology and representation. The later sections of this chapter covers searching techniques in graphs using DFS and BFS. This chapter also introduces in-order search in scenarios where nodes are conditionally dependent. The chapter also covers Dijkstra's algorithm widely used to estimate single-source shortest paths regardless of their directions. The concept of MST is introduced with algorithms such as Prim and Kruskal, which are covered to extract MST from a directed and weighted graph. The next chapter will extend of static algorithms to randomized algorithms, and it also introduces the fundamentals of programming.

9
Programming and Randomized Algorithms

In the preceding chapters, we covered some fundamental data structures and algorithms. The current chapter extends static algorithm (deterministic algorithm) concepts to randomized algorithms. Deterministic algorithms use polynomials of the size of the input, whereas random algorithms use random sources as input and make their own choices. The chapter will introduce the Las Vegas and the Monte Carlo randomized algorithms and their application using examples. The chapter will also introduce skip list and its extended version, randomized skip list, which uses randomization concepts to reduce the computation effort in an average case scenario. We will start with the fundamentals of programming, which can be used to reduce computational effort in intensive tasks. The current chapter will cover the concepts of dynamic programming and **directed acyclic graphs** (**DAGs**). The current chapter will cover following topics:

- Dynamic programming
    - The knapsack problem
    - All-pairs shortest paths
- Randomized algorithms
    - Randomized algorithms for finding large values
    - Skip lists

Dynamic programming

Dynamic programming can be defined as an approach that uses a recurrent formula (breaking a problem into a subproblem) to solve any complex problem. A sub-solution of any problem is reconstructed using the previous state solution. Dynamic programming-based approaches are able to achieve a polynomial complexity for solving problems, and assure faster computation than other classical approaches, such as brute force algorithms. Before we get into dynamic programming, let's cover the basics of DAG, as it will help with implementation of dynamic programming. DAGs are directed acyclic topological graphs, which are defined by a number of vertices and edges such that every edge is directed from earlier to later in the sequence. An example of a DAG is shown in *Figure 9.1*:

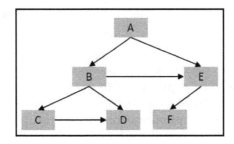

Figure 9.1: An example of DAG

Let's assume that the vertices represent cities and edges represent the path to be followed to reach a particular city. The objective is to determine the shortest path to node **D** from root node **A** in the preceding figure. This can be represented as follows:

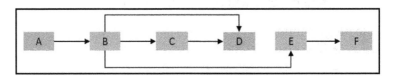

Figure 9.2: Another representation of Figure 9.1, with the objective to reach node D from the root node, A

Let $d(i,j)$ represent the distance from the ith vertex to the jth vertex, so in the example, $d(A, B)$ represents the distance from node A to node B. Also, $mdist(k)$ represents the shortest distance to the kth vertex. The minimum distance to D can be written as follows:

Shortest_Distance(A, D) = min{ mdist(B)+ d(B, D), mdist(D)+d(C, D)}

Similarly, *mdist(k)* can be further broken down into subproblems. DAG is implicit in dynamic programming, where each vertex acts a subproblem and an edge represents the dependency between subproblems. The approach of dynamic programming is very different from recursion. Let's consider an example for writing a function to calculate the nth Fibonacci series. The Fibonacci series is a sequence of integers such that every number is a sum of the preceding two numbers: *{1, 1, 2, 3, 5, 8, ...}*. The function for evaluating the nth Fibonacci number can be written using recursion in R, as shown here:

```
nfib<-function (n) {
    assertthat::assert_that (n>0) & assertthat::assert_that (n<50)
    if (n==1 || n==2) return (1)
    val<- nfib (n-1) + nfib (n-2)
    return (val)
}
```

Let's look at how the recursive approach processes the computation of the nth Fibonacci number. *Figure 9.3* shows how the preceding recursive function *nfibonacci* will evaluate the sixth Fibonacci number:

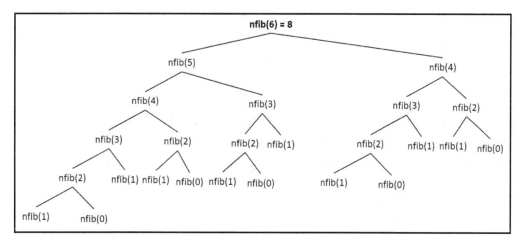

Figure 9.3: Number of times the nfibonacci function is called to calculate the sixth Fibonacci number

From *Figure 9.3* it is evident that in the recursive approach, the lower values are computed multiple times thus making the algorithm sub-optimal; however, computational time increases exponentially due to repeated computation of the same values, as shown in *Figure 9.4*:

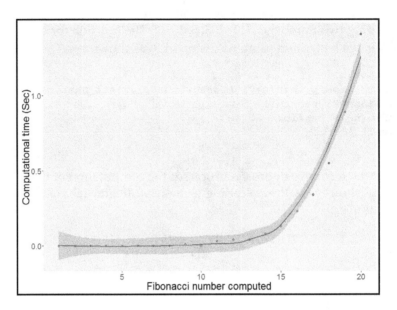

Figure 9.4: Computation time required to calculate the nth Fibonacci number using the recursive solution

The other approach to compute the nth Fibonacci number can be decided based on DAG. The Fibonacci DAG can be represented as shown in *Figure. 9.5*.

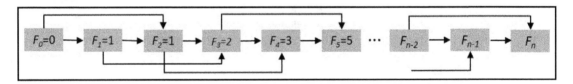

Figure 9.5: DAG representation for generating the Fibonacci series

Figure 9.5 shows that the nth Fibonacci number depends on the last two lagged values, so we can make the computation linear by storing the last two values, as shown in the following R script:

```
nfib_DP<-function(n){
  assertthat::assert_that(n>0) & assertthat::assert_that(n<50)
  if(n<=2) return(1)
  lag2_val<-0
```

```
    lag1_val<-1
    nfibval<-1
    for(i in 3:n){
      lag2_val<-lag1_val
      lag1_val<-nfibval
      nfibval<-lag2_val+lag1_val
    }
    return(nfibval)
}
```

The approach is very powerful for solving complex computations when the problem can be split into subproblems, which need to be solved repeatedly. The next sub-section will discuss the knapsack problem, which has many different variations, and how dynamic programming is used to address the problem.

The knapsack problem

The knapsack problem is a combinatorial optimization problem, which requires a subset of some given item to be chosen such that profit is maximized without exceeding capacity constraints. There are different types of knapsack problems reported in the literature depending on the number of items and knapsacks available: the **0-1 knapsack problem**, where each item is chosen at most once; the **bounded knapsack problem** puts a constraint on selection of each item; the multiple choice knapsack problem, where multiple knapsacks are presents and items are to be chosen from multiple sets; and the multi-constraint knapsack problem, where more than one constraint is present–such a knapsack having constraints on volume and weight.

The current section will discuss the 0-1 knapsack problem formulation and propose a solution can be addressed using dynamic programming. Let's consider an example storing a data file, n, with W total storage capacity available. Suppose F is a set of files to be stored where $F = \{f_1, f_2, ..., f_n\}$, $S=\{s_1, s_2, ..., s_n\}$ is a set of the amount of storage required by the ith file, and C is the computational effort required to get the files, and can be represented as $C=\{c_1, c_2, ..., c_n\}$. The objective is to select files so that it minimizes the wastage of storage capacity S, and to maximize the computing time for stored files so that the minimum time is required to recompute the files that are not stored on disk. This is a 0-1 knapsack problem, so a partial file cannot be stored.

The problem can be written mathematically as follows:

$$maximize \sum_{i \in F(*)} c_i$$

$$subject\ to \sum_{i \in F(*)} s_i \leq W$$

The aforementioned problem can be solved using dynamic programming, which stores the subproblem solution in a table that can be reused repeatedly while searching for an optimal solution. However, it will require more space to store the results of the subproblem. The implementation of this problem using dynamic programming is as follows:

```
knapsack_DP<-function(W, S, C, n){
  require(pracma)
  K<-zeros(n+1, W+1)
  for(i in 1:(n+1)){
    for(j in 1:(W+1)){
      if(i==1 | j==1){
        K[i,j]=0
      } else if(S[i-1] <= j){
        K[i, j] = max(C[i-1] + K[i-1, (j-S[i-1]))], K[i-1, j])
      } else
      {
        K[i, j] = K[i-1, j]
      }
    }
  }
  return(K[n+1, W+1])
}
```

The problem requires us to search for the solution in a two-dimension computation of the file and the storage required. The matrix K stores intermediate results, which can be reused to satisfy the objective under given constraints.

All pairs shortest paths

The **All Pairs Shortest Path** (APSP) problem focuses on finding the shortest path between all pairs of vertices. Let's consider a directed graph $G(V, E)$, where for each edge $(u, v) \in E$, the distance $d(u, v)$ is associated if the edges u and v are connected. For example, $d(A, B) = 8$ units, as shown in *Figure 9.6*:

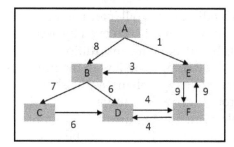

Figure 9.6: DAG representation for generating Fibonacci series

The APSP algorithm will determine the shortest path to reach from one edge to the other. For example, the shortest path to reach edge B from A is A -> E -> B with a distance of **4** units. The $d(u, v)$ in graph G is defined as follows:

$$d(u,v) = \begin{cases} 0 \text{ if } u = v \\ dist(u,v) \text{ if } u \neq v \text{ and } (u,v) \in E \\ \infty \text{ else} \end{cases}$$

One of the approaches to solve the APSP problem is by using the Floyd-Warshall algorithm, which uses dynamic programming. The approach is based on the observation that any path linking two vertices u and v may have zero or more vertices between them, defining a path. The R implementation of the Floyd-Warshall algorithm is as follows:

```
# Implementation of Floyd-Warshall algorithm
floydWarshall<-function(graph){
  nodes<-names(graph)
  dist<-graph
  for (n in nodes){
    for(ni in nodes){
      for(nj in nodes){
        if((dist[[ni]][n]+dist[[n]][nj])<dist[[ni]][nj]){
          dist[[ni]][nj]<-dist[[ni]][n]+dist[[n]][nj]
        }
      }
    }
  }
  return(dist)
}
```

The implementation begins by disallowing all intermediate vertices, thus, the initial solution is simply an initial distance matrix achieved by assigning `graph` to the `dist` list. The algorithm then proceeds by introducing an additional intermediate vertex at each step and selecting the shortest path by comparing it with the previous best estimate. The approach breaks the problem into subproblems, as the shortest distance $d(u, v)$ between the vertices u and v, passing through vertex k, is the sum of the shortest distance $d(u, k)$ and $d(k, v)$. The Floyd-Warshall implementation requires a computational effort of $O(n^3)$. The APSP problem output for the graph shown in *Table 9.1* can be determined using the following example script:

```
# Defining graph structure
graph<-list()
graph[["A"]]=c("A"=0, "B"=8, "C"=Inf, "D"=Inf, "E"=1, "F"=Inf)
graph[["B"]]=c("A"=Inf, "B"=0, "C"=7, "D"=6, "E"=Inf, "F"=Inf)
graph[["C"]]=c("A"=Inf, "B"=Inf, "C"=0, "D"=6, "E"=Inf, "F"=Inf)
graph[["D"]]=c("A"=Inf, "B"=Inf, "C"=Inf, "D"=0, "E"=Inf, "F"=4)
graph[["E"]]=c("A"=Inf, "B"=3, "C"=Inf, "D"=Inf, "E"=0, "F"=9)
graph[["F"]]=c("A"=Inf, "B"=3, "C"=Inf, "D"=4, "E"=9, "F"=0)
APSP_Dist<-floydWarshall(graph) # get shortest pair distance
```

The graph is stored as a list in R, which can be called using edge name. Similarly, the outcome is returned as a list object. The output from the Floyd-Warshall algorithm is shown in *Table 9.1*:

	A	B	C	D	E	F
A	0	4	11	10	1	10
B	Inf	0	7	6	19	10
C	Inf	13	0	6	19	10
D	Inf	7	14	0	13	4
E	Inf	3	10	9	0	9
F	Inf	3	10	4	9	0

Table 9.1: Output from the Floyd-Warshall algorithm as the shortest distance between nodes

The `Inf` in the preceding table shows that there is no direct or indirect connection between the two nodes.

Randomized algorithms

In scenarios where computations are very expensive, introduction of randomness can help reduce computational effort at the expense of accuracy. The algorithms can be classified into the following and are depicted in *Figure 9.7*:

- Deterministic algorithms
- Randomized algorithm

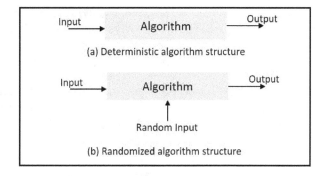

Figure 9.7: Different types of algorithm structures

Deterministic algorithms solve the problem correctly where computational effort required is a polynomial of the size of the input, whereas random algorithms take random sources as input and make their own choices while executing.

Randomized algorithms for finding large values

The computational cost of finding the largest value in an unsorted list is $O(n)$. Any deterministic algorithm will require $O(n)$ effort to determine the maximum value. However, in scenarios where time is essence, and n is very large, approximation algorithms are used, which, instead of finding the actual solution, determine the solution that is closer to the actual solution. Randomized algorithms can be classified into the following based on their goals:

- **Las Vegas algorithm**: The Las Vegas algorithm fails with some probability, so we could continue the algorithm until we get legitimate results, but it has an impact on time, which becomes unbounded. Thus, the Las Vegas algorithm usually uses legitimate results in defined time (it raises an error if the algorithm fails). Quicksort, covered in `Chapter 5`, *Sorting Algorithms*, is an example of the Las Vegas algorithm.

- **Monte Carlo algorithm**: With the Monte Carlo algorithm, we cannot test when the algorithm could fail; however, the failure probability can be reduced by increasing the number of iterations, and taking expected results.

    Generally, Las Vegas algorithms are preferred. However, there could be scenarios where Monte Carlo algorithms are useful, especially if we could bring down the failure probability and uncertainty is involved with the data itself. For example, say we want to determine the average height of a city using sample data. We have to run the Monte Carlo algorithm to estimate the average, using the sample, to get an expected value and the volatility factor involved. There is always some possibility of getting the wrong answer if the sample is a bad representation of the population, but we will not be able to detect it unless we have the population dataset.

The cost of randomized algorithms is based on expected bounds and high probability bounds. Expected bounds consists of the average outcomes captured using all random choices, whereas high probability bounds provide information on the upper bound of correctness, usually represented in terms of sampling size. Let's consider an example of finding the largest values from an n size array. The probabilistic algorithms could be very effective in a scenario where n is very large. The approach involves randomly picking an m element from the n size array, and deciding the max value, as demonstrated in *Figure 9.8*:

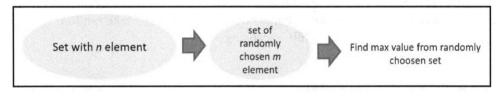

Figure 9.8: Randomized algorithm for max value evaluation

As we keep increasing m, the probability that we will get the max value keeps increasing. For large n, if we use $m \approx log_2(n)$, then the results are pretty good. Let's evaluate the performance of $m \approx log_2(n)$ using simulation. For example, with $n=1,000,000$, the number of random sampling done is 20. Splitting the whole data into ventiles (20 blocks), the probability of having a 5% error is $1-\left(\frac{19}{20}\right)^{20}$, which is equal to is 0.64, and the solution will be in the first two quantiles representing a 10% error, that is 0.87. Let's conduct a simulation to get an error distribution using Monte Carlo simulation for $n=10,000,000$ and m selected as 24 with 10,000 iterations. The error distribution is shown in *Figure 9.9*:

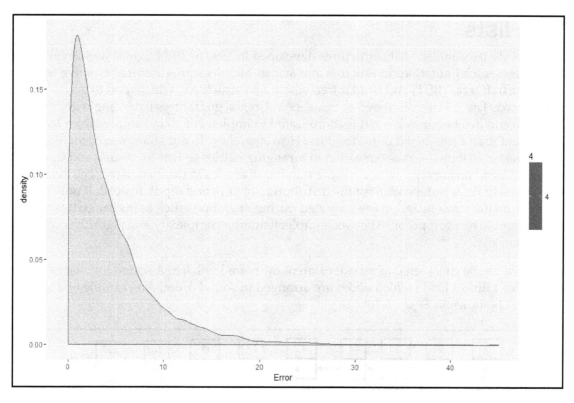

Figure 9.9: Error distribution with log m randomized sampling

A similar approach can be applied to other problem statements, such as picking a number from the upper half of n numbers. The probability of a number being in the upper half, when the greater of two number (n_1 and n_2) is picked, will be 3/4 as there are four situations:

- n_1 and n_2 both are from upper half
- n_1 and n_2 both are from lower half
- n_1 from upper half and n_2 from lower half
- n_1 from lower half and n_2 from upper half

The accuracy can be further improved by increasing sampling, with the probability of getting the right solution being represented as $1-\frac{1}{2^k}$, where k is the sample picked from n.

Skip lists

Skip lists are probabilistic data structures developed in 1990 by Bill Pugh. It was developed to address search limitations in link lists and arrays. Skip lists provide an alternative to **binary search trees** (**BST**) and similar tree-based data structures, which tend to get unbalanced. The 2-3 tree discussed in `Chapter 8`, *Graphs*, guarantees balancing with insertion and deletion; however, it is complicated to implement. Skip lists are easier to implement than a tree-based data structure. However, they do not guarantee optimal performance, as they use randomization in arranging entries so that the search and update time is *O(log n)* on average, where *n* is the number of entries in the dictionary. The average time in a skip list is independent of the distribution of keys and input. Instead, it only depends on the randomization seed selected during operations such as insertion. It is a good example of a compromise between implementation complexity and algorithm performance.

A skip list can be considered as an extension of the sorted link list. A sorted link list can be defined as a linked list in which nodes are arranged in sorted order. An example of a sorted linked list is shown in *Figure 9.10*:

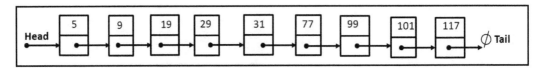

Figure 9.10: An example of a sorted link list

Any insertion or search operation in a sorted link list will require scanning the list with *O(n)* computational effort in an average case. The skip list is an extension that allows skipping nodes of a sorted link list. An example of a skip list is shown in *Figure 9.11*:

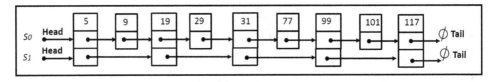

Figure 9.11: An example of a first order skip list

Figure 9.10 shows an example of a first order skip list, where there are two links: **S₀**, which connects each node, and **S₁**, connecting each alternate node of the sorted link list. The node of the skip list can be represented as shown in the following R script:

```
skListNode<-function(val, height=1){
    # function to create empty environment
```

```
create_emptyenv = function() {
  emptyenv()
}
# Create skiplist node
skiplist <- new.env(parent=create_emptyenv())
skiplist$element <- val
skiplist$nextnode<-rep(list(NULL), height)
class(skiplist) <- "skiplist"
skiplist
}
```

The `nextnode` in the `skipListNode` node function can be of variable length depending on the order of the skip list. A skip list can be of nth order; an example of a second order skip list is shown in *Figure 9.11*:

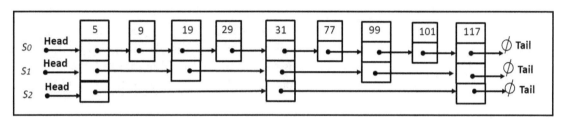

Figure 9.11: An example of a second order skip list

The higher order allows a larger jump in the skip list, which, in turn, helps to reduce the execution time of operations such as searching, insertion, and deletion. An example of a search operation for value **101** within a skip list is shown in *Figure 9.12*:

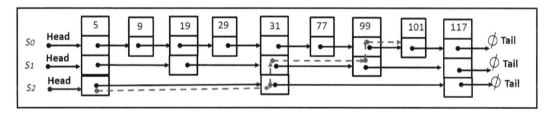

Figure 9.12: An example of search in a skip list

The dotted line in the graph shows the path that will be followed while searching for the value **101** in the skip list.

The script for searching a value in a skip list is shown next:

```
# Function to find a value in skip list
findvalue<-function(skiplist, searchkey){
  for (i in level:1){
```

```
        skiplist<-skiplist$nextnode[[i]] # head values
        while(!is.null(node) && node$element>searchkey){
          skiplist<-skiplist$nextnode[[i]]
        }
        skiplist = skiplist$nextnode[0]
        if(!is.null(skiplist) && searchkey==skiplist$element){
          return(skiplist$element) # Return element
        } else
        {
          return(NULL) # Element not found
        }
      }
    }
```

The skip list is stored as an array of environment in `nextnode`. The search operation starts with the highest level s_2 in case of example shown in *Figure 9.12*. The `while` loop keeps moving from the head to 31 and then to 117 before exiting the `while` loop. The search operation then switches to the s_1 level, and the search moves from 31 -> 99 -> 117. At 117, the nodes again exit the `while` loop, the pointer is set at node 99, and height is adjusted to s_0. The node goes to 117 before exiting and comparing with `searchkey` to stop at 101.

The preceding examples of skip lists fall into ideal skip lists where the s_0 layer connects n nodes, s_1 connects 1/2 nodes, and the layer s_k connects $\frac{1}{2^k}$ nodes. The distances are equally spaced and they are called a perfectly balanced skip list. However, maintaining this balance is an expensive process, especially during insertion and deletion operations, as all connections need to be updated accordingly to ensure a balanced skip list. To address the issue, a randomized skip list is created, which assigns a random level to the node.

Let S represent a randomized skip list with height h for a dataset D consisting of the series $\{s_0, s_1, ..., s_h\}$. List s_i maps to the subset of entries of D in a sorted order, starting at the head and ending at the tail of D. Also, S should satisfy following properties:

- List s_0 should connect each node of the dataset in a sorted order.
- For $i = 1, ..., h - 1$, list s_i consists of randomly selected nodes from D. The selection is conducted using geometric distribution, such as level s_1 assigned 50% probability of selection, s_2 with 25% selection probability, and so on. Geometric distribution can be simulated using the `rgeom(n, prob)` function from the stat R library.

An example of a randomized skip list is shown in *Figure 9.13*:

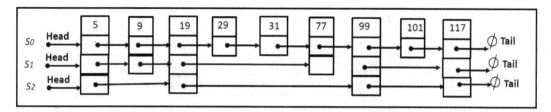

Figure 9.13: An example of a randomized skip list

The search algorithm holds for randomized skip lists. The operation for the Insertion of a node also uses randomization to decide the height of the new node. The search operation can be used to determine the place where the node is to be inserted. The search strategy is similar to the `findvalue` function to determine the insertion position. The connections are updated based on backward and forward scanning for randomized height. An example of the insertion operation is shown in *Figure 9.14*:

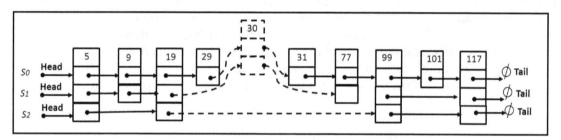

Figure 9.14: An insertion example of a node with value 30 in a randomized skip list with height 2. The dashed lines shows a new connection inserted into an already existing skip list

The randomized height is adjusted to a maximum value to ensure that any random value is not picked. The approach of having a fixed height to make it as a function of *n* such as *h = max(l0, 2logn)* or any other distribution constrained at maximum value. The deletion algorithm follows a structure similar to insertion, and is quite simple to implement, as the value will be removed and the incoming input is linked to the outgoing node.

An example of deletion is shown in *Figure 9.15*:

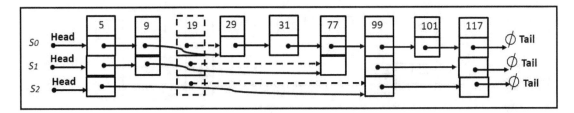

Figure 9.15: An example of the deletion of node 19 in a randomized skip list. The dashed line in the figure shows the connection removed and curved lines are extended to the closest node

Probabilistic analysis of skip lists

Skip lists are very simple to implement. However, skip lists may not be the best data structure in a scenario where insertion is not prevented from going above the specified maximum height, as it will lead to an infinite loop. Let's consider a scenario of a skip list with height h, and n entries. Then, the worst case scenario for insertion, deletion, and search operations is $O(n+h)$. The worst case scenario for a skip list is quite inferior to other implementations discussed in this book. However, this is highly overestimated, because operations are randomized. Thus, the analysis requires probability to get a better estimate for the computational effort required for insertion, deletion, and search operations.

The probability that an entry can be reached at height k is $\dfrac{1}{2^k}$ where $k>1$. In case of n entries probability P_k of an entry reaching k height is $\dfrac{n}{2^k}$. The probability that the height h of the skip list is greater than k is equal to the probability that the kth level has at least one position that is no greater than P_k, that is, h is larger than $3logn$ with the probability given as follows:

$$P_{3\log n} \leq \frac{n}{2^{3\log n}} = \frac{n}{n^3}$$

The preceding equation can be generalized for any constant c as follows:

$$P_{c\log n} \leq \frac{n}{2^{c\log n}} = \frac{n}{n^c} = \frac{1}{n^{c-1}}$$

For a skip list with 10,000 entries, the probability would be one in 100 million. Thus, with very high probability, the height of `skiplist` is $O(log\ n)$. Similarly, as time spent in scanning any height in a skip list is $O(1)$, and a skip list would have $O(log\ n)$ levels, which is high probability, the search is expected to take $O(log\ n)$ computational effort.

As we have shown, the expected number of entries at position k is $\frac{n}{2^k}$, which can be used to evaluate the space required for a skip list with n entries:

$$\sum_{k=1}^{h} \frac{n}{2^k} = n\sum_{k=1}^{h} \frac{1}{2^k}$$

The preceding equation can be reduced using geometric summation as follows:

$$\sum_{k}^{h} = 1\frac{1}{2^k} = \frac{\left(\frac{1}{2}\right)^{h+1} - 1}{\frac{1}{2} - 1} = 2\left(1 - \frac{1}{2^{h+1}}\right) < 2\ for\ all\ n \geq 0$$

Thus, the expected space requirement is $O(n)$.

Exercises

1. One of the classic problems is the Tower of Hanoi, inspired by Hindu temples, where priests are provided with three poles of 64 gold disks, and each disk is a little smaller than the one beneath it, as shown in the following figure:

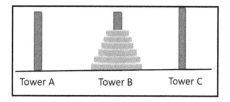

- The task is to transfer all 64 disks from one pole to another with two constraints, that is, only one disk can be moved at a time, and that they cannot place a larger disk on smaller one. Write a dynamic programming-based approach to solve the Tower of Hanoi problem.

2. Implement a function that gets the edit distance of two input strings, where the edit distance is defined as insertion, deletion, and substitution. The function should determine the minimal number of edit distance required to modify one distance to another.

3. Given a rope of length n, write a function to determine how to cut the rope into m parts with *length l[0], l[1]*, and so on until *l[m]* so that the product of each part is maximum. The rope needs to be cut as an integer with a minimum of one cut.

4. Construct an all-pair shortest distance matrix for the following graph:

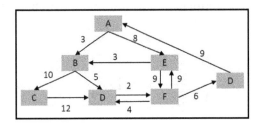

5. In a class, there are m students. An exam is conducted with 30 questions. The examiner picked random eight questions and graded them. The grades will be either A or D. A will be assigned if more than 50% questions are answered correctly; otherwise, grade D will be assigned. Set up a Monte Carlo simulation to determine the expected error for a person getting A instead of D.

6. Write a function to delete a node from a skip list.

7. Write a function to develop a skip list to contain numbers in the range *[1, m]* where m is not constant, and a support query to find an element e1 so that e1.key=q is a given pointer to an element e2, e2.key=p so that $p<q$ in $O(log\ k)$ expected time, where k is the distance between elements e1 and e2.

Summary

This chapter focused on the fundamentals of programming and randomized algorithms. The chapter built on the programming concepts of dynamic programming, and presented the difference between dynamic programming and recursion. The DAGs was also introduced in this chapter, and how it can be used to set up dynamic programming was discussed. Two popular examples of the knapsack problem and two APSP were covered in this chapter, and their solutions using dynamic programming were presented. Randomized algorithms, Las Vegas and Monte Carlo, were introduced with their application in determining max value using randomization. This chapter also introduced skip lists and the extension to randomized skip lists. The probabilistic analysis of skip list was covered for major operations and data storage. The next chapter will introduce functional algorithms concepts. Functional algorithms provide the ability to write clean and clear code by eliminating state during runtime so that output is always determined based on input.

10
Functional Data Structures

Data structures form an integral part of any algorithm. Heaps, queues, stacks, trees, and hash tables are various forms of data structures widely used across programming languages. Some of them are primarily used for look-ups, such as trees and hash tables, while others, such as heaps, queues, and stacks, are used for update modifications, such as insertions and deletions. The current chapter will build foundation to extend conventional data structure to functional data structure. In this chapter, you will learn the following concepts:

- Functional data structures
- Lazy evaluation
- Functional queues
- Functional stacks

Functional data structure

Functional data structures are special forms of data structure, which are implemented primarily in functional programming languages. R supports functional programming by providing tools for creation and manipulation of functions. For example, R support assigning functions to variables and passing them as an argument within a function. The R support generating the function dynamically and returning them as a result of the function is also known as a closure function. For example, the function which takes a function as an argument is shown as follows:

```
arg_function <- function(g) g(seq(1, 100, by=1))
```

The function `arg_function` can take functions as an argument, such as `mean` or `sd` as shown in the following code snippet:

```
> arg_function(mean)
[1] 50.5
> arg_function(sd)
[1] 29.01149
```

The functional data structure is also known as persistent data structure as they are immutable in the sense that any operation performed on function data structure will create a new copy of data structure with an updated operation. The original functional data structure will always remain intact. The functional data structure possesses different characteristics compared to traditional data structures. These are highly flexible in implementation and support the properties of immutability and persistency. In addition, they are thread-safe; that is, functional data structure ensures safe execution even in multithreaded environment during data structure manipulation.

The following are some benefits of immutability:

- It supports data hiding and data sharing. The former prevents any possibility of leakage of data (dynamically generated within functions) and the latter supports auto-sharing of data (based on pointers), as per the requirement within the functions.
- As functional data structures do not support mutations, it requires no external synchronization. However, some support modifications (additions or deletions) using controlled mutations.
- The pointers prevent long-distance coupling.

The following are some benefits of persistency:

- It augments mutation using constructive updates on the data structure instead of destructive updates. The modifications are incorporated constructively by replicating the whole data structure, keeping the older versions intact.
- It supports memory-efficient ways of replication, such as sharing of older versions instead of copying.

The following are some benefits of thread safety:

- It supports concurrent programming without any need to worry about data races without mutation

- During construction of new objects, mutations are performed only within the thread under consideration using pointers, and the original data is kept intact (immutable)
- It is memory-efficient as it supports thread-safe reference counting using shared pointers and is optimized as log-free

Lazy evaluation

Functional data structures used in functional programming languages support lazy evaluation. In lazy implementation, the arguments of a function are evaluated if and only if the computational results are used further within the function. Furthermore, once the arguments are evaluated, the computational results are cached and can be reused later, if needed again, using look-up instead of recomputation. This kind of caching (also termed as **memoization**) makes it highly difficult to estimate the asymptotic complexity of the algorithm as it is not straightforward to determine when a given argument (or a subexpression) will be evaluated.

Lazy evaluation plays a key role in the implementation of purely functional amortized data structures. It is extremely difficult to analyze the asymptotic performance of algorithms involving lazy evaluation. However, the following framework provides a basic support to calculate the asymptotic performances of algorithms involving lazy evaluation. Firstly, the costs of any given operation are classified, as follows:

- **Unshared cost**: This defines the actual execution time of an operation, provided every deferment pertaining to that operation was forced and memoized prior to executing the operation.
- **Shared cost**: This defines the execution time of all deferred operations, which were earlier excluded, while evaluating the performance of the operation under consideration. The shared cost can be further split into realized and unrealized costs. Realized costs evaluate the runtime of deferred operations, which are executed during overall computation whereas the unrealized costs evaluate the runtime of deferred operations, which are never executed during the overall computation.
- **Complete cost**: This defines the actual execution time of the operation if it is implemented using lazy evaluation. It is the sum of shared and unshared costs, excluding unrealized cost. The minimum value of complete cost is unshared cost, provided no deferred operations are executed during the overall computation.
- **Amortized cost**: This defines the shared costs of the overall computation that are accounted using the concept of accumulated debt. Initially, the accumulated debt is set to zero and it starts accumulating for each deferment created. Then, each

operation starts paying off the debt. Once the debt is completely paid off, the deferments can then be forced and memoized. Here, the amortized cost of an operation is sum of unshared cost of the operation and debt paid off by each operation.

Thus, a deferred operation can only be forced and memoized once the accumulated debt is completely paid off. As the total amount of accumulated cost is capped at realized shared costs, the amortized cost cannot increase beyond the total actual cost.

Functional stacks

A stack is a **First In Last Out** (**FILO**) form of a data structure, wherein both insertions and deletions usually happen at the beginning (or top) of the stack. These forms are widely used in **Depth-first search** (**DFS**) algorithms. In ideal scenarios, the insertion, removal, and peeking operations require very little time generally with an asymptote of $O(1)$ for the worst case scenario. Thus, during a worst case scenario, n insertions or removals would have an asymptote of $O(n)$, provided average asymptote of each operation of $O(1)$.

Now, let's understand the implementation of fully-persistent stacks in R. The implementation of a fully-persistent stack data structure is available in an rstackdeque cran package contributed by Shawn T. O'Neil. In R, mutability can be ensured using environment variables using side-effect-free interface functions.

In this package, stacks are implemented using unordered linked lists, wherein each node (list) consists of both data elements and reference to the next node. These stacks are S3 objects, accessible using the head stack node.

Let's consider a stack with five character elements:

```
a <- as.rstack(c("p", "q", "r","s","t"))
```

Analogous to a traditional push function, insert_top is used to return a stack with new elements at the top. Here, instead of creating a new stack, the head element of b is pointed towards the o element, which is in-turn pointed toward stack a, as shown in *Figure 10.1*:

```
b <- insert_top(a, c("o"))
```

In case of withdrawal of top element from stack (pop), the without_top function is used. Similar to insert_top, the primary a stack is not destructively updated, but the pointer of stack c is shifted towards right by one element, as shown in *Figure 10.1*:

```
c <- without_top(a)
```

The `peek_top` function is used to return the data element present at the top of the stack:

```
d <- peek_top(a)
```

The following *Figure 10.1* illustrates the implementation of fully-persistent stacks in R:

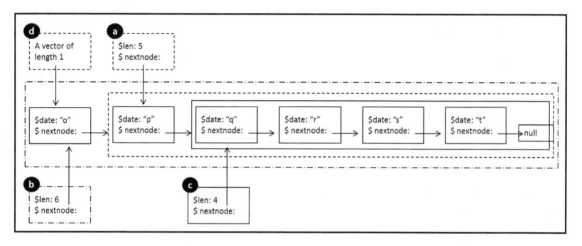

Figure 10.1: Working of fully-persistent stacks based on different types of insertion or deletion operations. (a) represents a stack of five characters, each character linked to another character as in case of linked lists. (b) represents a stack after inserting a new element o on top of the stack (a). (c) represents a stack after removing the top element of the stack (a). (d) represents a character vector with top element of stack (a).

Functional queues

A queue is a **First In First Out** (**FIFO**) form of a data structure, wherein deletions happen in the same order of insertion. One way of implementing queue is to insert elements from end (top of the queue) and delete elements from opposite end (bottom of the queue). Some queues support insertions and deletions from both the ends. These are termed as deques or double-ended queues. Queues and deques are used in **Breadth-first search** (**BFS**) algorithms. Similar to stacks, ideally the insertion, removal, and peeking operations require very little time with an asymptote of $O(1)$ for the worst case scenario. Thus, during a worst case scenario, n insertions or removals would have an asymptote of $O(n)$, provided average asymptote of each operation of $O(1)$.

Now, let's understand the implementation of fast, fully-persistent and slowly-persistent queues and deques in R using the `rstackdeque` cran package contributed by Shawn T. O'Neil.

Fast fully-persistent queues

Fast and fully-persistent queues are governed primarily by recursively-defined operations and delayed evaluations. In other words, these queues are implemented using lazy lists wherein the first elements are immediately accessible and rest of the elements are evaluated with a delay. This is helpful, in the case of recursive large lists where elements are only evaluated whenever accessed.

The R function to implement fast persistent queues is rpqueue. It comprises of three last lists: l, r, lhat. Here, the elements are inserted at the back of the queue and removed or deleted from the front of the queue. In other words, the insertion of new elements occurs at the top of the r list and the deletion of existing elements occurs from front of the l list. These lazy lists are implemented as rstacks and every node's nextnode elements are assigned using the delayedAssign function. These are subsequently memoized on first evaluation.

Traditionally, the queue tries to ensure that the length of l stack is at least equal to the length of the r stack. However, during any insertion or deletion operation, the lengths are disturbed. The length of r stack increases upon insertion and the length of l stack decreases upon deletion. Post these operations, the l and r stacks are readjusted by appending the last elements of r stack with l stack. This readjustment requires an asymptote of *O(1)* for any sort of insertion or deletion happening within l and r stacks. Upon readjustment, lhat is assigned with data of stack l. Then, for each subsequent insertion or deletion, the elements of lhat are removed one by one until the lhat stack becomes empty. Once lhat becomes empty, the lengths of l and r stacks are evaluated and the elements are readjusted, again delaying the time of iteration.

Let's understand the working of fully-persistent queues using an example. Consider a persistent queue of length four:

```
a <- as.rpqueue(c("p","q","r","s"))
```

The "p", "q", and "r" elements are assigned to left stack l, element "s" is assigned to right stack "r", and, elements "q" and "r" are assigned to stack lhat. The following *Figure 10.2* illustrates working of persistent queues based on insertion and deletion operations. The insertion operation is performed using the insert_back function and deletion operation is performed using the without_front function.

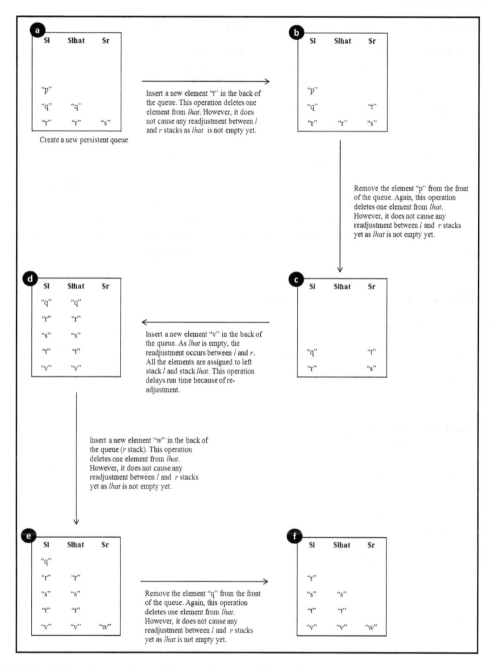

Figure 10.2: Working of fully-persistent queues based on different types of insertion or deletion operations. (a) represents a new persistent queue. (b) represents a queue after inserting a new element "t" in the back of queue (a). (c) represents a queue after deleting the front element from queue (b). (d) represents queue after inserting a new element "v" at the back of queue (c). (e) represents queue after inserting a new element "w" at the back of queue (d). (f) represents a queue after deleting an element from front of queue (e).

The following are R codes, which are used in the preceding illustration:

```
b <- insert_back(a, "t")   # insert a new element "t"
c <- without_front(b)      # remove front element "b"
d <- insert_back(c,"v")    # insert a new element "v"
e <- insert_back(d,"w")    # insert a new element "w"
f <- without_front(e)      # remove front element "e"
```

Slowly-persistent queues and deques

The queues are implemented as two stacks, that is, the left stack and the right stack. The left stack holds the first set of elements of the queue, which is used for deletion operations, and the right stack holds the last set of elements of the queue, which is used for insertion operations. On the other hand, the left stack can also be used for insertion and the right stack for deletion. The right stack holds elements in the reverse order as shown in *Figure 10.3*.

Let's consider an a queue with seven character elements:

```
a <- as.rdeque(c("p", "q", "r","s","t","u","v"))
```

The a queue is split into left and right queues, as illustrated in *Figure 10.3* and *Figure 10.4*.

Using the `insert_front` or `insert_back` functions, the elements are inserted at the front or back of the queue respectively:

```
b <- insert_front(a, c("o"))
c <- insert_back(a, c("w"))
```

Similarly, elements can also be deleted from the front or back of the queue using the `without_front` or `without_back` functions:

```
d <- without_front(a)
e <- without_back(a)
```

The following *Figure 10.3* and *Figure 10.4* describes implementation of slowly-persistent queues in R:

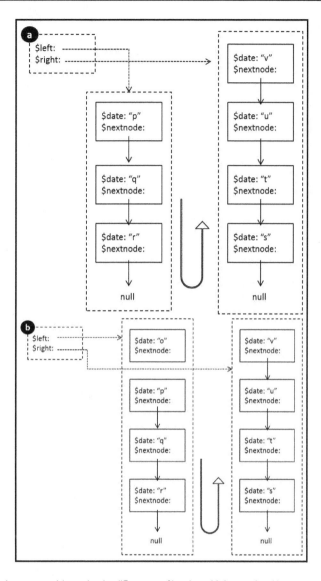

Figure 10.3: Working of slowly-persistent queues and dequeus based on different types of insertion or deletion operations. (a) represents a queue with left and right stacks. (b) represents queue after inserting a new element "o" at the front of queue (a).

The *Figure 10.3* presents how slowly-persistent queues stores initial seven character element passed to a. The left side of the queue can be extracted using a$l and similarly right side of queue can be extracted using a$r. The b part of image demonstrate how functional queue a will be updated when an element o is added using function insert_front(a, c("o")).

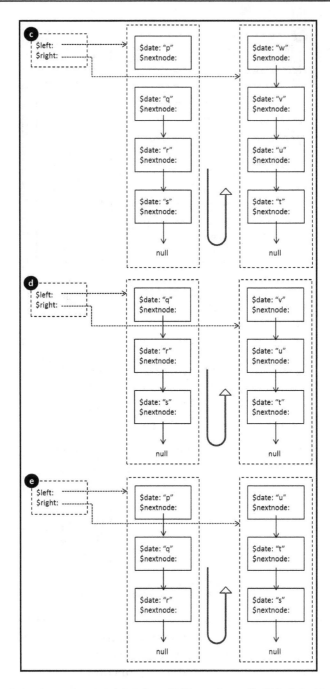

Figure 10.4: (c) represents queue after inserting a new element w in the back of queue (a). (d) represents queue after deleting the front element from queue (a). (e) represents queue after deleting the last element from queue (a).

In the current implementation, double-ended queues, which rebalance after every insertion or deletion, are used as shown in *Figure 10.4*. If both left and right stacks become highly unbalanced, then they are both first decomposed into a list and then recomposed back into two nearly balanced stacks.

Summary

Apart from academic purposes, functional programming has found its way into a wide range of industrial applications such as aerospace, telecommunications and robotics. Pure functional languages such as Haskell, Scala, F# are becoming popular across these industries. The properties of immutability and persistency make these data structures more robust in terms of transparency, simulations and efficiency. The current chapter primarily covers functional data structures, concepts of lazy evaluation and detailed analysis of functional stacks and functional queues.

Index

H

hash functions 152, 153
hashing
  about 151, 152
  closed hashing 157
  deletion 165
  open hashing 155
heap sort algorithm
  about 124, 126, 127, 128
  heap criterion 125
  shape criterion 124
heuristics, self-organizing lists
  count 146, 148
  move-to-front 147, 149
  transpose 147, 150

I

Indexed Sequential Access Method (ISAM) 169,
  173, 174
indexing
  linear indexing 169
  tree-based indexing 174
input key values
  non-uniformity 153, 154
insertion sort algorithm 109, 110, 111
integrated circuit (IC) 8
Integrated Development Environment (IDE) 16

K

knapsack problem
  0-1 knapsack problem 231
  about 231
  bounded knapsack problem 231

L

Last In First Out (LIFO) 84
linear indexing 169, 170, 171, 172
linear linked list 70, 72, 74
linked list
  about 68, 69
  circular linked list 76
  doubly linked list 75
  linear linked list 70, 72, 74
  types 70

linked queues
  about 98, 100
  and array-based queues, comparing 101
linked stacks
  about 88, 90, 91
  and array-based stack, comparing 91
list
  analysis 79, 80

M

memoization 249
memory allocation 34
memory management, R
  about 34, 37
  algorithm asymptotic analysis 44
  attribute pointer 34
  average case 40
  best case 40
  computer, versus algorithm 41
  memory allocation 34
  memory padding 35
  metadata 34
  node pointer 34
  problems, analyzing 54
  program, computer evaluation 50
  space bounds 54
  worst case 40
merge sort algorithm
  about 118
  analyzing 120
miles per gallon (mpg) 37
Minimum Spanning Tree (MST)
  about 219
  Kruskal's algorithm 221, 222, 224, 225
  Prim's algorithm 219, 220

O

object-oriented programming (OOP)
  class 66
  generic function 66
  method 66
  object 66
open addressing 155
operation costs
  amortized cost 249

---

www.ingramcontent.com/pod-product-compliance
Lightning Source LLC
Chambersburg PA
CBHW060529060326
40690CB00017B/3429